# mums on
# pregnancy

# mums on
# pregnancy

**Carrie Longton, Justine Roberts
and Rachel Foster**

**mumsnet.com**

CASSELL
ILLUSTRATED

The opinions relating to childcare advice and information contained in this publication are the expressions of individual parents and are not those held by the Publisher. Whilst the advice and information in this book is believed to be accurate and true at the time of going to press, no legal responsiblity or liablity can be accepted by the Publisher for any errors or omissions that may be made.

This book is not intended as a substitute for professional medical advice. It is therefore advisable for the reader to consult their doctor in all matters relating to health and particularly in respect of any symptoms which may require diagnosis or medical attention.

First published in Great Britain in 2004
by Cassell Illustrated,
a division of Octopus Publishing Group Limited
2–4 Heron Quays, London E14 4JP

Text copyright © Rachel Foster, Carrie Longton and Justine Roberts, 2004
Design copyright © 2004 Cassell Illustrated,
a division of the Octopus Publishing Group Limited

A CIP catalogue record for this book is available
from the British Library.

ISBN 1 84403 0717

Edited by Deborah Taylor
Designed by Helen Ewing
Jacket design by Jo Knowles and Abby Franklin

Printed in Spain

Jacket and inside image: Getty Images/Lise Metsger

## Dedication
To our mothers, Elizabeth, Sheila and Pat. They may not have had access to mumsnet.com in their day but they knew a thing or two.

## Acknowledgements
We're eternally grateful to Steven (Tech) Cassidy for his enduring tolerance in the face of gross technical illiteracy. Thanks also to Tigermoth, a Mumsnet oldie (in the membership sense only), for her help in researching this book, to Victoria at Cassell Illustrated for her unflappability and to Tif, our agent, for her endless enthusiasm. Special thanks to our partners Ian, Philip and Paul, who with great forbearance put up with us tapping away into the wee hours and only occasionally ask whether we are making any money. And as ever, thank you to the thousands of Mumsnet mums without whose wisdom and generosity there would, of course, be no book.

# Contents

# Introduction

Here you are, pregnant and though squillions of women have been here before – around 210 million every year (The Pacific Institute for Women's Health) to be precise – you've every right to be excited. And you're not the only one. Expect all and sundry to start treating you like a national treasure – to pat you, grill you on the most intimate details of your life and generally bore you to death about their own pregnancy and birth experiences.

Excited, and maybe just a little apprehensive, like it or not your body is taking over. Let's face it, for the next nine months you will become a highly efficient incubator and life-support system. For those who think pregnancy – and we'll admit to thinking like this once ourselves – is about getting a bit fatter with a few weeks of morning sickness thrown in, there's a shock in store. To put it bluntly, whilst you would be unlucky if you got all the 'minor ailments' that are painstakingly detailed in most pregnancy tomes, if you got none of them you'd most likely be preserved for the benefit of scientific research. Whether it's exhaustion, indigestion, constipation, piles, backache, nausea or insomnia everyone seems to have their own particular bugbear and most will have an unappetizing cocktail of a number of these complaints.

And the physical side effects don't stop there – when you find yourself weeping uncontrollably at *Pet Rescue*, it will dawn on you, if it hasn't already, that your hormones are in a frenzy. Plus, don't be surprised if your brain feels like it's turned into a blancmange – no prizes for guessing the answer to the old Trivial Pursuit teaser: 'What part of a woman's body shrinks during pregnancy?' He would never get away with it these days, but it's hard to argue with Gordon Bourne, who noted in his 70s bestseller *Pregnancy* that pregnant women, 'become emotional and irritable' and 'occasionally they will not even respond to logical argument'.

No doubt Victorian women suffered similar lapses but at the turn of the last century life as a mother-to-be was relatively simple. Two pints of milk a day was considered the only dietary change required – as long as you laid off the pickled onions of course, consumption of which (along with under-ripe fruit) was believed to give a child with a 'sour disposition'. Oh, and exercise was also out. Women were considered 'temperamentally unsound' if they even rode a bicycle when pregnant (Tommy's campaign research, commissioned by Boots the Chemist).

But things have moved on a bit since your grandma's, your mother's and even your big sister's day. Not only is it almost impossible to find time for the pregnancy yoga in amongst the aqua-aerobics and active birth classes, but it almost seems like you need a 24-hour newswire to keep you up to date with the latest guidelines on WHAT PREGNANT WOMEN SHOULD NOT DO – a list which seems to be as long as the queue of people ahead of you at the antenatal clinic. Blink and you'll miss the fact that shellfish are off the menu. Then on again – but only on if they are thoroughly cooked and piping hot all the way through... And without a degree in food science you might struggle to establish exactly which cheeses are pregnancy no-nos. You may know that soft ones are off limits, but you could find it hard to tell how soft is soft? Does feta count and what about the deliciously runny one at the local deli that claims to be pasteurized? Then there's liver, alcohol, bags of pre-pared salad, Parma ham, gardening, sitting cross-legged, sunbathing, bungee jumping, and even having your hair highlighted – all of which are on the current list of things to be avoided.

And those are just the first gusts in the hurricane of questions that will engulf you over the next few months. More testing questions will concern whether you should bother with antenatal classes. What tests should you have – and what should you make of the results? What kind of birth should you have? If you're planning to travel, how late is it safe to fly? What equip-ment should you buy for your newborn? Should you find out the sex of your child? How much maternity leave will you need? How will you know when you are going into labour?

Who is going to answer all these questions for you? Almost certainly not your frazzled GP whose advice is unlikely to run much beyond, 'don't forget to take folic acid'. Your mum might have some reassuring words of advice along the lines of 'I survived on peanuts and red wine and it never did you any harm', but the truth is that things have changed since she was in maternity knickers. What you really need is a bunch of mothers who have been through modern pregnancy and are willing to share their wisdom and experiences.

So, relax. Because if a bunch can run to several thousand, this makes a pretty good description of Mumsnet. The Mumsnet website is a vast, constantly updated archive of expertise – collected the hands-on way – by women who have negotiated pregnancy and given birth in many different ways and under many different circumstances. Whatever the pregnancy poser you are facing, the chances are that one of Mumsnet's members will have faced it already. From what to pack in your hospital bag (who'd have though of flip-flops?) to dealing with the news that you are expecting twins, our members share the solutions and advice that worked for them.

Though we have produced eight children between us (eight!) since meeting in antenatal classes five years ago, the three of us are emphatically not parenting experts: Justine is a football reporter, Carrie's background is in TV production and Rachel worked in radio. The initial idea behind Mumsnet was to create a place where parents could pool recommendations on family-friendly holidays. But almost immediately our users began swapping advice on a much wider range of subjects: they shared the pain of miscarriages, suggested ways of staving off pregnancy nausea, debated the pros and cons of birth doulas, and when they paused for breath, wondered if their private parts would ever be the same again.

Over the last four years, the Mumsnet chat boards have grown into a constantly evolving snapshot of every parental concern from MMR to Michael Jackson's parenting skills. We've even had a live birth, with thousands of members rooting for the mother and father as they waited for the midwife to reach their remote Swedish home. (The midwife didn't make it but the baby did, with help from the battalion of virtual doulas dispensing advice on the site.)

Most of the discussions on Mumsnet are less dramatic but nonetheless still packed with hard-earned know-how, advice and – just as important – wit. This book, the second in a series of Mumsnet guides, is an attempt to distil some of that wisdom in an easy-to-find and portable form. Since it is our members rather than us who are the real experts, we have tried to mediate their words as little as possible.

No single piece of advice should be read as 'a Mumsnet way of doing things'. One of the first things we learned from the site is that there really are different strokes for different folks. The aim of this book is simply to provide you with a bank of solutions discovered by the many thousands of our members who have encountered the same thorny dilemmas, problems and panics every pregnant woman faces. We're confident that, whatever the subject, you'll find some advice that works for you. And if you can't, or if you'd like to share your own ingenious cure for heartburn, or your inspired solution to the oxymoron that is maternity fashion, we're just a click away at www.mumsnet.com. Good luck!

# 1

# First Thoughts
# and Practicalities

# Introduction

There's no mistaking that thin blue line, you're pregnant, girl, and though you're probably feeling as tired as the lettuce in a hospital salad and sicker than any parrot, you still need to get practical. There are decisions to be made. Not least who to tell and when. Sadly, more than one in five pregnancies ends in miscarriage (The Miscarriage Association) but the risk of miscarriage decreases dramatically after the eighth week and as the weeks go by (womens-health.co.uk). So should you wait, as many do, for the second trimester until you break the news or should you just go for it in the knowledge that you're going to need a lot of support if things do go wrong?

If you're a first timer you'll probably consider attending antenatal classes and, given that some of them can be tougher to get into than the Ivy on a Saturday night, you need to decide soon whether they are worth the trouble and if so should you plump for those run by the NCT (National Childbirth Trust), the hospital or your GP?

Like it or not, as your girth expands, you'll also need to review your wardrobe. But it's hard to hand over cash for items that, however fancy, aren't going to stop you looking like a Christmas turkey. Might you just as well pinch a few of your partner's old shirts and pick up a donkey jacket from Oxfam?

Whatever you wear, by the time your bump's obviously more than a fondness for half a bottle of Chianti a night, you'll be noticed (unless of course you're standing in a packed Tube carriage hoping for a seat) and complete strangers will feel at liberty to interrogate you on the most intimate details – from how much weight you have put on, to what sex you're hoping for, and even your planned post-birth sleeping arrangements.

Worse still, some may even take it upon themselves to pat and stroke your bump as if it was their long-lost pet rabbit. How can you encourage the opinionated to keep their views to themselves and introduce the concept of personal space to the gropers without resorting to physical assault, particularly if the worst offender is your boss? The same person who you're expecting to talk to about your plans for maternity leave. When should you plan to stop work and if you're lucky enough to have any say in the matter, how much maternity leave should you take?

And what if you choose or find yourself pregnant and single. What's it like and is there anything you can do to make it easier? Single or with a partner, you may well covet a final holiday before the baby arrives and removes the likelihood of being able to sit back, relax and enjoy the flight for the foreseeable future. But is it advisable to fly and, if so, how can you make it more comfortable for yourself? How late in your pregnancy should you plan to travel and how far afield should you go?

If you do manage a break, no doubt much of it will be spent thinking of what you might call your progeny. It is a remarkable fact that however many hours parents seem to spend giggling over Balthazar and Beryl, the novelty of discussing names never seems to wear off. But then again there's loads to consider. Are Ruperts still destined to be the butt of the playground bullies? How will Granny feel if her new grandchild's given Grandma's name and can you really plump for Ellie if your best friend has already nabbed it for her child?

One thing's for sure unless you are super superstitious you'll want to do a bit of shopping for Ellie prior to the birth. Buying baby clothes may well be one of the high points of your pregnancy (in my case, possibly my life) and the urge to fill the box room with everything a baby could ever want becomes overwhelming. But what should you resist? Is the Winnie the Pooh nappy stacker strictly necessary and if not, what is?

And what about that hospital bag or, more realistically, hospital suitcase? What else, besides a bottle of hard liquor, is an essential aid? Do you really need to take the baby hairstyling equipment? Read on for the answers to all these conundrums and what's more, find out why you should definitely leave your best moccasins at home.

## When should you tell people you are pregnant?

**I chose only to tell** family and close friends when pregnant with my first, as I was a bit wary until after the first trimester. My parents-in-law, however, didn't have such worries and apparently rushed out to their local boozer and announced it to all and sundry – cue round of congratulatory drinks. My husband was very miffed when he strolled in there a few weeks later to break the news to be greeted with bored faces. With my second, the big grin on my face gave it away to everyone. Only you can decide when to tell but I would opt for telling those you are closest to and ask them to respect your privacy until you are ready for everyone to know.

*Snugs*

**With our first we didn't tell anyone** until after our nuchal scan at about 12 weeks. It was nice having a little secret (well, a big one really). Mind you, I was lucky, as I didn't feel ill. With number two we had to tell my parents at under two months pregnant, as I put my back out really badly and had to go and stay with them for a week. We had to explain why I couldn't take many pain-killers. It's really a personal matter.

*SoupDragon*

**I told some people at work** before the end of my first trimester in case I miscarried – I was sure that I would need some time off and a lot of understanding from my boss, so I thought it only fair that he knew about the pregnancy. Also, we moved offices when I was about two-and-a-half months and I didn't want to do too much lifting and packing!

*Sis*

> **Mumsnet tip**
> Don't tell people your expected due-date (i.e. 40 weeks) but give a 42-week date instead. That way you won't be inundated with well-meaning but irritating calls at 40 weeks from people saying, 'Have you had it yet?' or 'Oh – you're late then.'   *Mo2*

**With my first pregnancy** I was so excited that I told everyone straight away. I then lost the baby and it was horrible having to 'untell' everyone. But I'm glad I did, as they were very supportive and it hit me really hard. Second time round, I only told my mum and boyfriend. I lost this baby too. My boyfriend stopped talking to me (long story) and mum went to pieces ('Sorry, can't talk to you now dear, I'm too upset!') Hence with pregnancy number three and four, I did not tell a soul until the scans. I'm now pregnant again but have told my son and daughter and they are telling everyone for me. I feel so rotten, it would be hard to hide anyway and if I did lose this baby then I would want people to know.

I went to see a friend this afternoon to tell her the news only to find my sister-in-law had beaten me to it. It's so annoying when that happens – there is a lot to be said for spreading the news yourself, otherwise it's a big let down when you make your grand announcement.

*Hopeful*

**Both times I only told people** once I'd had the dating scan. I think keeping it a secret during the sicky/tired stage actually helped me to cope with those symptoms. Both times I ate lots of Hula Hoops though, so anyone observant enough would have clicked. I've just told a very dear friend who's had all sorts of complicated miscarriages over the years, has one daughter but would dearly love another one. She was the hardest person to tell – I can't help but feel guilty because I'm pregnant and she's not.

*Bundle*

**I always told as late as possible.** When I had my first two you couldn't get home pregnancy tests, so you waited until you'd missed two periods before you could even be sure yourself! It just isn't something I want to share with all and sundry – I prefer to mull over it for a bit. It did mean that no one except my husband knew when I had a miscarriage but I preferred to keep that to myself as well. It's horses for courses, really.

I think the worst 'telling' I had to do was informing my 21-year-old son that I was pregnant. He reacted as I expected – not a happy bunny.

*Baabaa*

**I told my parents and my hairdresser** (only because she asked: 'Any kids on the way yet?' and caught me off-guard). I also told a girl who was pregnant too, because I wanted her opinion on something. Other than that, we waited until I had had the scan. We also made my parents keep quiet until we gave them the all-clear. I was terrified of miscarrying and was worried about jinxing myself by telling too many people. I am really bad about keeping secrets, so the strain was enormous!

*Chinchilla*

**I felt really awkward about telling** and didn't until about 16 weeks. First, I didn't know myself until 10 weeks; also I was a bit embarrassed about the whole thing – I'd always been adamant that I never wanted children, so I felt a bit foolish having to admit that I'd changed my mind, especially as everyone said I always would. And at 42, I also felt a bit past it. I left it to my husband to tell most people and particularly dreaded telling my mum. In the end I blurted it out over the phone as she was pontificating about someone else she knew who was having a baby at well over 40 and calling her a fool. Mum was over the moon!

*Lindy*

**We told people as soon as we knew** ourselves. My mother had died two weeks before I found out and I knew that if anything went wrong with the pregnancy I was going to need support big time. Several people guessed anyway because I went to a Christmas party and was still sober at the end of it...

*Sobernow*

**We'd decided to go public,** but I still got irrationally upset if my husband told family and mutual friends that I was pregnant. I remember seething in the background whilst I heard him telling one of my close friends I was eight weeks. I knew the news would result in questions about my morning sickness and what sex we hoped for, etc. As soon as people know you are pregnant, in my experience all sorts of things become public property. I feel that it's my body, so my news.

In the first trimester we agreed to tell on a 'need to know' basis, plus close family. The very first time I was pregnant, age 34, I had a miscarriage at 10 weeks. We told lots of people I was pregnant and the news was greeted with great surprise – most people had assumed I didn't want children. Therefore news spread fast.

I was still coming to terms with the idea of motherhood (and quietly panicking) when I lost the baby. I then had mixed feelings about the miscarriage, especially since it was an early one. I felt very confused and this was not helped by the fact that total strangers, people who knew my husband or a friend of mine, came up to tell me how sorry they were that I had lost my baby. I felt like a rabbit frozen in front of a car's headlights and didn't know what to say or do. So I'd say tell few people until after the first trimester, and if possible, tell them yourself.

*Frank1*

**I had a rule of thumb** that if I was happy to tell people IN PERSON that I'd miscarried, then I could tell them I was pregnant. This included most of my workmates. As it happens I was sick about five times a day from nine weeks, so it wouldn't have been much of a secret really.

I didn't mind my partner telling people, especially his family. His mum cried when he told her – that was a beautiful moment between the two of them.

*Philippat*

**Both my previous and my current** pregnancies have been miracles and each time I was told not to get too excited, but I felt that if anything did go wrong I would need people's support anyway. Pregnancy can be such a wonderful experience and it only lasts nine months so enjoy it as soon as you can and don't worry too much about something that may never happen. I was five weeks when I told my family and telling your family usually means the world and his dog will know within days anyway.

*Nona*

**What the experts say**
If you don't tell your closest friends that you are pregnant, how else do you explain why you no longer have the energy to lift your gym bag, let alone take a 90 minute aerobics class?

Vicki Iovine (*The Best Friends' Guide to Pregnancy*)

**We arranged to go out** for a meal with both sets of parents plus siblings and partners at seven weeks and my husband told them there. I would have waited longer but it was summer and with holidays and things it would have been a long time before we could see them again. That was Friday evening and we asked them to keep it to themselves for the rest of the weekend so that we could visit the grandparents and let them know next.

My mother-in-law immediately blabbed to her neighbours, which wound us both up but it didn't really matter. After that weekend pretty much everyone knew except the people at work. I don't really socialize with work colleagues so there was no chance of them finding out by accident. I told my boss at three months and then let it filter through the rest of the office. I think in future I might wait a bit longer because I quite enjoyed having a secret that just my partner and I knew about. And it also means fewer weeks of the inevitable sex and name questions.

I do think that sometimes people can be a bit insensitive and 'pinch' your news. That's partly why we made the decision to tell the close family first and to let everyone know immediately afterwards rather than to let the news leak out.

*Bozza*

**We told our parents at eight weeks** but swore them to secrecy – they kept to it and we were surprised when we saw other relatives at eight months and they didn't know. We didn't expect our parents to keep the secret after 12 weeks – but clearly we weren't explicit enough!

*Scatterbrain*

**I told my parents straight away**, as I hate keeping secrets from them but didn't tell anyone else to start with. However, by 10 weeks most of my family had guessed – mainly because I was not drinking or smoking and was eating food like it was going out of fashion. Most people at work guessed because I kept running out to throw up!

*Ghosty*

**When I got pregnant the first time** I wanted to tell everyone, and practically did. But unfortunately I did miscarry and on top of all the personal pain and agony I was going through I was worried about telling everyone what had happened and facing them feeling sorry for me. I was glad though that I had told my parents because they were very supportive. This time round I waited until about 16 weeks, until I had had my dating scan and a few check-ups before telling anyone.

*Pjay*

**As I've only conceived with IVF** treatment, it makes keeping things a secret a bit more difficult. First time round was easy: we started telling people once we had had two scans showing a heartbeat (at six and eight weeks). This time it was more difficult: my mother-in-law looked after my son whilst I was in hospital for egg retrieval and my mother looked after him for a few days later during embryo transfer – so no chance of any secrets.

I also had various friends looking after my son for the numerous appointments in the run-up. Confusingly when we tested, the result was negative, and as the phone started ringing immediately we let people know. A week later when I realized that I still hadn't had my period, I tested again to find that it was positive. When we saw the heartbeat a week later we started putting the record straight.

*MiriamW*

**We weren't going to tell anyone** until 12 weeks, but the fact that I wasn't drinking was a bit of a giveaway. I had a threatened miscarriage at six weeks, so had to go in for an early scan. I rang my husband excitedly to tell him it was all clear, and he came home shamefaced that evening and admitted to telling everyone at work because he had been caught dancing around with the telephone still in his hand.

*Slug*

**I think it is superstitious** not to tell – it's not like the *telling* will cause a problem. If anything, not telling would have stressed me out more. As it turned out I couldn't help myself and told family first and close workmates at about eight weeks, as well as my boss. I had severe morning sickness more or less straight after that, which meant weeks off work and time in hospital on a drip, so then everyone knew. The passing of the first trimester seems to be like some magic 'sign' or something, but really I think it's better to assume all is well from the start, be positive and go from there.

*Mollipops*

**Someone I work with announced** that she was off for a pregnancy test at lunchtime! I admit that with my last pregnancy I only waited until eight weeks and then had to tell as my stomach muscles had given up and I looked six months but I think telling people even before you take the test takes away some of the *je ne sais quoi*.

*Lilibet*

## Maternity leave – when should you take it and how long should you take?

**I'm 35 weeks** and in theory have this week and the next before I start maternity leave. I have a 20-month-old son who isn't sleeping well and I'm so exhausted I can't concentrate on anything – I just want to sleep. Being at home wouldn't be a breeze with a 20-month-old but I think it might be easier than pretending to do some work! I'm useless and really want to go earlier than I said I would.

*Niceglasses*

**I stopped working at 36 weeks** but was lucky to enjoy very good health and not much tiredness in the later stages of pregnancy – a lot depends on how you feel. I found the full month at home before my son was born really enjoyable (lying on a creaking sofa watching Wimbledon, mainly).

*Clare2*

**I stopped at 35 weeks** – I commuted to work, which was a good reason for stopping but actually I think it was too early. I got quite bored sitting around at home 'waiting'. On the other hand, I did appreciate having that time to get things ready.

*Katmam*

**I finished two weeks before my due date.** I was working full time and commuting 20-odd miles but I found doing nothing was a bit tedious. I think it's a good idea to wind down slowly. For example, to go half-time at about 34 weeks for four weeks and count this as two weeks' leave.

*Bozza*

**I stopped at 37 1/2 weeks** as I didn't want to go right up to the line – I have a fairly long commute and didn't fancy having to get home in a hurry if anything happened unexpectedly. I felt that was early enough, as I only had 18 weeks off in total and in fact I found two weeks of just waiting for something to happen, without work to take my mind off it, was quite long enough.

*GillW*

**Mumsnet fact**
Eighty-five per cent of pregnant women wish they could quit their job earlier and return later. *Junior* magazine

**I stopped at 38 weeks** and my son arrived two days after. The thing I was most gutted about was that I had planned to finish knitting a patchwork cot blanket. It never did get finished. I was glad to have more time with him after the birth though. I took almost nine months' maternity leave and I felt it was just right. I was ready to go back to work by then.

*Bobbins*

**People have no idea what's in store** when they have their first baby. I was set to go on maternity leave at 38 weeks but ended up having to leave work (bed rest) at 34 weeks, was in hospital at 35 weeks and was induced at 361/2 weeks. So I ended up having a baby 11/2 weeks before I was due to go on maternity leave.

I went back to full-time work when the baby was three months old. This was not nearly enough time off for me, but due to financial constraints I had to go back.

*Chelle*

**I think the newborn stage flies by** and has gone just as one is getting to grips with it. I always advise pregnant friends to wallow in the early days because it is never the same again. I do think that physically and emotionally you need time to adjust to be able to enjoy your baby. You probably won't know yourself how long you'll need until after the baby has been born and your life has settled down a bit. (Does it ever?) Whatever you do, make the decision that is right for you.

I went on maternity leave at the first opportunity because I was having so many problems with colleagues and my pregnancy, but I was not desperate to return to work (although we needed the money) at the point my paid maternity leave ran out. However, within a couple of months I was climbing the walls and started looking for employment. Some friends who'd planned to return to work after their babies were born found it an enormous struggle and one in particular returned to work only to throw it all in a few weeks later because she hadn't been ready for it. Others thought they'd want to stay at home but quickly found they weren't cut out for it. It depends on the individual and it's not always as you'd expect.

*Winnie*

**For my first baby** I went to great pains to stress to my employer that having a baby would interfere as little as possible with my job. After six weeks off I made myself available via a networked PC. Looking back I was mad to bother as it was all fairly pointless and caused me a lot of stress and upset.

I returned after 14 weeks and I felt it wasn't enough. My baby was born two weeks late and I found it quite traumatic leaving him at 12 weeks. It was made worse by the fact that he was not yet sleeping well at that stage. Also, as I wanted him to be solely breastfed until six months, I had to use a breast pump extensively at work, which was not fun.

Inevitably, if you are a valued employee, people will forget quite quickly how long you had off and I think it's better to have a longer break and return at a time when you can focus on your job properly and be happy with your decision to leave your baby during the day. Next time I will definitely take six months.

*Ringer*

**I had six months off and that was just right,** as I was getting a bit bored with the monotony of the house by then and my son was ready to socialize! But at 16 weeks, he was not sleeping through and I would have missed him too much had I gone back then.

*Lil*

**It takes time to recover physically** and emotionally from a birth. And if you choose to breastfeed, it takes time to get this established. So, just from the mother's point of view, going back to work too soon is not desirable.

Even if you do struggle in to work, still sore and befuddled from lack of sleep, what sort of professional image are you going to put across? Isn't it better to wait until you can hit the ground running?

*Frank1*

---

**What the experts say**
I worry when mums return to full-time work in those early months after birth. I do not believe any newly delivered mother is physically fit for this.

Dr Christopher Green (*Babies!*)

It takes about nine months for your metabolism to return to normal after a pregnancy.

Dr Miriam Stoppard (*New Pregnancy and Birth Book*)

---

**I took my full 16 weeks** with my first son (having worked up to my due date) and six months with my second. The first time round I thought I would breeze back to work and was really taken by surprise at how hard it was – lots of doubts and howling. Second time around I thought going back would be easier because he was older and we still had the same nanny. But I was totally floored again!

*Lara*

**I only had 14 weeks maternity leave,** which I had to start early as a result of illness. It was a shock, therefore, when they changed my baby's due date at the last moment but if he hadn't been born early I would have had to have left him at six and a half weeks. As it was, I had to leave him at nine weeks, which was hard. Fortunately, they had tissues and sympathy all ready at work. I am now expecting my second; I'll miss out on the full entitlement I think by one week so I am thinking about leaving and then finding another job. Though I love where I work, I know I need more time with my baby.

*Peachey*

**I think it is very difficult to make definitive plans** with your first baby as you simply do not know what the birth will be like and how you will react to motherhood.

I know we all have to make our own choices but it seems such a shame to pressure yourself to go back to work early if you don't need to.

*Molly1*

**After my first son I had to go back to work** as soon as my paid maternity leave stopped so he was about four and a half months. I wasn't happy about this but we couldn't afford to live on one wage. I gave up work altogether after having my second.

Some people need to work for their own sense of self worth and sanity. I've heard of people craving to get back to work within a few weeks of the birth. Others, like me, are happy to stay at home and find other things to do.

Whatever you decide, it must be your choice but don't feel guilty if you do decide to go back sooner rather than later because you will probably be happier in yourself and more able to be a happy caring mother to your baby. Bear in mind that babies often become more clingy at around seven months – leaving them with someone else at this stage would be much more difficult.

*PamT*

**I went back to work four days a week** when my daughter was four and a half months old and although ideally I would have preferred only three days, I felt good going back. Whether or not you're ready will depend a lot on how well your baby is sleeping by then. I was lucky and my daughter was just starting to sleep through the night by the time I went back.

*Rkayne*

**My son is now six months old** and while I have days where I feel I would enjoy being at work, most of the time the idea of going back and leaving him is hard. I know that my employers would not welcome me going part-time, so that would mean my son would be in childcare for long hours as I have to be in by eight and the journey takes an hour. I also know that the job would bring lots of stress as we are over-worked and under-staffed and have to work at home each night. I can't see how I could do all that, then come home, do all the housework and look after my son and still be up and ready and out the door to work on time in the morning.

*Carrieboo*

**Mumsnet tip**
You don't know how you will feel about maternity leave until after you've had your baby and been at home for a few months so try to delay the decision if at all possible.

**I went back to work full time** when my daughter was four months as I was not entitled to any more time off. I found the hours and pressure very difficult to deal with on the amount of sleep I was getting. My daughter would wake at 5.30 am, which meant that once I had fed her and put her back to sleep it was not worth my while going back to bed. I seemed to spend all day at work and all evening preparing for the next day. What's more, because I went back to work early, I did not get the chance to meet other mothers and form friendships.

*Minks*

**Those first months are the toughest time** – not only establishing feeding and sleeping 'routines' but just adapting to the whole change in identity. It affects everyone differently. It's important I think not to 'judge' your experience of motherhood by those early months, as things change so quickly after that and soon it is not only about feeds, naps and nappy changing, but about smiles, laughs, sitting up, playing and before you know it they are crawling, talking and walking.

If you are lucky enough to have options, don't feel pressured to go back and don't hurry back too soon; return when you think you are ready and only for as many hours as you want to.

*Mollipops*

## Antenatal classes – which ones and are they worth it?

**The best thing about antenatal classes** are the friends you make – they are invaluable for sharing information and good/bad times with post-birth. I couldn't get on to the local NCT classes – I would have had to book it as soon as conception took place to get a place. All the other mums at my GP's classes were local, which was handy for coffee and restorative spritzers. I didn't actually learn any more from these classes than I did through the internet or from books but I felt a lot less isolated.

*Bettys*

**I went to hospital classes the first time** round and also for refresher classes with my second. The most valuable part was the tour of the hospital delivery suite and meeting other mums-to-be. It is nice to hear the midwives' stories rather than just reading the facts in a book, so they are worth going to even if you don't actually learn anything new. I didn't really feel prepared for the births, though, as I wasn't really taught enough about breathing and I didn't have a clue what to do with the baby once I got it home but you manage somehow.

*PamT*

**I went to GP and NCT** classes as I like to know as much as possible about everything in advance (perhaps I should have gone before the conception!). My top tip is to be proactive about suggesting meeting up with the other mums for coffee before or after the classes, or even for exercise classes. The help and friendship of the people I met was worth far more than anything the midwives told me.

*Berries*

**I went to the NCT** classes having tried the GP ones, which seemed a bit basic – I'd read it all in books by then. The NCT classes were more informal with people talking about their fears and emotions. It was a natural progression from this to the coffee mornings and I'm still in touch with some of the mothers now.

*Katherine*

**Mumsnet tip**
Sign up for antenatal classes early. I left it too late and only got a last-minute place because someone moved out of the area. I don't know how I would have coped without the support of the other mums I met there.

*Holly*

**I went to NCT classes** when expecting my fourth, more to meet people than learn anything. But actually I found the classes were incredibly informative and helped me to have a very positive experience, which I'm pretty sure I wouldn't have had if I'd just attended NHS classes. I went to those as well, but they were very basic and the midwife so obviously wished she was elsewhere.

*Baabaa*

**I heartily recommend NCT classes** to all parents-to-be but I do think the NCT pushes a particular philosophy. Yes, the facts were presented about what can happen during labour but certain options were definitely 'favoured', i.e. the more 'natural' the better. I topped up my knowledge myself, which I'm glad about because I ended up having an emergency c-section, which was only covered briefly.

I thought we did a bit too much grunting, which I never understood – I don't think anyone needed lessons in making a noise. However, I'm still in touch with the antenatal group two years on. I think it's a shame when people are disappointed by their births. One couple I know felt very down after their experience – lots of intervention in hospital following the failure to progress at the midwife-led centre – but they have a lovely baby boy. I try to remember I had a baby, not a birth.

*Bundle*

**The NCT isn't everyone's cup of tea.** It can be a bit 'middle-class' for some. I tried to go to NCT classes but left it ridiculously late to book and they were full up. So I just did NHS ones and did a separate tour of the hospital. The hospital tour was useful, as were most of the classes, but the midwife who ran them just kept saying in a soothing Irish accent, 'Ach don't worry about it, you'll be fine, dear' – actually, I wasn't fine but that's another story.

My antenatal group didn't really meet up much but I did a postnatal course and exercise class and still meet up every week with my group four years on. The children are all the best of friends too and we have second children of similar ages.

I'd say do *something* to meet people in your area, whether it be antenatal, postnatal, exercise, aqua-natal or yoga classes. It's good to know that you're not the only one who can't get out of the house before 11 am. Remember pregnancy doesn't end with giving birth – what happens afterwards is far more important.

*Titchy*

**My NCT class was invaluable** as I gained four really good friends from it. We're still meeting up and our babies were born in 1999. How useful the actual class is depends on the teacher. The two NCT teachers I've had (first time and then refresher classes) were both down to earth but I have heard the 'knit your own placenta' comments from close friends who did their classes at different branches.

In our classes we covered all forms of pain relief from breathing to epidurals and saw rather more of the 'intervention' equipment than we'd have liked! C-sections were briefly discussed but I think you have to accept that not everything can be covered in short classes, which need to be geared to everyone's needs and wishes.

*SoupDragon*

**The good thing about ante-natal** classes is that partners can go too. Yes, I knew everything (near enough) from reading and surfing the Net but my husband was not so well-informed and rather than me lecturing him, he came to classes and learned from an outside source.

*Bozza*

**I went to NHS classes** and felt I learned very little. Partners were expected to attend and my husband loathed them; because of his work he was genuinely only able to attend a couple, one being the hospital visit which was good but the image of him sitting in a community centre doing 'quizzes' on 'how you know when you are in labour' will last for ever! I would have preferred 'women only' classes. Ours were very much oriented towards 'natural' birth and the midwives were very disappointed when seven out of 10 of us had to have caesareans.

*Lindy*

**My NCT classes were definitely more useful** and informative than the NHS ones – but so they should be at nearly a hundred quid. I think the focus of the NCT classes depends on what the group wants to discuss and when it's your first baby you are obsessed with labour and how you'll get through the pain. Somehow, you don't seem to dwell too much on what you'll do once the baby actually arrives. It was only afterwards that I thought, 'Why didn't we talk a bit more about the first few weeks POST birth?' There was also a whole session devoted to breastfeeding. In my NHS class the midwife had to rush through this bit because of time and so we covered breastfeeding in about five minutes. Thanks to the NCT class I knew a bit more about what to do when I got mastitis – boy, am I glad I did!

*Catt*

**I had a fantastic NCT teacher** who coached us through every aspect of labour and birth and I went on to have my first child at home in water. For me meeting people was secondary to getting the right, unbiased information on pregnancy and birth.

*Rozzy*

**I was quite disappointed** by the antenatal classes I went to. They were at the hospital and they did not include a tour of the facilities. I found them quite scary. I was not given the information on how to arrange a water birth by either the classes or my midwives, so I missed out. There were no reunions or postnatal groups at all in my area. In fact there was nothing at all for new mums to do and I ended up quite lonely.

*Juliet*

**My baby-life would have been very different** if it wasn't for the NCT. I remember going to the classes and hating the first one and thought I had nothing in common with the five others but stuck at it, and all these years later, two of the mums are two of my best friends. Days with baby number one would have been so different without it. The three of us and babies discovered the world of motherhood together; I would have been so lonely if I hadn't gone.

*Maisy1*

**Every cliché was lived out** during my course of NCT antenatal classes. My teacher was totally negative about any form of pain relief during labour (except gas and air, if we were really desperate), instead advising us all to inhale lavender oil and try to get through most of it with 'pelvic rocking'. Whilst careful to go through all the alternatives, natural and managed, she made absolutely no attempt to hide her (very strong) viewpoints.

At our get-together after all the births, she was horrified to discover that I was expressing milk to feed to my baby in a bottle rather than breastfeeding because I absolutely didn't like the feeling of breastfeeding and it just wasn't for me. I was made to feel like a leper, an 'unnatural mother'. It finished her off altogether to discover that I had tried almost every form of pain relief going, had asked for an epidural and had furthermore agreed readily to the use of forceps and to an episiotomy. I think the moral of my story is join another group if you are uncomfortable.

*Heidi*

**I'm with all those people** who have found the NCT a useful introduction agency. I have to say that I thought the actual 'teaching' bit of it was fairly useless. Being bent over the teacher's kitchen units breathing through pretend contractions simply does not prepare you for labour! In fact it is slightly misleading because you think that you are prepared because you have been to these classes and you are not.

I thought the hospital antenatal classes were much better from that perspective. However, I have made some really great 'local' friends through the NCT who I would probably never have found otherwise. Through my local doctor's surgery I was asked to join another 'new mum' group and it was horrendous. So, it really is luck whether you find these things a help or hindrance.

*Molly1*

## Other people's reactions – what did you have to deal with?

**Why is it that when you are pregnant**, people take it as a free-for-all to make comments about your weight, clothes and any other area they care to think of? One of my managers said to me the other day that she hadn't realized how pregnant I was until she saw me 'waddling' across the car park.

At a work Christmas party one of the directors of the company said to me: 'Of course, you're hoping for a boy, aren't you?' With hindsight I should have said: 'Not if it turns out to be a chauvinist pig like you!' But naturally I only thought that up afterwards.

I also hate: 'You're so huge, are you sure there's only one in there?', particularly as I don't think I'm huge and my GP doesn't think so either. It was very interesting this morning that although to friends and colleagues my bump is HUGE, it is invisible to strangers, particularly those who have seats on the tube in rush hour.

*Pamela1*

**What annoyed me most** were the constant dire warnings from other parents about forthcoming sleepless nights and how horrendously miserable everything was going to be. Then came the ghoulish satisfaction with which each approaching milestone would be treated – wait till he starts crawling/walking whatever, then life will be much more difficult.

---

### What the experts say
When people react to your pregnancy, it's not about you, it's about them. If they say negative or rude things, it comes from their own experience or their own personality, their own fears or their own problems with body image, babies, their mother, whatever.

Kaz Cooke (*The Rough Guide to Pregnancy and Birth*)

---

People can be incredibly insensitive. I got quite upset with the constant remarks about how 'small' my bump was. This made me very worried that our baby would be underweight (he weighed 8 lb). The nadir for me, though, came on day three after the birth during an ill-fated expedition to Sainsbury's. The first woman who stopped me to admire our newborn told me to look after him as she had 'lost three of her own', the second woman told me, 'enjoy it as it's all downhill from here' and the third, wait for it, informed me that I shouldn't be out and about with him so young as she had done the same and as a result became paralyzed from the waist down for three weeks. Not surprisingly I had a good cry by the bakery counter before completing my shop.

*Croppy*

**It is a few years** since I was pregnant but the thing I hated most was when people patted my stomach like they had every right to touch me.

*Morag*

**It's when people you only know** on an acquaintance basis (such as work colleagues) start asking if you plan to breastfeed and for how long that you really wonder where the comments will stop. Every person you meet has some kind of opinion on the whole aspect of childbirth, childrearing etc. I just used to smile in a vacant kind of way and say, 'I'm sure you must be right, I'll suggest that to my midwife,' and that usually shuts them up.

*Molly1*

**Elderly ladies were always coming up to me** in supermarket queues when pregnant with my first and informing me that life would never be the same. Drove me completely nuts. One of the advantages of having one already must be that total strangers leave you alone more.

*Frances*

**I used to hate it when people would comment** on the effect my hormones were obviously having on my hair/skin etc. One day my patience at work ran out, and when someone commented on how bad my facial eczema had become since I'd been pregnant. I replied, 'Yes, I think people must be coming down with problems in sympathy, because your mouth hasn't half got big as well.' Felt a bit mean, but strangely better!

The worst comment was from someone with two children who really should have known better. She asked if I knew if I was having a boy or girl (I didn't), then said, 'I wouldn't be surprised if it's a little girl in there, because with girls you often tend to carry a lot behind.' She may as well have said: 'Strewth your backside's got big.' My husband's non-married friends used to pat my tummy, so I used to pat theirs back. They stopped then.

*Pootle*

**It was afterwards that I got annoyed** – when everyone started asking you how long it took to get back in your pre-pregnancy clothes.

My eldest sister went out a few days after the birth of her son. A shopkeeper commented, 'So you've not had it yet then?' She wouldn't have minded, but she was pushing a pram at the time!

The other classic comment immediately after birth was, 'So, when are you going to have another one?' Right, yeah, I've just endured nine months of pregnancy, hours of labour and stitches, I don't want to see a *penis* again for a good long while, let alone have another baby!

*Emmam*

**I couldn't believe the midwife** talking about contraception just when my bum hurt more than I ever thought possible, going for a wee took an hour of positive talking to myself and I'd had no sleep. After my third I just laughed and said, 'don't you think three under fives will sort that for me?'

And how do people know when they tell you it's a boy/girl because you're all out front/out sides? I was exactly the same shape with my 7 lb 7 oz boy and 6 lb 15 oz girl and then much smaller with my 7 lb 15 oz girl.

I also got really fed up with people, seeing me with my two and my bump, telling me, 'You're going to have your hands full.' What did they think I was doing all day with two? As for patting tummies, please arrest me if I ever do it someone...

*Emmy*

**I would have gone bananas** if anyone had had the nerve to pat my stomach. The last time I was pregnant a guy who was a total stranger said, 'What have you got hidden in there then?' Why can't people behave themselves?

My standard answer to 'are you hoping for a boy or a girl?' was 'actually, I'll just be happy if it's a baby'.

*Javarose*

**One good piece of advice from my mum** was not to listen to other peoples' birth stories as every birth is different. I wish people would be careful about sharing their sad stories as I felt compelled to listen to them and on occasion it really upset me.

My funniest pregnancy moment was when the supermarket cashier commented on my huge size. She wished she hadn't when I informed her that I only had two days to go and felt fit to pop. Her face was a picture and she put the goods through pretty quickly. One of the rudest questions asked of me was 'WAS IT PLANNED?'

*Kate71*

**Despite choosing to have my two** close together (17 months gap) everyone assumes the second is a mistake. And everybody from strangers on the bus to family members said constantly, 'Oh, so close together. You're going to have your work cut out for you.' Not particularly helpful or reassuring. Do these people just not think, or are they deliberately trying to infect the world with their Dr Doom philosophies?

*Allschwil*

**Mumsnet tip**

As a mum of six, I've made a special delivery half a dozen times and every one has been totally different. No one can guess what it will be like for anyone else so don't listen, prepare well and try and enjoy it!

*Jackiann*

**People do feel they can ask** the most personal things when you're pregnant, but on the positive side don't you agree that most people make you feel really special? Whatever's going on in a room, a pregnant woman seems to be a focus of attention and curiosity and that's great if you're a bit of a show off. I particularly loved answering single, childless, women's curious questions. I made sure my answers were really gross and off-putting – I just loved seeing their faces turn a funny shade of green.

*Catt*

**The worst moment I had** was when my sister-in-law's boyfriend stood behind me and reached round to cuddle my bump. Far too intimate. I jumped a mile.

*Hmonty*

**I resented being asked if it was twins** – I had the most colossal bump. When he went transverse it seems he placed his hands and feet on my spine and braced himself (that's how he was found by the surgeon!)

*Clare*

**I had problems at the three to four month stage** when it was a toss up as to whether I was fat or pregnant and nobody dared say anything. It was a positive relief to have someone ask if there were two in there.

Although I was extremely ill through both my pregnancies, I still loved the way people seemed to think they have to 'look after' you when you have a huge bump. Working in a profession with lots of blokes and being expected to lug around large amounts of heavy kit all day, as well as frequently crawling around under desks etc, it made a lovely change. And at least if people comment about you looking huge it must mean that you look slimmer when you aren't pregnant.

*Scooby2*

**Today, at work, a colleague** of mine said, 'You seem a lot shorter than you used to, it must be all that extra weight you are carrying around.' Bloody great, I thought I was doing quite well. I've still got two months to go, so I'll probably be looking like a midget by the time I go on maternity leave. Incidentally, I am 5ft 7, so not exactly short.

And then there are the pregnancy police. I was even warned about getting my hair coloured in case the bleach managed to get into my blood supply.

*Joz*

**When I was 42 weeks pregnant** I was at Tesco's and the very friendly checkout woman was attempting to have the 'When is it due? Oh careful I'm not delivering it, hahaha' conversation with me. But as I could hardly stand up and had not slept in weeks, I was not in a good mood. By the time she got to, 'Is it a girl?' I could take no more and snapped, 'I don't care if it's a rat, I just want it out!' There comes a point when you can take no more 'ahhing' as in 'ahh you're pregnant', 'ahh, how you're glowing'. I always wanted to say, 'Yes and so are my piles.'

*Snowy*


**I am 30 weeks pregnant** and am beginning to dislike going to work because every day this week someone I don't know very well has rubbed my pregnant tummy and I HATE it. My tummy seems to be a free-for-all zone! I don't mind if friends who know me well ask if they can feel the bump but I really don't like acquaintances just reaching out to touch it. It kind of gives me the creeps.

*Jasper*


**Maybe a quick, 'Excuse me,** what are you doing?' as they reach out? They wouldn't feel your boobs, would they? Or maybe that'll be next.

*Baabaa*


**I've only had people I know** touch my bump. I think it would annoy me if it were someone I didn't know very well. I mean your body is your body, bump included.

As for remarks, people seem to be obsessed with saying you are big or small. Why do they feel the need to say anything at all? I've had a huge variety of comments from being small (usually other pregnant women) to 'oh, so you can't have far to go then?' from someone who was young, childless and obviously stupid – I was only 25 weeks. I prefer it when people just ask how I am feeling.

*Eulalia*


**I don't mind at all having good friends** try to feel the baby. Some of my single male friends were really chuffed when I asked them if they'd like to feel – I think it's just totally out of their league and they were really interested but obviously would not have a chance normally. Two of them were just thrilled – quite emotional really – when they felt the baby move. But definitely invitation only!

*Amber1*


**The worst comment made to me** was just hours after I had given birth. I had been induced three times and on the third evening gave birth very quickly with no time for any pain relief. However, there were complications after the birth and I had to go down to theatre for surgery and ended up having an epidural after all. I finally arrived on the darkened ward at 2.30 am and was left with my baby in a bassinette next to the bed.

It was a terrifying night – I felt abandoned and couldn't feel my body from my neck down. When the baby cried I could only hang onto the side of her bassinette and hope a nurse was nearby and could hear her. I'd lost an awful lot of blood and was very weak and probably still dazed by it all.

By morning I still had very little feeling – I had not had a shower yet (or a pee). When a slim, young, healthy-looking teenager bounced over to my bed and said she was here to talk to me about exercises and asked if I had 'done my pelvic floor exercises yet?' and if I could 'get up on all fours' on the bed so she could 'run through the sheet', I was so dumbfounded, I just mumbled that I couldn't move yet.

*Spring*

**I well remember** the totally ludicrous questions asked of me mere hours after I'd finally managed to heave the little darlings out. 'Have you thought of contraception?' was always a favourite. I was never sure whether this was a comment on my child or a genuine concern!

*Lara*

## Maternity wear – when do you need it and are there any alternatives?

**Everyone shows pregnancy** in different ways and at different times anyway – I know people that didn't show for a good four months, but looked enormous at the end; and I'm one that showed pretty much straight away, but then just sort of stayed looking the same until there was about a month to go. It doesn't matter a jot what you wear, so long as you're comfortable.

*EmmaM*

**Being pregnant is uncomfortable** enough without adding to it with too tight clothes. I am normally quite thin and gained lots of weight very quickly in both my pregnancies, so both times I was in 'fat people' sweats (I was too cheap to buy maternity wear) by six to eight weeks. I couldn't wear even my baggiest clothes by 10 weeks. I'm 36 weeks now and finally broke down and bought a couple of pairs of maternity trousers a few months ago as I couldn't even fit the 'fattest' sweats.

*SofiaAmes*

**I didn't show so quickly** or have as big a bump second time round but couldn't wait to get into maternity clothes at around 12–14 weeks. I hated that tight feeling I was getting from my ordinary clothes – I just wanted to be comfy.

*Peanuts1*

**Mumsnet tip**
Haberdashers and stores like John Lewis sell 'button-hole' elastic. Use a strip (with a button sewn on one end) to extend skirts and trousers in the early part of pregnancy.

*Mo2*

**I started to show** with my second pregnancy earlier than with the first – second time around your stomach muscles don't have so much fight left in them. Wear whatever feels the most comfortable. My dark secret is that I had one maternity skirt that I never stopped wearing in between my two pregnancies.

*Azzie*

**It's well worth investing** in some comfy stretchy clothes early on. You have to face the fact that they're not just going to be useful for the next few months but probably for ages after the birth as well, so you will get your money's worth from them. Then you can either go for obvious maternity stuff or just invest in some stretchy larger sizes. I got some gorgeous dresses, which I've continued to wear ever since.

*Katherine*

> **Mumsnet fact**
> Seventy-eight per cent of women spend up to £300 on maternity wear, 15 per cent spend between £300 and £700 and 2 per cent spend over £700.
> *Blooming Marvellous*

**I recommend drawstring** or elasticated waists. I was happily wearing a pair of drawstring trousers I'd bought years previously right through to nine months.
*Philippat*

**I practically lived in sarongs** – very, very comfy indeed. You can buy nice silk ones that look good over black tights or maternity leggings in winter. I also invested in one nice black velvet skirt with an elasticated 'hipster-fit' waist in two sizes bigger than normal, and that with long tops lasted me through – sitting under my bump at the end. Plus I bought one pair of drawstring trousers, and they're still being worn.
*FrancesJ*

> **Mumsnet tip**
> Contact your local NCT branch to see if they sell maternity wear for a cheap way to expand the expanding wardrobe.
> *Ems*

**I bought jeans in a larger size** in stretch denim for the 'just fat' stage of pregnancy and the 'still fat' stage of motherhood. I also lived in some drawstring trousers. Hennes were great for cheap maternity stuff which looks different from the usual things on offer and aren't so large they make you look like a tank.
*SoupDragon*

**Shirts that have big splits** up from the bottom of the side seams are very useful. I have several from well before pregnancy life, which I've worn throughout both pregnancies and afterwards. They're particularly good for 'slimming down' during the 'just looking fat' stage at the beginning, and the 'still looking pregnant' stage after the event.
*Wmf*

**Menswear did the job for me.** You do need the cooperation of a larger husband/partner. I spent most of my time in my husband's jeans and fleeces. Luckily, as you can probably tell, I never had to look too respectable.
*Berta*

**I picked up a HUGE man's raincoat** from a charity shop and it did me the whole way through my pregnancy. It was lined, so nice and warm.
*Pamela1*

### What the experts say

Resist the temptation to swamp yourself in tent-like dresses or squeeze into things that are too small.

Dr Yehudi Gordon (*Birth and Beyond*)

It's a wonderful boost to your morale to invest in one or two really smart or glamorous outfits.

Dr Miriam Stoppard (*New Pregnancy and Birth Book*)

**I felt so over-heated** most of the time, I never really needed a 'full-time' coat, even in winter. If I went out I had a fantastic maternity fleece jumper, bright red, with a big scarf and loads of layers and that did the trick.

*Maisy*

**I bought a swing coat** from Nicole Farhi while I was pregnant with my first, in the days when I had a proper salary and still went to shops. It's a bit too stylish to fit in with my current jeans-wearing, buggy-pushing, grocery-toting persona, but I keep telling myself that one day soon I'll go back to wearing clothes I've selected for their look rather than their machine washability.

*Dannie*

**When I was pregnant** a few Christmases ago I foolishly stretched my usual coat around the expanding me (and I don't just mean the bump, sadly) and went supermarket shopping with my sister. We got followed by a security guard most of the way round – presumably he thought I'd shoved my Christmas turkey up my coat. Don't think he had the nerve to stop us though, as my sister was giving him daggers, and he was aged about 17.

*ChanelNo5*

# Pregnancy no-nos – what should you not do and what's realistic?

**It's difficult to keep up** with all the things you shouldn't do when you are pregnant. On my list I've got wearing underwired bras, visiting birthing sheep, using electric blankets, spraying garden pesticides and gardening without gloves.

*Grommit*

**I resisted having my hair highlighted** for the first four months of pregnancy. Some people say that you shouldn't have it done in the first trimester due to the strong chemicals. Apparently highlights are okay after that as the dye is not actually touching your scalp and can't be absorbed, unlike other hair dyes. I eventually had mine done and felt like a new woman.

*Jzee*

**I would avoid paint fumes**, especially during the first trimester. If you have to paint then I would make sure to open the windows.

*Oakmaiden*

---

**What the experts say**
Today's paints don't contain lead or mercury and therefore probably aren't dangerous. But because you don't know what hazard may turn up in paint next, it's a good idea to consider painting an inappropriate avocation for an expectant mother.

Murkoff, Eisenberg & Hathaway (*What to Expect When You're Expecting*)

---

**Heatstroke suffered by the mother could be harmful,** so be careful when sunbathing. Aerobic exercise is okay if you are doing it pre-pregnancy, you just have to watch for joint strain, dehydration, sunburn and fatigue. Don't change the cat litter (at least, not without gloves). Don't go near ewes about to drop their lambs. Avoid any reptile or bird that might carry salmonella. Say no to most insect repellents (they contain DEET or diethyl toulamide, which causes birth defects).

Also say no to many over-the-counter drugs. No to dental x-rays. No to working with lots of specific chemicals found in certain work places. No to painting with paints with high VOC (Volatile Organic Compound) levels.

I wouldn't worry about underwired bras during pregnancy. But they can pinch milk ducts post-partum and cause infections when breastfeeding. Also remember that pregnant women should avoid people with shingles, chickenpox or rubella, unless you know you're immune.

Having said all that, when I was pregnant, sometimes because I didn't know I was pregnant, I have got drunk, had a dental x-ray, applied DEET (because I didn't know DEET was diethyl toulamide) and worked with ionizing radiation. I never bothered with gloves in the garden because I grew up drinking raw cow's milk and chucking cat poop out of sandpits. If I haven't had toxoplasmosis before now, it's not possible for anybody to catch it.

I reckon you do your best to avoid things and hope for the best. Some things are important to avoid (like heatstroke), others are just preferable to avoid. But there's no point in stressing about it if you can't avoid it – my two children only have three heads between them!

*Zebra*

---

**What the experts say**
There are heaps of potentially harmful substances at home and in the work-place, and even in the food you eat. Read labels and avoid using toxins. Definitely avoid 'fumy' cleaning products, including oven-cleaners and dry-clean-ing solvents, most paints, lacquers, thinners, paint strippers, pesticides, herbi-cides, petrol, glue, many manufacturing chemicals and waste products.

Kaz Cooke (*The Rough Guide to Pregnancy and Birth*)

All of today's environmental risks combined (alcohol, tobacco and other drugs excepted) are far less of a danger to you and your baby than one untrained birth attendant was to your ancestresses.

Murkoff, Eisenberg & Hathaway (*What To Expect When You're Expecting*)

---

**It is estimated around 30 per cent** of the UK population have antibodies to toxo-plasmosis, whereas in France the figure is around 80 per cent. The main risks of catching it come from cat faeces and eating raw meat. If you've always eaten raw meat and always handled cat faeces, the chances are you have already had toxoplasmosis.

*SueW*

**You need to avoid Ibuprofen/Aspirin-type** drugs, which not only thin the blood but also can damage the baby's circulation. When a baby is born the blood has to stop flowing into the placenta and instead be rerouted to the lungs. Taking these drugs can prevent this from happening properly.

*Susanmt*

**When I was pregnant** I wasn't allowed on the water slide.

*Jac34*

**It's tough shaving your legs** when heavily pregnant – that's not to say I didn't give it a try.

*Flippa*

**I can't paint** my toenails.

*Angelmother*

**Ironing, cleaning, making dinner.** That's what I told my husband anyway!

*PandaBear*

**You can't bungee jump**...or stop peeing!

*Mum2toby*

**Sitting with your legs crossed** or even your ankles is really bad. And you should make sure you keep your knees together when you get out of bed or out of a car – it helps keep your pelvis in one piece. It's all too much in my opinion. Bloody men!

*Dahlia*

**But no one's forcing you** to avoid certain things, they are just informing you and leaving you to make your own decision. Personally, I'd much rather have the information. It's only nine months of your life, surely it's not going to kill you to avoid a few things? I think these days, in the western world, because maternal and infant mortality is low we tend to treat pregnancy much more like normal life than historically it ever was. A couple of centuries ago one in 10 women died in childbirth.

*Philippat*

**During my first two pregnancies** just about the only no-no was smoking. By the time I was expecting numbers three and four there were whole raft-loads of 'Things Pregnant Women Must Not Do'. I think this is one of those issues in which common sense is required. An occasional drink isn't going to harm a baby, the same as the occasional Paracetamol for a headache won't do any damage.

*Baabaa*

**I know we can't all live in a bubble** but in defence of those pregnancy books that have lists as long as your arm of what you shouldn't do (it was those books that got me so wound up about the possibility of cot death that I practically froze my daughter for her first six months of life), 30 years ago a lot more babies either died or were born with birth defects. I've found that a lot of people pooh-pooh my abstinences with comments about what they used to do in the past – well, figures show that they used to die. I think we happily forget how successful pregnancy is now. Okay, so now we have tons of rules for when we're pregnant but that's because science is moving forward and we are understanding more and more about the development of our bodies.

I'm probably a little too sensitive because I've had a miscarriage, which has left me feeling raw and frightened. I am therefore a lot more passionate during this pregnancy about doing my best. I miss alcohol like crazy because, frankly, I'm sick to death of mineral water but don't really like other soft drinks. But I think it would be nice to be supported rather than be seen as neurotic when all I'm doing is trying my best given current knowledge.

Oh and by the way, ironing is definitely out. The bump might get burnt, for goodness sake!

*Wills*

**You can only do what you think** is best for you and your baby. One person's anxiety levels may well be lower than another's simply because of their situation and experiences. In my case, becoming pregnant after IVF meant that I was willing to give up pretty much anything. Having said that, I did read that being anxious in itself is a problem, which seemed like such a no-win situation that I started having the odd glass of red as a relaxant.

*Eeek*

**I was able to give up smoking** straight away when I fell pregnant with no problems at all. I know the risk that smoking poses for MY body, but it is my body. When I am pregnant it ISN'T just MY body, it is someone else's as well, someone who doesn't have a choice about what I put in it.

*Ghosty*

**How you handle yourself in pregnancy** is just like the rest of life, a matter of balancing risks. But when you are pregnant the balance is slightly different, because most people would choose to take fewer risks when they are responsible for two lives instead of one. But you can only do as much as is realistic and get on with your life. Should you stop driving once you are pregnant because if you had a crash you'd kill yourself and the baby – and not just yourself? I'm all for being sensible in pregnancy but some people completely martyr themselves to it.

*Princesspeahead*

## Going it alone – what's it like being single and pregnant and what can make it easier?

**I faced pregnancy and birth alone** and did pretty much everything before the birth (antenatal classes, appointments) on my own because, being quite a proud madam, I'm not the sort to ask for help. But my mother moved in about a week before the due date and some friends were there for me at the birth. Just having to make all the decisions about everything, such as tests for Down's syndrome etc was the hardest part plus being asked at my antenatal appointments about family diseases and having no idea about 50 per cent of the family.

Other tough things were: braving it out at work when I knew I was the subject of gossip; completely panicking about money because I just didn't earn enough to pay for childcare (my mum helped financially) and just feeling very, very lonely throughout the whole pregnancy. And yet, I do feel immensely proud that I've done it and I have a tremendous sense of having achieved the best thing in the world on my own. I have much more confidence and know that should I ever be completely alone again with a child I would cope.

My best advice would be to accept any offers of help. People genuinely do care. Don't be proud, take all the loans of cots, high chairs etc. and accept bags of clothes. I hardly bought anything new. Also be sure to maintain contact with the adult world – I was lucky enough to have a job to give me adult contact, which I think is vital. It's not the end of the world to find yourself pregnant and alone, just a temporary blip. I would never have chosen this route but it's not been the disaster I (and my mother) anticipated.

*Tinker*

> **Mumsnet tip**
> Have support lined up early on in case the worst happens. I ended up in hospital having miscarried, but had told no one I was pregnant, so there was no one to phone work for me, no one to turn to for help and support etc.
>
> *Emily100*

**My pregnancy was unplanned** and my partner was initially pleased, but walked out on me when I was eight weeks pregnant, leaving me with a house that needed to be completely renovated. At the time I was devastated and very anxious about finances, especially as I hadn't been in my job long enough to be entitled to full maternity benefits. But just knowing that I was carrying another life inside me gave me the strength to get through it all.

In practical terms I worked lots of overtime to try and save some money so that I could still pay the mortgage when I was on maternity leave. I sacrificed a lot and my lifestyle completely changed, as my main concern was to have the money to tide me over until I went back to work. I don't feel I really enjoyed the pregnancy as much as I should because I was worried about coping, and also I suppose I was embarrassed to say that I was going to be a single mum. I managed to get the house decorated so that at least I had somewhere nice and cosy for the baby.

When labour started and I couldn't stand the contractions I called a friend who took me into hospital and my sister arrived later. When I went home the next day it was just me and my new baby – very daunting but I knew I just had to get on with it. I didn't tell the midwives that I was on my own as I thought that they might try to interfere so I used to make excuses as to where my partner was. I got told I was doing too much and that I should rest (tricky when you're on your own with a new baby). I tried breastfeeding but this just made me more tired and took up too much time, so I gave formula after a week.

I went back to work when my little boy was four months old and put him into a full-time nursery, which, I think, in a strange way helped. It gave me back some of my identity – I wasn't just a mum – even though it was really tiring at times. Also there is the social aspect of work (sometimes being at home all day and evening can get a bit lonely). I'd highly recommend making sure you go to post-natal groups, play groups etc. I met some great people there. Ideally I would have liked to work less hours but would never have been able to afford to do this. I was fortunate that I had lots of friends that I could talk to, although a lot of the time we only spoke on the phone, because by the time I'd picked my son up from nursery, fed him and put him to bed I was shattered.

Mostly though it's just very difficult having to make all the decisions on your own and having no one to discuss things with or to share the pressure or worries. You always have the fear that maybe you're not doing the right thing, but you can only do your best. My mum died 15 years ago so I don't even have her to call on, BUT my lovely son is now six and he makes life worthwhile.

*Matty*

> **Mumsnet fact**
> One in four families in the UK is now headed by a lone parent
> www.Gingerbread.org.uk

**I think that if you're a single parent** and have the money (unlikely I know!) then it would be worth buying in all the help you can get for immediately after the birth – a maternity nurse, doula or mother's help. In the longer term I think a good nanny is a huge boon to the single parent – much better than the average husband, in fact. Sadly, I don't have either and have to make do with a nursery but that's another story! The most important thing is the getting time for yourself any way you can. It's really hard for any mother but especially so for the single one.

*Sheila*

**I'm not a single parent** but because of my husband's work taking him overseas for the vast majority of our life, I have pretty much brought up our daughter single-handedly. From my experience I would say the hardest things are:

- You don't want to go to couples' ante-natal classes because you've reached the point where you are fed up of partnering the teacher.
- It's lonely being stuck in hospital for five days and watching everybody else's husband/partner coming in and helping out with the baby.
- There's no one to turn to in the middle of the night when the baby wakes and cries again and you still haven't dropped off to sleep from the last time.
- There's no advantage to bottle-feeding because there's no one else to give the bottles.
- You have times when you feel so utterly, utterly alone and everyone you meet assumes that you know how to look after this child you've just had.

On the up side:

- There's no one turning up at six o'clock expecting dinner on the table.
- You only have to do laundry for yourself and the baby.
- If you are breastfeeding and baby's having a feed-fest, you can just disappear to bed with baby and feed and rest.

*SueW*

> **Mumsnet fact**
> A study comparing both single and married women who had undergone donor insemination to get pregnant found no difference in the quality of parenting between solo and married mothers, or between the two groups of children in sleeping and eating difficulties.
> Family and Child Psychology Research Centre, City University, London

**I found out that I was pregnant** at five months and after telling the daddy was quickly presented with, 'Well, the only option is to have it adopted.' Hence I did the pregnancy thing on my own.

I stayed with my parents through the whole thing and they were very supportive, but not in a way I felt the dad could have been. I would have loved to have somebody to share all the newness with and to ask advice from someone who was new to the experience as well. Although my mother was always there to chat to, it was difficult as she always had 'the voice of experience' in her corner.

The hospital staff was very condescending to begin with. The obstetrician was the worst. When my dad came with me for the first scan, he assumed he was the child's father then went on to ask many questions, knowing that I couldn't answer them and making me feel awful. There was one fantastic midwife though who was a shoulder to cry on, a friend, a professional and who really encouraged me to feel good about doing it alone. Likewise, the health visitor is also great, even helping me to arrange returning to university.

I found the actual birth really strange. It was a bit of an ordeal (nearly three days' labour then an emergency Caesarean) and I felt overwhelmed with emotion that I wanted to share with the child's father – although in some ways I'm glad that he wasn't there. It sounds selfish but it was nice to have the experience of our child all to myself.

*Jo82*

**I went it alone.** I chose not to tell the father about the baby and therefore there has been no contact since conception. I have been fortunate in having my family around right from the start and I don't know how I would have coped without them. I'm a stay-at-home mum and at times have felt a bit isolated. Despite living in a town where there is a high percentage of teen/single parents, I know very few, and it's more difficult to relate to people who have their 'perfect family' set up.

I just wish people had been more supportive and trusted in my ability, whereas in reality everyone made me feel like I was completely crazy to be going ahead. I was lucky that despite their disapproval, my parents were really supportive and the support really kicked in when it was discovered at my 20-week scan that the baby had a cleft lip and palate. Suddenly everyone rallied round, and I suppose that was when I needed them most.

Hospital for me was absolute agony, both after the birth and once my son was in hospital for the operation. I found the attitude of the staff appalling, but perhaps that was more because of my age (I was 17) rather than the fact that I was single. They tried to do everything for me and assumed I wouldn't be all that interested in my baby.

Both my parents were at my son's birth. It wasn't planned that way, it just happened, and it was nice. They felt incredibly honoured to be able to witness the birth of their grandson.

I've found the parts of parenting books directed at single parents to be both patronizing and dismissive and they tend to give a really bleak view. It seems everyone assumes I shouldn't be happy. Apparently, I should be leaning on the shoulders of anyone I can find in the community by day and sobbing into my pillow by night. Well, excuse me, but there are certain advantages to being a single parent. It's hard work, but I have a family and whether or not people choose to accept that, I am happy and we are happy.

*Anais*

**I made the decision to have a baby** on my own when I realized that it would be quicker than waiting for the right man to come along. I had 30 attempts at getting pregnant with donor insemination resulting in three pregnancies though the first two ended in miscarriage. When I finally did get and stay pregnant I was lucky enough to get massive support from everyone. No one I met was negative. I was always up front about how I'd got pregnant so it was on my records and I didn't have to keep justifying it to everyone.

The pregnancy was great until the last month when my feet became so painful I couldn't walk. I'd had lots of offers of help for after the birth, but felt bad asking for help at this stage. In the end I did a deal with a pregnant friend. I did her ironing (sitting down) and she did my shopping.

When I finally gave birth they found I had eclampsia and I was given massive doses of Valium–type drugs, which left me unable really to take anything in. Breastfeeding was a nightmare and going home with a week-old baby was a real shock. My sister, who had also been my birth partner, had said she'd be there every day, but she meant for an hour or two whereas I think I needed help all the time. I spent almost all of the first six weeks in the chair feeding and dozing; I hardly made it to bed and my son only slept for 20-minute stretches. I made good use of the NCT breastfeeding counsellors and would call them day or night for help – invaluable when there's no one else around to offer support.

In an ideal world I'd suggest having a calendar of availability for friends for the first few weeks – with two people (if possible) for each day. They also need to be the sort of friends who won't mind if, on the day, you don't actually want them. Having too much pre-planned might mean you have people hanging around when you'd rather be alone, but if you can have a heap of people to call on in a flexible way, that's much better. Obviously you also need to be able to fend for yourself so a freezer full of ready meals is a good idea.

I'd done ante-natal classes at my local health centre and avoided the NCT groups, which seemed full of women swapping wedding day stories – we didn't have much in common. After the birth I started my own single mothers group – putting ads in the NCT newsletter and in my health centre. I would really recommend doing this if there isn't already one in your area. I made great friends that I could really relate to.

I also contacted www.dcnetwork.org, an organization set up for women trying to get pregnant by donor insemination (DI) or those who have had babies by DI. They organize support groups and eight years on we still all meet every month. Not only is this great for the mothers, but it lets the children know there are others who were conceived in the same way and gives them a forum to talk about any issues if they need to. Though, to be honest, they usually end up talking about TV!

*Emily100*

## Equipment – what you need and what you don't.

**Obviously I went out and blew a fortune** on baby things, deciding I needed everything and it all had to match. Pregnancy does something to your brain cells, I think! With hindsight you need something for the baby to wear, somewhere for them to sleep, something for them to travel in, some way of feeding them and something to 'play' with (more for the parents at first really). My 'must have' list includes:

- Pram, cot and car seat – don't skimp too much on these as they get a lot of use. If you can lay your hands on a second-hand cot, buy a new mattress.
- Baby sling – I loved mine but you could try to borrow one. You could also borrow a rocking seat. Ours lasted for ages – it can be used for weaning at six months and napping/playing in when they're small.
- Muslin squares – which protect your clothing, mop up a multitude of messes, act as emergency bibs, can be made into a sun hat, sun shade, comforter, etc.
- For bedding I went for a 'one on, one dirty, one clean' approach, so bought three of everything (fitted sheets, flat sheets and blankets).
- If you're breastfeeding you may want a pump, in which case you'll need most of the equipment for bottle feeding, such as a sterilizer, bottles and teats.
- Whether you need a baby monitor depends on the size of your house. In a small flat you can hear your baby from everywhere and may not need one in a house you may not be able to hear in some rooms. You can use an ordinary rucksack as a changing bag but make sure it's a large one.
- I wouldn't bother with a baby bath – they are a real pain to use. Borrow one or get a bath float.
- A Moses basket – borrow one if you can as you'll only use it for three months, if that, and then it will be in your loft.
- Avoid buying too many clothes – you may well get a lot as presents. Just invest in some vests and some sleepsuits.
- And the number one item: a Do-It-Yourself vasectomy kit.

*SoupDragon*

**In my opinion the only essentials** are a cot, a pushchair, a sling and a sterilizer, as even if you're breastfeeding it's good to be able to express and store milk and take a break. I found the baby bath useful but not essential and used the top of a fridge-freezer as a changing table.

The thing I wish I hadn't wasted money on was cot blankets – I should have just got a sleeping bag plus one or two cellular blankets. You don't need cot bumpers, nappy stackers, baby toiletries, baby towels and all that jazz. But, as with everything in life, if you have unlimited amounts of money, some of those things can be fun and occasionally even useful.

*Amber1*

**I wish I'd had a proper pram** for the first few months as I hated pushing my pushchair and not being able to see my precious baby and I wanted him lifted away from traffic fumes and cosily protected from draughts. However, you do need to swap to a pushchair for convenience and to let the baby sit up and see, so I wish I'd bought a cheap and not necessarily very trendy pram with a mattress. I also loved the baby gym and activity arch for the pushchair, which gave my baby something to look at when we were out.

I found a bouncy chair vital for putting him in whilst I had a shower and I liked the listening device. We also got a fantastic little cardboard black-and-white mobile. I put it over the changing table and my son loved it. It took his mind off wailing miserably through all his nappy changes and changed our life!

My advice is to bug all your friends with babies for stuff. Most of it is outgrown so quickly and you'll regret spending a fortune. My son hated his Moses basket – I wish I hadn't bothered and just gone straight for the cot. In fact, I wish I'd got a cot-bed, which would have lasted longer. And I have never used baby lotion or baby oil (what is that for, anyway?)

*Aloha*

**Mumsnet tip**
NCT sales are brilliant ways of buying second hand. Contact your local branch for details.

*Claire1*

**Buy a book/journal to write down all those 'firsts'** and special memories. I do Birthday Letters for my daughters in a book each. I just write about the previous year, how they've changed, trials and tribulations and the good bits. I'm going to give it to them when they're 18. It's a good 'grounder' for me when I'm struggling with them and think they're being their worst. I look back and see actually it has been harder and we got through the teeth, the tantrums, the clinginess, etc. so we'll get through the current thing.

This isn't the usual 'baby stuff' but if you are due in the winter you'll need a decent, waterproof coat with hood. It's impossible to hold a brolly and push a buggy for more than a few feet.

Non-essentials which are dead handy are a cordless phone and remote control for the TV, so you don't have to get up when feeding. Oh, and a partner who will see to your every whim!

*Batey*

**One of the best tips I was given** was to buy a five-year diary. Keep it to record all your child's achievements and so forth. You vow you will never forget, but it's amazing how quickly, as a busy mum, you do. And it's wonderful to look back on it later.

*Jenny2998*

**The best advice I was given** was not to buy fitted sheets for crib mattresses – cotton pillowcases will slip over most mattresses. We wish we hadn't bought a bottle/food warmer – it took too long and we ended up using jugs of boiling water after about a week. We also regretted a car seat that didn't fit on the pram chassis so we often woke a sleeping baby when moving him from the car to the pram.

If friends or relatives are likely to be buying you things, don't be afraid to say what you would like. We have so many soft toys and baby rattles and I wish we'd been given some 6–12 month clothing instead (everyone buys diddy newborn, or at least 0–3 month stuff and when you get to six months the drawers are bare!).

*MotherofOne*

**I still have four unopened bottles** of talc and four of baby lotion – I never ever used either of them. Borrow a Moses basket – I bought mine and am now doing sterling work lending it to friends for the six weeks or so it is needed. The microwave steam sterilizer is a marvellous thing whereas a bottle warmer is waste of money, as it takes too long.

*Zoe*

**What the experts say**
Preparation for the birth: have all the baby essentials in stock: cotton wool, baby oil, nappies, nappy and moisturizing creams, baby wipes, soft sponges, bath brush, bath oil and baby shampoo.

Gina Ford (*The New Contented Little Baby Book*)

**I'd recommend a sleeping bag.** From six months our son has gone to sleep cheerfully in beds all over the UK because he was in his familiar bag. As he's got older his folding booster seat has been invaluable – it's much better than his expensive, impossible highchair.

*Clare2*

**I'd say dummies** – goodness knows how I'll get rid of them but they've certainly helped me get some sleep. Intercoms are a great invention (and the soaps would lose half their storylines without them). Oh, and those foldable changing mats – invest in one of those.

*Berta*

**The baby sling and then the backpack** were two of the best items we had. We also had my big pram from when I was small, and I used to take it outside when I went to feed a shed full of heifers and tie it to the gate. The heifers used to nuzzle the handle and rock my daughter back and forth until she fell asleep in the afternoon – cheap childcare!

*Tigger*

**My vote goes to those triangle-shaped** pillows. They're absolutely divine for those uncomfortable hospital beds and at home for getting comfy to breastfeed. Plus they're useful for keeping newborns snuggled on the sofa and to put behind six month, olds just learning to sit up.

*Madasahatter*

**I couldn't have lived without bouncy cradles** that you can just rock with your foot – and later feed them in. Also, the baby bouncer, which gave us our only 20-minute spells of peace.

*robinw*

**The baby swing was our saviour** giving us some hands-free 'time off'. My first hated being still for any amount of time – I still find myself rocking and swaying around Asda!

*Rosilee*

**We had a swinging crib** and he slept in that for six months in our room but as soon as we put him in the cot bed in his own room he slept much better as he had more room. See how big the baby is before you buy anything and then get your partner/relative to run round like a blue a***d fly whilst you're in hospital.

*Selja*

---

**What the experts say**
Don't feel you have to buy everything brand new; look out for second-hand items advertised in local papers or on notice-boards in the local baby clinics.
Dr Miriam Stoppard (*Your New Baby*)

---

**I think a cot bed wins hands down** over a cot. We bought ours seven years ago. It has been a cot, a bed for an up-to-six-year-old, and now it's back to being a cot again for son number two – certainly the most useful and hard working piece of kit we own. Even if your baby ends up sleeping in your bed, you know you can still get your money's worth from it as a bed later.

*Frank1*

**We liked having a bath** and used it for quite a few months, but it would probably have been easier to borrow one as they take up so much space afterwards. Buy the bare minimum of clothes. People we barely know bought us clothes and toys and it was a pity that we didn't get to use some of them. Even now, my mother and grandmother-in-law would dress our daughter completely if they could!

Do buy a sling – when my son wanted to be held I could strap him in and still get on with jobs.

*BCawthorne*

> **Mumsnet tip**
> Don't buy a baby bath. You won't use it for long and they're a pain to fill and empty. You're better off with a bowl or adult bath with a small amount of water in it.
>
> *Angie677*

**I'd get two changing mats** – a travel one for your changing bag and a standard one. I do all nappy changing on the floor – they can't fall off the floor. It gives you peace of mind to be able to use your own mat, even in mother and baby rooms, and you always have it for those park bench/in-the-car type changes.

*Demented*

**It's really difficult to be ready** for anything beforehand, because all babies are different and your child might hate a certain product that others swear by. (I know someone who found a bouncing chair an absolute waste of money.)

Buy as little as possible to begin with. I waited until I was sure I'd need it. I did not buy a cot until my daughter was three months and then a friend of mine gave me hers. I borrowed a pram and backward-facing pushchair, which was good until four to five months when we bought a new lighter one.

After the first week or so, the need to do some shopping may get you out of the house, which, however much you may not feel like it, will be good for you and your baby. Don't worry too much about buying stuff. Just enjoy your first pregnancy, it'll never be the same again!

*chiara71*

**I would have quite happily purchased** nothing until the baby was born but luckily my husband (who had three children from previous relationships) dragged me out a month before I was due and made me buy a few babygrows. I ended up having an emergency C-section and wasn't able to do any shopping for almost a month after the birth.

*SofiaAmes*

# Flying in pregnancy – is it a good idea and how can you make it more comfortable?

**I'd be reluctant to do a long flight** late on in pregnancy, though I did a 24-hour flight at 23 weeks with no problems. At 32 and 36 weeks I flew to Europe and I made up my mind that I was prepared to have my baby overseas if necessary (I didn't think Germany and Switzerland were terribly bad options). I thought it was highly unlikely that I'd actually have the baby on the plane, it being such a short flight.

The 36-week flight was an absolute shocker. I remember nearly passing out after standing in the customs queue at Heathrow for nearly an hour. I was bent double most of that time having incredibly strong Braxton Hicks, but nobody even asked if I was all right, let alone offered to let me go to the front of the line. Looking back, I should have done the 'I'm going to have a baby right here if you don't let me out' routine, but I was having enough trouble standing up without causing a scene. I was also travelling by myself and had all my luggage to deal with, which didn't help.

The things you need to consider are: (a) what if you have the baby overseas? and (b) what if you go into labour on the flight? If you're reasonably relaxed about either of these things happening – and it is a small risk – then go for it. But personally I'd go somewhere closer to home after 32 weeks. Although you can get travel insurance, it just won't cover anything pregnancy/birth related.

*Amber1*

**We went to Ibiza** a couple of months before my daughter was born. It was a wonderful break as it was full-board with a crèche for our little boy, but I wasn't very comfy on the plane and that was for only two and a half hours.

*Rhiannon*

**Pregnant women are much more at risk of DVT** when they fly. Presumably, if you give birth abroad without insurance you are liable for the costs – which could be considerable with a premature 32-week baby, and you could be in for a long, expensive stay before he/she was fit enough to fly home.

*Baabaa*

**I was around 30 weeks** when I went on a pre-arranged holiday to the Caribbean. I know we are all different but I would not recommend it. The flight was oppressively long, my feet swelled so I could hardly get my shoes on and I did feel it was a waste of what to us was an expensive holiday – it was an all-inclusive deal and I could not enjoy a lot of the activities, not to mention the alcohol. I had really looked forward to it, and had no qualms at all about going but ended up being quite homesick and not really enjoying it, although the resort was really lovely.

*Jasper*

**I had to go on a business trip at 32** weeks but it was only a short haul flight. Ironically I got all these letters from my doctor and checked the work insurance situation, etc. and no one from the airline even noticed I was pregnant.

*Molly1*

**I flew to New York** on business at 25 weeks. I would advise getting as much rest before and after the flight – I flew back overnight without a wink of sleep and was a total zombie for ages afterwards. I also managed to pick up a nice flu bug on the way back.

*Pamela1*

**I travelled to California** when I was 27–28 weeks and everything was fine, except I perhaps overdid it and felt queasy for a couple of days after getting there (unlike most people, jetlag normally affects me very badly going West). I took my medical notes with me and phoned the midwife once to check on some symptoms. The flight staff tried to make me as comfy as possible – bringing me my own large bottle of water, extra cushions, etc. – but in reality I spent much of the flight walking up and down as I couldn't get comfy. In retrospect the distance was a little too far – a flight of up to four hours might have been better.

*Bundle*

---

**What the experts say**
Popping over to the other side of the world on any long flight, especially in economy, is not a great idea. A long-haul flight will multiply the discomfort and side effects of anything you may already be experiencing, such as fluid retention and puffing up.

Kaz Cooke (*The Rough Guide to Pregnancy and Birth*)

---

**I checked with BA about pregnancy** and they're happy for pregnant women up to 36 weeks to fly as long as they have a letter from a GP confirming their due date and that they are fit to fly. Wear stockings, drink plenty of water and avoid all alcohol. Oxygen levels on board are slightly lower than normal atmosphere so that's why some people feel much more tired on flights, especially if their diaphragm is compromised by a wee one, so practise some deep breathing exercises before you go.

My week in Grenada at 30 weeks was absolutely fantastic. No problems with the nine-hour flight, although I didn't sleep on the return leg. I made the most of the free daily beauty sessions, facials, massage and pedicures and didn't miss the alcohol. No one seemed to mind a 30-week bump on show in my bikini, so I got over that initial embarrassment very quickly.

*Honeybunny*

**I flew to St Lucia** at 26 weeks- pregnant and even though the flight out lasted 15 hours – we had to stop in the Azores for a medical emergency – I was fine. I moved about the whole time and on the overnight on the way back didn't even think about sleeping – I just watched bits of movies and went to the loo.

I wore the support tights, drank loads of water and went to bed as soon as I got home. I recovered in no time. I'm really glad I went as it was our last big holiday for a while and I really wanted some intensive time with my two children before the baby. Having said that, I wouldn't have wanted to go any later – by 30 weeks I think you feel a lot bigger and more breathless, and long-haul travel is a whole different prospect.

*Berta*

**Mumsnet tip**
Make sure to pre-book an aisle seat and move around as much as possible.

*Nelly*

**I went to Italy at 30 weeks** when pregnant with my first and had a great short break – it really felt like a final fling. The flight was fine, shorter and no less comfy than a lot of car rides I'd been on and at least on a plane you can get up and go to the loo!

I went to Tobago when pregnant with my second, at around 27–28 weeks. We had to move the holiday by a week and I admit I was getting a bit anxious. We flew out Club-class (because my husband's firm had cocked up the holiday and there were no economy seats left – they paid!) and I'd thoroughly recommend that, if it's at all possible. I still wore those special anti DVT tights and wandered round a lot – I just had more room to wander in. We flew back economy and overnight, which was a bit grim. A pillow to prop myself into a more comfy position would have helped, and I'd definitely insist on an aisle seat for everyone else's sake as well as yours as you need to keep going to the loo. This is a good way of keeping the blood flowing though as you have to keep mobile. I'd make sure you have childcare the next day as you may well be wiped out. For me, the benefits of wallowing in warm water and having some quality family time before the arrival of the baby completely outweighed any slight discomfort or imagined risk.

*Biza*

## Maternity nurses – are they a good idea?

**I had a maternity nurse** for two months to help with my twins. The second month she just did nights. They were very premature and I'd had a C-section so we needed some help. It's not the easiest relationship because you're so hormonal and instinctively you want to do everything for newborns yourself. But she was very supportive with breastfeeding and saw her role as much to look after me as the babies. She helped to get them into a good routine and they subsequently have always been good sleepers.

She also taught me lots of tricks of the trade – so I was much more competent when she left than I would have been otherwise. As I was breastfeeding I still got up in the night but she did all the settling afterwards (she slept in their room) so I got a lot more sleep than I otherwise would. It was quite nice to have the second month where she was still around for the nights, but I flew solo in the days, as it meant it wasn't too terrifying when she left. Of course it all cost an arm and a leg (I can't even bring myself to add it all up!).

If I hadn't had twins, I wouldn't have had a maternity nurse because I like the idea of bedding down with your baby for a couple of months with no one else getting in between you. Also, having someone living with you when your hormones are up the spout can be quite testing and if you have some specific ideas about the way you want your baby looked after (e.g. dummy/no dummy, breastfeeding, routine) spell them out during the interview. I've had friends who had difficult experiences because the maternity nurse just took over.

*Berta*

**It is very hard having someone living** with you at such an amazing time of your life when you just want to be your 'new family unit' and it didn't help that I didn't get on with mine at all. She picked at a lot of things I did and gave my son formula when I wanted to breastfeed only. I spent a huge amount of time on the phone to my mother for reassurance that I wasn't going mad. In the end I got my husband to speak to her (I was very emotional) and a couple of times I actually lost it with her myself. I tried to remember that it must be a very hard job moving from place to place where your boss is always a very tired and teary new mother.

On the plus side I managed to sleep a lot, which was great for getting over a C-section and by the time she left, my son knew the difference between night and day. So I would have another maternity nurse (obviously not the same one) but I would be much clearer about what it was that I wanted help with.

It's a good idea to interview with someone whose judgement you trust, to think out all possible questions you want to ask beforehand and to make it absolutely clear how you wish things to go when she is with you. If she doesn't like it, then find someone else. Better to find that out beforehand.

*Tinkerbell*

**It depends on the individual maternity nurse** as to how much non-baby help they're prepared to give. Mine took over all the washing, took my three-year-old to the park with my twin babies, picked him up from nursery, made me lots of snacks and cups of tea and even meals. I was very anti having help the first time round, but with twins I think it's essential. The babies slept in her room so I only got up to feed during the night. She also took them out for a long walk twice a day, which gave me time to rest or to spend time with my older son.

I would recommend it as long as you stay in control. You don't want to feel vulnerable when she goes, so don't let them do everything. I encouraged mine to leave me on my own for the odd afternoon/night etc. so I could feel confident that I would be okay when she finished. They are expensive, though. An alternative is a night nurse, which is cheaper.

*Lauraw*

**Mumsnet fact**
The average weekly wage for a maternity nurse is between £550 and £700 – or between £12 and £15 an hour.

Tinies.co.uk

**We have three-month-old twin girls** and had a maternity nurse for the first six weeks, living-in five days a week. They're expensive, but well worth it. Ours did all the night feeds, which meant that for those first six weeks I could get a good night's sleep. By the time she left, we knew exactly what we were doing and the girls were into a regular feeding routine. Choosing a suitable maternity nurse can be tricky – I fully intended to get a 'motherly-type' with age and experience behind her, but ended up going by gut feeling and employing someone fairly young but very experienced, who fitted in perfectly with our way of life. Ultimately, you just need to choose someone who you can live with. I would certainly recommend employing someone professional rather than relying on family help – it's not easy trying to be firm with family. Save your mum's help for those special times.

*RoseAnne*

**I used a maternity nurse to help out** from 6 pm until midnight for a couple of weeks after my daughter was born. My husband was working abroad, my mum was ill, the baby was colicky and my older son needed a fair amount of settling down in the evening too. I found her very helpful but would not have enjoyed her company 24/7. She was unable to offer any great insights into how to prevent or help colic, which I found hugely disappointing given that Gina Ford says none of her babies have ever suffered from colic. You can hire a maternity nurse at very short notice, so if you're at all unsure I would wait and see how you are getting on. If you need one, hire one when you are ready to start paying.

*Molly1*

**I think it's worth waiting to see** how you get on, and hiring someone at the last minute if need be. No one knows how they'll feel after birth. You may hate the thought of letting anyone else even hold your baby for the first month (I know plenty of people who've been like that).

I think the best support comes from others in the same situation. My antenatal class had eight couples – all first-time mums. We met weekly to begin with (then more often) and spoke on the phone regularly. We all reassured each other that we didn't have the faintest idea about what we were doing, but that it was probably going to be okay. Cheaper than a maternity nurse and more fun!

*Jimjams*

**I think whether or not to have** a maternity nurse must be horses for courses. I would hate someone coming in and sorting my baby into a routine – sounds like programming the video (which I can't do, so maybe that's not a good analogy!). I think it would be utterly pointless to have one who annoyed you, or did things you didn't want her to do. Help with burping and settling and taking for a walk is very useful – but that's what dads and grandmothers are for, not a maternity nurse. Of course if there's no other adult around, I can see a need.

*Tiktok*

**I loathe the idea of a maternity nurse** as I cannot imagine someone else sleeping in the room with my newborn baby and watching over me at such a special time. I also really don't like the fact that so many of them seem to measure their success by getting the baby to sleep through the night at a very young age.

I know quite a few people who have used them and while many have raved about them, there are lots of horror stories ranging from actively discouraging breastfeeding to causing trouble between husband and wife.

Aside from anything else, you may be blessed and have a very easy baby. I remember thinking that employing a maternity nurse for my daughter would have been just like setting fire to £20 notes as she was a dream as a newborn. Personally I would prefer to use the money on a good holiday.

*Ringer*

---

**What the experts say**
As well as providing welcome help with the baby, maternity nurses are invaluable teachers.

Dr Miriam Stoppard (*Your New Baby*)

---

**The best person** to know what a baby wants are its parents – you will soon learn what to do, however daunting it feels at first. Help with meals was most useful for me. My mum filled my freezer and the local takeaways were well used.

*Prufrock*

**Get a cleaner/mothers help/doula** rather than a maternity nurse. You may have a very easy baby and it could be a waste of money. On the other hand, having someone around to do the housework and make meals, wash clothes, etc. is a godsend no matter how good the baby is.

*Enid*

**I have known people complain bitterly** about the bossiness of their maternity nurse, who did all the fun stuff with the new baby whilst they still had the housework to do. A friend whose husband is permanently away on business hired a housekeeper to come in for a few months. She did all the housework, ironing, etc. and was also there to mind the baby whilst my friend had a shower/nap etc. If I had another, I would get my cleaner to come in three mornings a week so I didn't feel so overwhelmed by the house. Most maternity nurse agencies recommend they come in for at least a month, which is terrifyingly expensive. A doula is cheaper, will support you in caring for the baby if that really worries you, as well as helping cook and do housework, which most maternity nurses definitely won't do!

*Aloha*
•

**I can live with a dirty house,** but a tired, windy, crying baby is one of the most tiring and stressful things on earth. Give me a maternity nurse over a cleaner any day for the early days. It would have been so nice to hand the baby over to someone else to spend an hour burping/jiggling/patting/walking them around after a feed instead of me doing it and getting into tears of exhaustion, plagued by the insecurity of first-time motherhood and wondering if baby won't settle because I'm doing it wrong. And the sheer relaxation of getting into bed knowing that I was not going to be disturbed until the next feed would be bliss. I don't care who is with my baby whilst I'm asleep – I'm hardly missing out on quality time when I'm unconscious!

Also it must be reassuring to have someone experienced on-hand to bounce ideas off – do you think he's hungry? Do you think he's sleepy? Is there anything I can do to help with this problem, etc? Having had two babies that were not easy to feed, were dreadfully hard to settle afterwards and not great sleepers, I didn't find the weeks after the birth a lovely intimate family time. They were exhausting, overwhelming and stressful – studded with some lovely soft cuddles. Plus I find it very difficult to sleep if the baby is in the house because the slightest whimper and I'm up like a shot. Someone to take the baby out for a walk would have really helped me relax. Whilst I'm feeding, they could bring me food and drinks, tidy a little and maybe even defrost the dinner! Wooohooo! I'm getting excited here... Maybe next baby... (And pigs might fly!)

*Bloss*

# Second time around – is it different?

**I'm 37 weeks pregnant with my second** and it has been a miserable pregnancy. My husband seems to have forgotten that I'm pregnant and keeps saying dumb things like, 'why are you so touchy?' Duh! And chasing after a toddler is so exhausting. I didn't enjoy being pregnant first time around, but at least there was the novelty and magic of it all.

Although this baby was planned and I'm thrilled to be having her, this pregnancy has been really depressing and I've done a lot of crying. I'm sure once my daughter comes out, I will be thrilled to meet her and it will have been all worth it and I will finally get my body back. No more acid indigestion, insomnia, rashes, cramps, fat, sweaty head, frizzy hair, sore breasts, big belly, nausea...

*SofiaAmes*

**I'm missing the excitement** and magic that I felt about pregnancy first time round. This time round it seems to be more of a hindrance – mainly because I'm running round after a toddler.

*Mog*

**I remember being obsessed** with how many weeks I was with my first – this time they are just going by without me. I feel guilty as I was much more in tune with my body the first time and it makes me worry about bonding with a second child.

I can't help thinking that I am disappearing with this second pregnancy – my life as a person in my own right is well and truly gone. I felt the baby moving today though and felt guilty for being selfish – we can't win. My son is only 17 months so is keeping me busy, as is severe sickness. I think I'll feel better when I am more obviously pregnant as at the moment you can't really tell and as I seem to be in denial, I'm not really telling people. I feel guilty about this too!

*Hughsie*

---

### What the experts say

Of course you're thrilled to be expecting again. But you may notice that the excitement level (and that compulsion to tell everyone you pass in the street the good news) isn't quite as high. This is a completely normal reaction... and in no way reflects on your love for this baby.

Murkoff, Eisenberg & Hathaway (*What to Expect When You're Expecting*)

---

**I spent the whole of my second** pregnancy running round after my daughter and would go whole days without remembering I was pregnant at all. Mind you, now I have two children, I am even busier.

*Susanmt*

**I wasn't sure how I felt** when I found out I was pregnant with number two. We had planned it and wanted a brother or sister for our son but I was still shocked. I didn't tell anybody for a few days, as I felt I needed to get my head round it. I kept thinking, 'are we doing the right thing?' and hundreds of worries went through my head. However, I have found time to bond with this little person as the weeks have gone by and although I haven't really kept up with how it's developing week by week, it was still great to see it moving around on the scan.

*Peanuts1*

**I am only eight weeks pregnant** with my second (first is 16 months) and feel over-whelmingly gloomy. I hate it when people tell you how hard it is with two children. Of course it is, but it's not exactly a helpful thing to say, is it? Frankly I'm terrified of coping with two, even though my first is pretty good, and I feel life is passing me by. I took voluntary redundancy last time from a job which I really didn't like and haven't regretted being at home with my first. However, I'm now panicking that I will be past it when the next one is old enough to go to pre-school. I expect it's all hormones.

*Bun*

**Wait till you get to number four** – no one is happy for you, including your husband. His exact words were, 'Oh no!' Everyone else thought it was a mistake. From being ecstatically happy at seeing that blue line one morning, I was miserable for weeks. First time round, my husband used to feel the baby move at every opportunity. Fourth time round, I used to have to ask him to do it. It wasn't that he wasn't sup-portive, just that he's so used to seeing me pregnant, it isn't a novelty anymore.

*Mears*

**This weekend my husband waved** as he drove past me half a mile from our house carrying our two-year-old home. I'm 24 weeks pregnant and had taken my daugh-ter for a longer-than-expected walk. His comment: 'you looked like you were doing okay!' Then on Monday a colleague gave me a massive pile of books to carry upstairs because he was a bit out of breath. I am 'blooming' at the moment and as he is overweight and a smoker, I thought I'd better do it before he col-lapsed on me and I had to carry him too.

In general I have been much more tired, worried and emotional second time. I think it's because I have spoken to lots of mums and know more about what can go wrong – last time I was blissfully ignorant. It's the same with the birth. It wor-ries me more this time. Luckily I don't have too much time to think about it as I've just started potty training my first.

*Lollypop*

**I spent most of yesterday afternoon weeping**, in fact sobbing so loudly my part-ner got out of the bath (I haven't had time for one of those for months!) to see if I was okay. I am nine weeks pregnant with number two and feel awful. Much sicker, fatter and more hassled. (I cried last time too, but mostly at watching animal documentaries and children's hospital programmes.) I scared myself because I contemplated running off to Spain with my son and leaving everyone behind and went as far as calculating my finances as a single mother with two kids. I have never thought of leaving my husband before or felt as much resentment. I hope this temporary madness wears off. It broke my heart that my son was stroking me better and trying to clean the snot off my nose.

*Clucks*

**Mumsnet fact**
The average gap between pregnancies is 27 months.

*British Medical Journal*

**I too am nine weeks pregnant** and feel much sicker, more tired, more irritable and more tearful. I went to bed at 8 pm on Friday night as I was feeling so rubbish – my husband, instead of laying on sympathy and TLC, told me I was very annoying because I knew the way to feel better was to eat something and I wasn't doing it. The next morning I was feeling rather tearful about this episode and he lovingly told me that he thinks, 'I exaggerate for effect'. Let him try being nauseous every evening for five weeks in a row. When he has a bloomin' hangover you would think the world was coming to an end!

*Percy*

**Early in my pregnancy I was a mess.** I, too, had a plan to leave and take my son abroad. One day I decided things were getting too dire, so went to my doctor and told him I couldn't cope anymore. He put me in touch with a psychiatrist, who dealt very well with my depression, without using medication. This, plus the inevitable shifting of hormones by the second trimester, made me feel much, much better. Now I'm 38 weeks and feeling very positive. Either pursue treatment, as I did, or just wait for time/hormone changes to sort things out, which may be just as effective.

*ExpatKat*

**I also felt guilty that my second pregnancy** was not 'special' – I'm now sure that I had pre-natal depression, although I hadn't heard of it at the time. I gave my partner the complete runaround and was horrible to be with. However, if anything, it made me bond more quickly with my second as I was conscious I had to do my absolute best for her. She still has to fight for attention with the 'Toddler from Hades', but she seems pretty self-sufficient and when she grins at me I know she doesn't mind that I was rubbish at being pregnant with her.

*Sobernow*

**I am 36 weeks with my second.** I felt terrible through most of this pregnancy – sick, tired, emotional, moody, anxious. But I seem to have found a new calm in the last couple of weeks, and I am really looking forward to the birth. The joy of a new baby seems to have come at last, and it's even sweeter second time round when it's based in reality, rather than the unknown of the first pregnancy.

*Enid*


**I agree that pregnancy number two** is not as special as number one. I also think I am more emotional this time, maybe due to tiredness, but silly things make me cry, even one of my daughter's books called: *There's a house in mummy's tummy.* I felt pretty pathetic with my daughter patting my arm saying, 'Okay, okay?' I can tell you.

What's more, my husband has asked me recently to help push a window frame up a ladder and take the other end of a boiler so he can move it into the garage. I am 38 weeks pregnant! His father has told him to get me to give him back massages as he pulled a muscle, and asked if I ever cook when my husband mentioned he was making an omelette – I can't remember the last time he cooked.

I feel like an old pack horse who can withstand all loads and when I said this to my husband he said, 'But you are a tough old bird and that's why I married you.' I can't wait to get this baby out so I can kick his a*se into touch!

*Queenie*

# What do you need to pack in your hospital bag?

**First time around** I packed an enormous holdall to cover all eventualities. As a first timer I'd been told I'd probably be in labour for ages so had CDs, magazines, a special 'giving-birth' nightie, snacks and drinks. (I was hoping for a water birth so I also had a brand new sieve to fish out any poo – sorry!) In the event I arrived fully dilated and ready to push, so no time for birthing pool or soothing CDs.

The things I recommend taking are: a camera (with black-and-white film in the camera which helps cut out those blood pressure blotches – vain, I know) – those first snaps are so special. Lipstick – having been appalled by the way I looked in all the pictures after my first was born, I made sure I put a bit on for the second. Drinks and snacks came in very handy as no one thought to tell me that breakfast was a DIY affair and anyway I could hardly move post-op. A pillow from home is lovely too, as they seemed to be rationed and they really help when breastfeeding.

My other top tip for ward attire is a sarong and a man's shirt. They're comfy on the saggy waist/C-section scar and there's easy access to the top half. My sarong is dark and brightly-coloured, so didn't show up any blood/leaks and the shirts were all old so I didn't care about milk stains.

Make sure the sanitary pads are industrial strength – no one tells you how much you bleed. If you have another child coming in to visit, wrap up and pack a few little gifts in advance. I knew I would be in for a few days and having some gifts helped keep my daughter happy.

*Cll*

> **Mumsnet tip**
> Pack energy tablets in your hospital bag. I found them the perfect thing to suck on during labour. It gives you something to do, they are thirst-quenching and energy-boosting to boot.
>
> *Jona*

**If you live fairly near the hospital** and will have people coming in each day, I would recommend taking the bare minimum – visitors can bring more. With my first baby I had the most enormous bag ever – it looked like I was going away for a month. I'd even packed a snowsuit for a baby who was born on midsummer's day!

*Annwyl*

**Take food.** I gave birth at 8.30 pm after 20 hours of vomiting during labour. Hospital suppers were over and there was nothing to eat until breakfast.

*Eemie*

**If you take drinks** and would like to keep them cool, freeze them beforehand – the frozen drinks helps to keep any food cool as well.

*SueW*

**I took a tiny radio** and hand-held TV with earphones and found they were invaluable. One of my best friends went into labour at home and called me to help. As she phoned her husband to drive her to hospital, she asked me to bring her bag downstairs. All she'd packed was a half bottle of Famous Grouse.

*Sobernow*

**Take something good to read.** After giving birth to my son, I asked my partner to get me a magazine. He came back with a slimming mag – just what I needed to read at that point!

*Viksy*

**I'd wished I'd had a water spray** – I got very hot – and energy food like bananas. I survived on Maltesers... but there's nothing in them but air, is there?

*Agaazaa*

**Homeopathic arnica pills for bruising** 'down there' really helped me. They reduce the swelling and you can take them whilst breastfeeding too. You must take them as soon as possible after the birth. You think it'll be the last thing on your mind but I remembered as soon as the throbbing started.

*Lizzer*

**I suggest a large bottle of something alcoholic,** a large box of chocolates and batteries and film for your camera – when my first daughter was born the batteries went at the crucial moment!

*Batey*

**This is the time to get rid** of all those greying knickers lurking in the back of your cupboard. Wear them once, then bin them! Food for your birth partner is also a good idea. I'd recommend packing the hospital bag yourself. I got rushed off to hospital and my partner had to follow with a bag for me. When the nurse unpacked it, I discovered he'd put in an old floor cloth as my face flannel. Personally, I've never had to take in anything for the baby as it's always been provided.

*Baabaa*

**I had an emergency C-section** and normal knickers sat right on the wound and hurt like hell. Disposables were much better.

*Elwar*

**This sounds grim** but I wish I'd taken a pair of cheap flip-flops instead of slippers, so I could wear them into the bathroom/shower/loo – the floors at my local hospital were disgusting.

*Mo2*

**I would suggest a sachet** of antibacterial wipes. I never went anywhere near a loo or bathroom without them in my hand. Gawd, the bathrooms were gross!

*HuncaMunca*

**A car seat is a must** for coming out of hospital. The best ones are those that you can carry quite easily and have a little rocking action, then you can use it as a day-time chair/cradle at home. Sanitary towels with wings are good because they stay in place better and I'd take in a pack of breast pads just in case you need them. I leaked a lot during the first few days and would have been drenched if I hadn't taken any with me. My hospital gave out Bounty packs with loads of baby toiletries, but we were asked to provide baby clothes, nappies and cotton wool.

*PamT*

**Think about what** you are going to wear to come home. My husband brought me a skirt and trainers but no tights or socks – it was February and snowing. For the baby I was provided with one nappy and five cotton wool balls. The cotton wool balls didn't even clean up the first lot of meconium.

*Bozza*

**Our hospital came up with clothes** for my baby – we forgot 'her' bag so she ended up with a hospital nightie for the first day (we can tell which are the very first photos from that!).

*Bundle*

**Pretty much the only thing given away** at our NHS hospital was an infection. I think the first maternity pad was free, but that was it. Bear in mind you'll probably need more maternity towels than you thought. My husband got sent out for additional supplies, much to his embarrassment! I had a labour bag and a separate 'me' bag, which we left in the car until our son was born. It made it easier to find things.

My top suggestions are: your own pillow – it's wonderful to have something homely for labour and afterwards – you can hug it on the journey to hospital and it's great to sit on in the car on the way home. Plus the softest quilted toilet paper money can buy and a dark bath towel!

*SoupDragon*

**I took some ridiculous things** in my hospital bag when I was going in for my first. Most notably a baby's hairbrush that's not been used to this day.

*Bon*

**I took four babygrows** into the hospital and on day two my husband had to bring more as we'd run out.

*Chiara71*

**I wished I'd bought in more** than the recommended three changes of clothes for the baby – he went through three changes of clothes a day at first. I'd also recommend a baby blanket and cot sheets – the hospital ones were harsh and it was a job to get them changed when my baby messed them.

*Eefs*


**I'd suggest nighties instead of babygrows** for the first couple of weeks (for boys too). Then you can change baby without fiddling around with poppers in the middle of the night.

*Enid*


**You need to check your hospital's policy.** In ours, babies have to wear hospital-provided clothing so that they can be identified as newbies (a security precaution). All we had to take in was a going-home outfit and nappies, wipes, nappy bags, baby towel and toiletries. Also, check what the telephone system is at your hospital – in ours it was phonecards and we didn't have one.

I'm also planning to take in a blanket this time for the baby so that he has something familiar around him when we take him home to his own bed. As well as spare pyjamas, lots of moisturizer (hospitals usually have very dry atmospheres) and the softest towels that can be found.

*Harrysmum*

## Choosing a name – what should you consider?

**I sat with my husband last night** going through the baby name book to see if we can make a better effort of deciding on a name *before* our second is born. The problem is the only two we can vaguely agree on are Dylan and Thomas, which would be quite silly. The poor child is going to be with us before we agree at this rate!

*Harrysmum*

**My two best friends** both had baby boys within about six months of each other and have both called them by the same name. It has caused untold hurt to the friend of the first baby and the mother of the second baby won't even talk about the matter. These were friends who saw each other three to four times per week and it has ruined their friendship.

*Paula1*

> **Mumsnet fact**
> 2002 saw the birth of 65 babies called Chardonnay after the character in the TV series 'Footballer's Wives'.
> Office of National Statistics

**Boy's names are so difficult.** When I was pregnant we decided on Felix in the event of a boy. When he came along he was Alfie for about a week, then we decided on Guy – we thought it short and macho enough to prevent a beating in the playground whilst still being a little bit out of the ordinary.

*Spacemonkey*

**Someone I know** has just called her child by exactly the same name as my daughter – first and middle name. They'll never see each other and I suppose I should feel flattered but, somehow, I'm a little peeved.

*Tinker*

**If you don't use the name** you'd always wanted because a friend has already used it, you might resent it later. If your children grow up to be friends they'll probably like being called the same thing. Do watch out for initials, though. My husband's are PMT and as everyone in his office is known (on emails/circulars, etc.) by their initials, that's what he's called day in, day out – good thing he wasn't a girl really!

*Biza*

**What the experts say**
A strong argument can be made against any name.

David Narter (*Don't Name Your Baby*)

**I don't think I'd choose the same name** that a close friend had chosen, even if it was a personal favourite – it just doesn't seem very original. It's not that I think it's a particularly big deal, just that I'd want my baby to have a special name at least amongst close friends. Isn't it amazing how children grow into even the most bizarre names? First time you hear them, you think no! A few meetings later and you couldn't imagine them called anything else. I guess I'd be quite flattered if a friend named their child the same as mine – but I wouldn't think them particularly imaginative.

*Alex2*

**Am I missing something here?** Why on earth should anyone resent someone else calling their child the same name? You don't get a copyright at the christening and it's rather flattering, actually.

*Javarose*

**Me and hubby could only agree** on one girl's name so we called our daughter that name even though we knew that two other people (who had become good friends) were also going to call their daughters the same. Why change it for anyone else? It's your child and besides it won't matter in the long term as lots of people have the same name.

We ended up sharing a nanny with one of our those friends, which was fine when both girls were babies, but as they became older it became a tad more tricky ('Give that toy back X, it's X's!'). So nicknames are now used. I would not change my choice of name even with a crystal ball as both girls suit their names (and nicknames).

*Blt*

> **Mumsnet fact**
> Jack was the favourite name for boys in 2000, as it has been for the last six years; while Chloe was the favourite for girls for the fourth year running.
>
> (The *Guardian*)

**You might want to check** out the Top 10 names of the year, which are produced by the Office of National Statistics (they have a website) to ensure yours isn't the most popular name. There are nine boys in my four-year-old's class at school and three of them are called Harry.

*Suew*

**I called my second child Tallulah** because it was a name that I loved and also I thought it unusual enough not to hear that often. When she was born we discovered that there was another child in the next road with the same name. It really shouldn't matter how many are called the name you pick as long as you love the name and it suits your baby. The two Tallulah's are almost opposites of each other and it suits them both. Mine is blonde and blue-eyed and the other has jet-black hair with brown eyes.

*Lou33*

**I was worried about my second child's name** 'going with' the first one's – luckily it was a girl as even at due date we could not decide on a boy's name. I prefer old-fashioned names and ones that don't shorten so the 'going with' bit just made it even harder (so many criteria to fulfil). Anyway, after all that thought we still managed to pick two names that my mother doesn't like!

*Clary*

**Names are such an emotive subject.** I spent months agonizing over what to call my boys. I soon learnt that no matter what name we came up with, someone was bound to dislike it. Then you have to think about what the name could be shortened to (I couldn't call my boys Richard as I dreaded them being called 'Dick' – apologies to any Richards out there), and what the initials stand for (I have a friend whose initials were WAS so she was always known as a 'has been'), and then the names have to sound good with the surname. Oh, and don't forget to throw in your favourite uncle's name so he won't get upset. What a minefield!

In the end we stuck to our guns and went for the names we liked. Strangely, once you've lived with a name for a while it becomes much less important anyway. The baby just becomes that person, if you know what I mean.

If anyone picked the same names we've used I'd be really flattered (after all, isn't this why you name your children after members of your family and friends that you admire?).

*Hmonty*

**My husband's best friend** had a visit from a salesman named Dick Scratcher. This is no lie – I've seen his card. You'd think he'd use Richard, wouldn't you?

*Willow2*

**My partner was dead set** on the name Yoda for a boy or a girl – until we discovered that it is a bit similar to the Spanish f-word. Lucky escape...

*Lucy123*

**2**

# Health Issues

## Introduction

One of the most ludicrous bits of most pregnancy tomes is the chapter devoted to so-called 'minor ailments'. As you lie there in the small hours of what seems like the 104th week of your pregnancy with ankles the size of coconuts, raging indigestion and a groaning back, you'll most likely be plotting a whole host of vile tortures to inflict on the bloke (it *has* to be a bloke) who came up with that description.

Maybe he could start with a spot of nausea – lasting all day and night of course (second on the list of those deserving some hands-on experience would be whoever coined the phrase 'morning' sickness.) Next, you could lob in a cluster of migraines, rapidly followed by full-blown insomnia, complete exhaustion, and a range of attractive stripes across the stomach, thighs and chest area (think pink zebra here) and just for good measure an inexplicable craving for Pot Noodles.

To top it all, how about a spot of hyperemesis, otherwise known as 'unrelenting, pregnancy-related nausea and/or vomiting that prevents adequate intake of food and fluids' (Hyperemesis Education & Research Foundation)? Even he might struggle to classify this paralysing pregnancy symptom that affects many thousands of women in the UK annually as minor.

Hey, and let's not forget to remind Mr Minor Ailment that for a mere nine months he absolutely must (another human life depends on it) abstain from a sizeable proportion of life's pleasures – smoking, boozing, gardening, sitting crossed-legged, eating runny cheeses and bungee jumping. Instead he must lug around an extra few stone, suffer undignified kicks to the pelvic region at the most inopportune moments and give up any hope of seeing his toes, let alone tying his shoelaces.

If by this point you were beginning to feel a twinge of sympathy for our master of understatement, you could point him in the direction of this chapter, where at least he'd get an idea of how best to cope with his ailments and privations. And if all this sounds depressingly grim, cheer up, there's the birth to look forward to!

# First signs of pregnancy – what are they?

**For me it was overwhelming** PMT-like symptoms. I was ratty, tired and had very sore breasts. And this was all before my period was due. A strange taste in my mouth and ridiculous amounts of saliva appeared about a week later.

*Clare2*

**I took my nightshirt off one morning** to see these strange things attached to my chest! My period wasn't due for a couple of days. We weren't trying to conceive so I wasn't expecting it. Looking back over that month, I also remember falling asleep at friends' houses a couple of times after Sunday lunch (they were very good friends!).

*SueW*

**Going from a 34B to a 38C** virtually overnight, going off tea and coffee and a strange metallic taste in the mouth.

*Mabs*

**With my two pregnancies** I had a strange metallic taste and sensitive boobs before my period was due. Nausea didn't kick in until about week six.

*Caroline5*

**Overwhelming tiredness** – I was completely wiped out.

*Jasper*

**Sore boobs!** Plus tiredness, a funny taste, nausea and needing to pee a lot!

*Demented*

**At three to four weeks pregnant** I was very, very tired and, joy of joys, by six weeks I was chucking up, as I was for the next 34 weeks actually, but that's a whole other story.

*Batey*

**Um...a positive home pregnancy test** when my period didn't appear. And very sore boobs.

*SoupDragon*

**A vivid red, sore and itchy rash** on my arms and legs, which I put down to putting on sun cream too soon after shaving my legs, but my GP spotted as an oestrogen surge. Followed by chronic fatigue.

*Zoe*

**I was really, really tired!** I could have slept all day and night and still felt tired.

*Hilary*

**I felt off colour, a bit queasy** straight away and so very tired. Also my boobs were very tender, I felt bloated, needed to pee a lot and felt like my period was about to start (not much help that one!).

*Hopeful*

**First time round I was very dizzy** – couldn't walk in a straight line. Second time round I had a shocking headache, nausea and went totally off my food.

*Pamela1*

**The biggest clue** for me was that I became VERY emotional!

*Chinchilla*

**I knew I was expecting my third** very soon after conception. I had a very strange feeling – I don't know how to explain it, I just knew. But the first physical sign was the need to pee six or seven times a night.

*Ariel*

---

### What the experts say
Most second-timers are more attuned to the early symptoms of pregnancy, and are more apt to recognize them.

Murkoff, Eisenberg & Hathaway (*What to Expect When You're Expecting*)

---

**Producing lots of saliva,** sore breasts (first time, but not so much the second) and extreme tiredness. I also had a very bad headache that didn't go for days when I was just pregnant.

*Bundle*

**My breasts went first,** tender within two weeks of conception, quickly followed by my waistline – my stomach felt bloated. Soon the heavy stomach was counterbalanced with light-headedness, progressing to constant feelings of nausea. Oh joy!

*Frank1*

**I just knew!** The first time I knew so early I had about five negative tests and the second time I wasn't even late, I just suddenly thought I'd buy a test. I was on the Pill and wasn't trying. I must have known subconsciously as I had an ear infection and decided not to take antibiotics. I was about two weeks pregnant at the time. My first physical sign was weird boobs.

*Tracyhay*

**Sore boobs, nausea** and going off booze and cigs – that was a dead giveaway!

*Grommit*

# Early pregnancy tiredness

**I remember being on holiday** with friends when I was six weeks pregnant and I could hardly get out of bed, I was so tired. Every time I woke I planned to get up and before I knew it had nodded right off again – I never surfaced before lunchtime. It was quite hard to explain, as I didn't want to tell them about the pregnancy but I also had a splitting headache and just pleaded migraines. The good news is that by about twelve weeks I stopped feeling so weary – I still felt nauseous though.

*Roberta*

**I'm just six weeks pregnant** and am having terrible bouts of tiredness. It really hits me like a wave and I feel so groggy I can hardly function.

*Janus*

**I took antenatal supplements** and found they helped, plus napping in the day. By three months it does improve.

*Pupuce*

**I recommend eating lots of fruit** and good carbohydrates like pasta and rice that are slow releasing. Chocolate is good for energy but the effect doesn't last long. I was very nauseous the first few months but found eating little and often, and napping when I could, a help.

*Tillysmummy*

**I found Lucozade helped me** – but I don't know how healthy it is.

*JaneyT*

**I was utterly exhausted when pregnant** with number two (number one was only five months when I found out). I found eating a bowl of cereal with chopped banana set me up first thing, then I would nibble at flapjacks because they were easy to grab on the hoof and weren't crisps. I would go to bed as early as possible and sleep as much as I could. It did get much better at the 12-week mark.

*Sobernow*

---

**What the experts say**
One of the most commonly held beliefs is that women bloom throughout pregnancy, shine with health and feel better than they ever have before. This does happen sometimes but most women experience a combination of high and low energy.

Dr Yehudi Gordon (*Birth and Beyond*)

**I really suffered with tiredness** from about six weeks until 14 weeks. The only thing that helped me was to turn in much earlier to bed each night and at work I would go and sit in a cubicle and shut my eyes for 20 minutes.

*Nics1stbaby*

**I was totally shattered in the early months** of my second pregnancy though being sick every day didn't help. But to be honest, running after a 22-month-old little boy, is exhausting in its own right – a few months on and I still have days of total exhaustion. I think all you can do is go with the flow and let your body tell you what it wants. When I started doing that, things became a lot easier.

*Peanuts1*

**Dried apricots** were about the only food I could face between six and 12 weeks – maybe the sugar levels gave me enough energy to cope?

*Sis*

**I was exhausted when pregnant** with both mine, but the second pregnancy was definitely harder. Floradix is a good vitamin supplement as it's got lots of iron. If you have an older child and can afford it, now might be the time to get some help. My first started nursery just before I fell pregnant so I'd crash out in bed whenever she was out, in between chucking up, that is!

*Batey*

**I am 18 weeks pregnant** with number two and still tired. Not as tired as I was (I literally dropped off in meetings) but not as energetic as I felt at this stage with number one. The morning and evening hours and the weekends are enough to do me in. Lots and lots of early nights needed.

*Harrysmum*

**Acupuncture** worked for me.

*Mk*

**I'm 36 weeks pregnant** and I only got my energy back at 30 weeks (just when most people start to feel tired again). This too is my second pregnancy and quite different to my first, when I felt fine most of the time, and seeing as I have some-one to help five days a week, I can't even blame the tiredness this time round on my toddler.

The things I found helped to alleviate the tiredness/nausea were:

- Muesli in the morning. Combine 1/2 cup rolled oats with milk or fruit juice the night before, and put it in the fridge. Eat in the morning with fresh fruit or sultanas, tahini, etc.
- Exercise after breakfast, even when you're feeling very tired – just a short walk to the park or something.

- Take a short sleep at lunchtime (or whenever your toddler sleeps) but only around 40 minutes.
- See if you can find a pregnancy yoga class in your area – I found gentle yoga helped quite a bit with tiredness.

*Lorien*

**Drink plenty of water.** Also eat little and often and try not to eat too much sugar – it will contribute to sudden 'waves' of tiredness. Take it very easy for the first 12 to 14 weeks and once you start feeling a bit better (hopefully in the second trimester), take some exercise – it really helps. I did pregnancy yoga but found all the bending and stretching impossible with low blood pressure (spent half the class in a faint). I recommend swimming as an alternative.

*Enid*

**My second pregnancy** has been completely different from my first. Number one was a 'give me that mountain to climb!' experience. Number two is proving to be a 'do I really have to walk up that step?' experience. My complete exhaustion stage was between 13 and 18 weeks – the smallest thing was the biggest effort. I think there is very little you can do, you have to let your body lead you. The one thing that did and still does help me is pregnancy yoga (talk to your doctor about when you should start though). It helps me shut off from the outside world and its madness and it's also invigorating and helps the energy flow (beginning to sound like an old hippie now!).

*Emilys*

## Morning sickness – how long does it last and what can you do to help?

**I threw up my entire breakfast in the toilet** at work. I can't hide the pregnancy now as my vomit stopped up the toilet and they had to call the engineers in to unclog it. I'm green and have constant nausea. The thought of this happening for the next few weeks is making me miserable. I feel like I know what it is like to be severely disabled, as all you can think about is how not to get sick and how to make it to the toilet as fast as possible in case you do. I can barely work or think about feeding myself, much less my partner or child. The terrible thing is that the only thing that makes me feel better is to eat a little something, but I have no appetite and all smells are putting me off right now. I think though that if I can make it through until 12 weeks when the nausea stopped last time, I will have a much more positive outlook and be able to look forward to having another baby.

*Tinyfeet*

**With both my pregnancies** my morning sickness stopped almost overnight at around 14–15 weeks. Before that I was puking five times a day and nothing helped. They soon learned to quickly clear the halls at work when I headed towards the toilets. In the States pregnant women eat Saltines, which is a dry, salty cracker. I found that eating small amounts of food all day long helped a little.

*SofiaAmes*

> **Mumsnet tip**
> Keep morning sickness at bay by stashing ginger biscuits by your bedside for a nibble whenever you wake up.
>
> CarolineG

**I had sickness all the way through my pregnancy,** although the first 16 weeks were by far the worst and I also lost a stone and a half in weight. I got terribly depressed – I couldn't function and got no further than the bathroom most days (there were three particularly bad weeks). The sickness does go – you just can't see the wood for the trees at the time. I wasn't hospitalized but was given anti-nausea drugs. I even heard the opinion bandied about that morning sickness could be psychosomatic. I would beg to disagree!

*Alli*

**I felt pretty rotten** until around the 13-week mark, both in terms of severe nausea (not so much actually being sick) and fatigue. I used seabands and tried to keep a little something in my stomach. I would keep an open packet of Hula Hoops in each pocket just in case.

*Bundle*

**With both my pregnancies** I had extreme nausea for 12 weeks, although I only actually vomited once at the very beginning. Eating (anything) helped.

*Cam*

**With my first pregnancy** the morning sickness got progressively worse until 16 weeks – I was vomiting every day, several times a day by the end – and then it stopped pretty much overnight. Second time, I was very nauseous but only sick a couple of times. I used seabands and had acupuncture but nothing really cured it. The best feeling was that half an hour after I had been sick and could relax until the feelings came back!

*Susanmt*

**My sickness came and went** and wasn't necessarily in the morning either! My stomach was totally in knots – I had cramps/bloating/constipation too.

*Jessi*

**I had no nausea at all with my first,** felt like death with number two (but never actually threw up), was not too bad with the third and was rough (but not as bad as with the second) with my fourth baby. All of my nausea was from around the sixth to the thirteenth weeks.

*Janh*

---

**What the experts say**
Not everybody gets it, but most pregnant women experience some form of nausea, usually in the first trimester, and half will throw up at least once.

Kaz Cooke (*The Rough Guide to Pregnancy and Birth*)

---

**I had nothing at all** with my first but am now 19 weeks with number two. Up to around 12 weeks, with a blip at 14, I definitely felt worse. I wasn't actually sick but needed the ginger pills and biscuits and a cold flannel on the back of my neck, especially in the wee small hours. I just think every pregnancy is different.

It is certainly an interesting phenomenon, as no one really seems to know what causes sickness and why some women aren't affected at all whilst others end up in hospital.

*TigerFeet*

**I've just discovered that lemon** and lime cordial helps with nausea.

*Lemonmumma*

**Not very healthy but something salty** worked for me. All I could eat were crisps and apples!

*Snowqueen*

**I swear by acupuncture.** Also ginger, a diet high in zinc (seeds, wholemeal bread, small amounts of eggs, red meat, cheese, etc.) and remember to nibble every two hours.

*Sibble*

**My nausea is coming to an end** but it has really brought me down. My best hint is to carry mints everywhere. As well as being convenient to carry, it is useful to have a few if disaster strikes and you are actually sick outside the house – they freshen up your breath without the need to carry a toothbrush everywhere!

*JayTree*

**My morning sickness evened out** at around 13 weeks first time round. This time I'm 17 weeks and it is still going strong. When I was eight weeks I was admitted to hospital. I was so sick and they only let me leave when I started to keep my fluids down. My advice is not to worry too much about the food, some of it will stay down but keep your fluids up. If you feel really awful, don't be afraid to see your GP and give them a urine sample to check if your body is not getting enough nourishment. Morning sickness is par for the course for most pregnancies but don't just put up with it if you are feeling awful.

*Pie*

**My nausea occurs mostly in the evening** and thankfully, at 10 weeks, is easing a bit now. Someone told me to drink flat Coke – which does sort of work but I can't really face it first thing in the morning.

*Grommit*

> **Mumsnet tip**
> A big bowl of porridge last thing at night is great for 'morning sickness' that lasts all day and all night. It keeps your blood sugar level high and saves you waking up in the middle of the night feeling sick.
>
> *Biza*

**I found that chewing** stopped me thinking about the nausea so much – Starbursts and Fruitellas were my favourites or you could try gum. I'm into my 11th week and the nausea seems to have worn off, except occasionally. When it does surface I have a slice of dry toast and a glass of water and I'm fine after about 20 minutes.

*Rachael17*

**My saviour was low-dose vitamin B6** (available behind the counter) taken just before going to bed at night and first thing in the morning. It was certainly better than the 24-hour vomiting that I had, and it's amazing how much difference just a little can make.

*Sueanna*

**I found that eating little and often** helped a lot. Digestive biscuits worked well and I always carried a secret stash in my handbag. Food shopping was hell and I would only manage to make it round the supermarket by sucking boiled sweets and breathing calmly.

*Daffy*

**I was incredibly ill for two months** – off work, bucket by the bed stuff. I think I'd have been hospitalized if my mum hadn't come to live with us and sorted me out (she had it with me too). Anyway the following helped:
- Don't let anyone cook in the house – everyone must eat salads and sandwiches.
- Don't go in the kitchen, ever. Even the sight of the fridge made me ill.
- Don't eat meals, eat snacks.
- I could tolerate: cheddar cheese, slices of peeled apple and pear, crackers, toast, breadsticks, celery, lettuce and radishes. Also fairy cakes. Later on I managed more variety.
- I drank water, diluted fruit juice, strawberry and banana milkshakes.
- A house rule was 'never ask me what I want to eat' as just contemplating food set me off. My mum used to bring me a selection, which I could take or leave.
- Occupy your brain. I do think it's partly psychological, my mind would torment me with thoughts of the most nauseating food. I did puzzles and crosswords to keep my thoughts away from nauseous things.
- Liquorice Allsorts went down well, but they always do with me and when all else fails, try Eccles cakes.

*Emwi*

**For me, the best thing was cinnamon balls** – remember them? They are hard-boiled sweets. I went through bags of them for the first 13 weeks.

*Mum2Toby*

**Ginger cordial and soda helped me,** as did peppermint tea. The main thing is not to let your blood sugar drop too much. In the first three months I ate a digestive biscuit whenever I got up to the loo (frequently) in the hope this would help in the morning. The other thing I found helpful was chewing gum, which stimulates saliva.

*Philly*

**When I was pregnant** with both of mine I had very bad sickness and sipping either ice-cold water, tonic water or ginger ale seemed to work for me.

*Chiccadum*

**I had acupuncture for morning sickness** and it was brilliant. I found the seabands worked a bit but were not as good as the needles. I used to make fresh ginger and lemon tea (the bags weren't good enough) by steeping about 2.5cm/1 inch square of ginger and the juice of one lemon in about a pint of water, then leaving it about 10–15 minutes. Strain it and drink lukewarm. It made a big difference.

*Susanmt*

**I had really bad morning sickness** until 16 weeks, to the point that I ended up in hospital three times, but at 14 weeks I found something that worked for me: mints, mints and more mints.

*Sliverx2*

**If your sickness is bad,** get it checked out by your GP, as you could have dehydration problems. I actually found drinking water could make me vomit but it's important to keep trying, and once I'd got a bit down I did feel better. I also kept track of when I was actually most likely to vomit, as I was more likely to be sick at certain times of the day, so I'd try and eat at other times, notably before I went to bed, which at one point was the only way I could be sure of digesting anything – by going to sleep straight away! Apart from that I just stuck to eating what I actually fancied (strangely, it was usually ice lollies) and eating little and often.

*Tamz77*

**I discovered by accident** that I felt better lying in the bath: also in the swimming pool for a short time but I had to give that up after a while because of the smell of chlorine. Eating small amounts of something starchy quelled it a bit: it took me a while to cotton on to this because it's so hard to think of food when you feel sick. I found I could keep liquids down better if they were bland, tasteless and chilled. Also, sucking on a sweet suppressed nausea for a while, which helped on journeys in the car/train, or to get through an ultrasound scan. I had most success with mildly-flavoured ones like buttermints.

Sleeping in the daytime also helped, at least whilst I was actually asleep. My aunt also recommended sitting on the bathroom floor wailing, 'oh please just let me die'. I felt more comforted by her telling me that than by all those who offered more conventional advice. Another thing – it's bad enough being vilely sick without also blaming yourself (is it because I ate that toast/didn't eat that toast/ didn't get enough sleep/am a pathetic wimp?). Remember. it's not your fault.

*Eemie*

# Hyperemesis – what can you do to help and how long does it last?

**I had hyperemesis with my son** and was constantly sick throughout my pregnancy. I had it from about six weeks' pregnant until the day I gave birth. I was in and out of hospital all the way through, having to go on a drip due to dehydration. The day after giving birth I was fine, cured. It obviously didn't affect my baby, so there is no need to worry as long as you don't become dehydrated.

*Jeb*

**I had hyperemesis with both of mine** – it is a reaction to the pregnancy hormones. I left it until nine weeks with my first before I did anything about it, as I didn't really know what 'normal' morning sickness was like, and ended up in hospital on drips for two weeks, but quite often, rehydrating the body will alleviate a lot of the symptoms. There are anti-nausea drugs which can be given but most doctors/midwives will just tell you that sickness is a feature of pregnancy and it will wear off, so you need to stress how bad it is. Unfortunately, mine didn't really go until I'd had the babies, but on a positive note, I felt much better after the pregnancy than my friends who had sailed through.

*Scooby2*

**Anti sickness drugs worked wonders** for me during my first two pregnancies. For my second two pregnancies I was prescribed the drugs again, but I wasn't quite as bad (i.e. I could manage to sit upright sometimes) so got some seabands, which did a really good job at keeping the sickness to odd bouts. They work by acupressure. I kept them on constantly until five months just to be sure.

*Lou33*

**I was very badly sick with both my daughters** all the way through – the only days I wasn't sick were the days I went into labour. I tried pretty much everything and I have to say very little worked but acupuncture did help a bit. I got some relief from crunching ice. I was like a woman possessed if the ice tray was empty. I used to take a Tupperware, with sealable lid (!) for chucking up while driving and have thrown up in the oddest of places. In the end I got used to it, I suppose.

*Batey*

> **Mumsnet tip**
> If sickness means you can't face cooking, then buy everything ready-made to save the rest of the family from starving.
> *Nck*

**I had hyperemesis from week five** of my pregnancy, part of which included very strong aversions to most smells (my husband couldn't wear deodorant, I couldn't go to the supermarket because the smell of fresh fruit and veg would make me sick). It may sound odd but the best times were when I was admitted to hospital as the loneliness of having to stay at home being so physically incapacitated was unbearable. I did have it particularly badly and went through most anti-nausea drugs (most of which had horrible side effects) until I found one which worked.

I didn't put on any weight until about 22 weeks but they kept telling me not to worry – the sickness was a sign of a very healthy pregnancy and I had a lot of scans to reassure me that everything was okay. I now have an exceptionally healthy baby so no harm was done to him at all.

It's not conventional morning sickness and none of the usual remedies helped at all (ginger, etc.) – it does need proper medical intervention. It is miserable – there were days when I didn't think that I would make it through the next hour, let alone to the next day and far less an entire pregnancy. I think the level of sickness and debilitation plays with your mind and I wouldn't wish some of the blackest days on anyone. I can still remember it very vividly and it does make me think twice about going through another pregnancy.

Now I can say I love my baby more passionately than I could ever have imagined but at the time of being ill it wasn't something I was able to focus on. Until I got the medication I needed, I didn't cope with it very well.

*Harrysmum*

**I had hyperemesis during both my pregnancies** and was being sick 12 to 14 times a day. Things like ginger, flat Coke, etc. made me even sicker. I used to go everywhere with plastic bags and would frequently pull over to be sick when driving. What helped me a lot was a tape called Morning Well, which works on electrical impulses in the brain to reduce sickness. One thing to watch out for is anaemia caused by keeping no food down. My GP prescribed me tablets which, as I couldn't keep food down, I didn't even bother taking. However, my consultant arranged for me to have iron injections and a blood transfusion, which were painful but worked well.

*Eve*

**If you are worried that you might** have hyperemesis, then take a urine sample to your doctor. If there are ketones present, then your body is beginning to burn muscle and you need treatment. Be warned that the presence of ketones is usually sufficient reason alone to admit a pregnant woman into hospital for rehydration and treatment with anti-emetics. This may be tough if you have younger children, although I have to say that when I went in 10 weeks ago (I was eight weeks' pregnant), it was rather nice to not have to run around after everyone else.

*Pie*

**What the experts say**
Most studies show that there is no health or other difference between infants of women who experience hyperemesis gravidarum and those who not.
Murkoff, Eisenberg & Hathaway (*What to Expect When You're Expecting*)

**With both of my pregnancies,** everything made me sick and I mean *everything*, including water and anti-sickness tablets so I was hospitalized and on a drip both times. I found that my sickness stopped almost totally as soon as I passed the four-month mark, though. Munching on a ginger biscuit first thing in the morning, sucking glucose sweets and drinking peppermint tea, can all have some effect but what I really found helped most was lots of rest and eating and drinking what I fancied even if I was then sick – not that I fancied much – I lost a stone and a half and even my tights were too big! With my second pregnancy, if they'd offered to cut the baby out and throw it away I'd have probably agreed, especially after having an allergic reaction to the anti-sickness drugs in hospital, but once she'd arrived it's amazing how easily I forgot about it all!
*Candy*

# Alcohol – how much is okay?

**My teetotal mother was made to drink red wine** through her whole pregnancy by her doctor. I tried to drink the odd glass of wine when pregnant but found that it tasted like shampoo and gave up.

*Bruntwig*

**I drank beer and wine whilst pregnant** (very infrequently during the first trimester, maybe twice a week afterwards). The doctor didn't seem to think it was a problem – she ticked the 'non-drinker' box when I said I had a couple of glasses of wine some days.

*Lucy123*

**Mumsnet fact**
Twelve per cent of women drink alcohol every single day of their pregnancy whilst over 30 per cent drink every weekend.
Survey conducted by Eisberg

**I didn't drink any alcohol** during either of my pregnancies nor when breastfeeding. On holiday in France the waiters were very surprised when I refused wine at dinner despite the fact that I was very obviously pregnant.

*Cam*

**In both my pregnancies** I completely avoided alcohol (and caffeine, painkillers, etc.) during the first trimester. After that I probably averaged a few drinks a week. I found that, particularly later in the pregnancy, it calmed my baby down enough at night to let me get a few hours' sleep. None of my doctors, American or English, suggested that I was harming my baby.

*SofiaAmes*

**I also didn't drink in the first three months** but after that I used to enjoy the occasional glass of wine or beer (I gave up the G & Ts though). I went to a wine tasting with a group of friends when I was about seven months' pregnant. I probably had one glass of wine in total all night but had a sip of most. You should have seen the faces as I went up to get a taster of each.

*Sjs*

**I too couldn't stay away** from wine altogether – I just felt I wasn't me anymore. I only ever had one or two tiny glasses at a time, and only twice a week at most – except on holiday at seven months' pregnant when I had a tiny glass every night. No G & Ts though and I must say the lack of hangovers made nice change.

*Aloha*

**Mumsnet fact**
Over 30 per cent of women admitted that they missed alcohol when pregnant, with 16 per cent craving it often.
Survey conducted by Eisberg

**I drank my usual three or four glasses** per day for the first 10 weeks of pregnancy – I had no idea I was pregnant. Due to my age I thought it was the start of the menopause. I then went off alcohol altogether for three months but by the last three I was drinking a glass of wine most nights and continued whilst breastfeeding. My son loves wine and beer now – I still allow him the odd slurp!

*Lindy*

**I too drank a glass of wine an evening** in the second and third trimesters of my pregnancy. I think it has a lot to do with how well your body processes alcohol and my body has a lot of experience and seems to process it rather well! And just think of the millions of women who drink alcohol in the first few weeks of pregnancy because they don't even realize that they are pregnant.

*Batters*

**What the experts say**
There is no evidence that light or occasional drinking during pregnancy will harm your baby.
Kaz Cooke (*The Rough Guide to Pregnancy and Birth*)

There is no safe level of alcohol consumption in pregnancy.
Dr Miriam Stoppard (*New Pregnancy and Birth Book*)

**I was in total denial** for the first four weeks and drank a lot. I marked my birthday with a half-bottle of champers followed by a positive pregnancy test. My daughter is the most alert child I've met so I don't think an early binge is a problem.

*Motherinferior*

**I too drank like a fish before I found out** I was preggers. Then I had about two or three units a week. This time I am having one unit a week until I'm 12 weeks when I will raise my allowance to two or three units.

*Rhubarb*

**I came back from a long holiday** to find out I was five weeks' pregnant. Not only had I drunk every single night but I was also taking malaria tablets. In the end there was no harm done to the baby but I did worry up to the day he was born.

*Whymummy*

**I am on my second pregnancy** and have a few glasses of wine a week without problems. On holiday, I happily had a glass most days. My first pregnancy was more or less the same and I have a healthy two-and-a-half-year-old. I have investigated the research somewhat and the data available concludes that a bottle of wine or equivalent a day will definitely harm your baby (doh!) but other than that there is no evidence to suggest drinking is a problem. Basically, wine is a healthy part of our diet and if not abused will go a long way to a happier pregnancy and baby.

*Emmalou*

**I drank wine during the middle part** of my pregnancy – two glasses most days. My doctors were outraged about this and treated me as if I were a bad and irre-sponsible person. The midwives suggested one glass a day but two was fine for me and my daughter is perfect, or near as damn it!

*Scoobysnax*

**I had the odd drink here and there** but never more than a glass at a time. I used to make the most of that one drink on a night out. I told my partner that if I could only have one, it had to be a good one – normally a lovely glass of champagne.

*Claireandrich*

> **Mumsnet tip**
> Because I drank wine by the vat-load before becoming pregnant, everyone wondered what on earth I would do afterwards. I decided to mix one small glass of white wine with mineral water so that I had an 'adult-flavoured' glass to last me the whole evening.
>
> *Sobernow*

**I'll put my hand up to being another** non-absolutist about alcohol in pregnancy. If I'm honest, I probably believe that it is better to abstain completely, but in the scheme of things (i.e. life is not a risk-free activity), I think small amounts of alcohol are unlikely to have a measurable effect. The strange thing is I am not a big drinker when not pregnant, but I do enjoy it and don't want to stop completely.

*Elliott*

**I used to think that** since, during the first few weeks (most of first trimester), the placenta and cord weren't formed properly that I could get away with eating and drinking normally. However, when I spoke to an obstetrician he explained that it's during the first few months that the genetic code is laid down and that it's through those months that damage could happen. Later on in pregnancy the baby is merely growing, putting fat on and finishing bits off, etc. Saying that, most books/articles seem to tell you not to worry if you drank like a fish before you found out you were pregnant. I suspect it's long-term exposure that is really harm-ful rather than a single binge.

The way I see it is that I know that the alcohol goes across the placenta to the baby, that's fact. I don't know how much goes across but since I would never give my three-year-old a glass of alcohol, I probably shouldn't do the same to a child even younger than her.

*Wills*

> **Mumsnet fact**
> In the womb a baby's brain gains more than a quarter of a million cells every minute and at birth it contains 100 billion brain cells.
> *Practical Parenting Magazine*

**Oh, someone please tell me** the odd glass of wine isn't going to cause foetal alcohol syndrome? Blimey, there's enough guilt once you've had the baby...

*Wickedwaterwitch*

**Foetal alcohol syndrome** is a recognized, well-documented syndrome that results from excessive alcohol consumption in pregnancy.

*Princesspeahead*

---

**What the experts say**
If you have more than two drinks a day there is a one in 10 chance that your baby will develop foetal alcohol syndrome... Binge-drinking can cause the same damage.

Dr Miriam Stoppard (*New Pregnancy and Birth Book*)

---

**I worked on the assumption** that as long as I had the wine on a full stomach and had a big non-alcoholic drink afterwards, a daily glass or two in the second and especially the third trimester was okay.

Isn't there a theory that states if a mother feels stressed, upset or angry this is bad for the growing baby inside her? And that stressed mothers produce hyperactive children? I decided that if a glass of wine helped me to chill out, it was doing more good than harm.

*Frank1*

## Smoking – how easy is it to stop and is there anything that helps?

**I actually found it really easy** to stop smoking when pregnant because luckily (!) it made me feel so sick. It's amazing how I went from 10 a day to not being able to tolerate the slightest whiff. First time around I packed it in as soon as I found out I was pregnant, second time it must have been just days after conception – I'd been cutting down anyway because we were trying to conceive. My problem was staying off the damn things once the kids appeared. I lasted about a year with my first child but have slipped back on the slippery slope the second time and my baby is only three months.

*Roberta*

**When I got pregnant** I gave up the day after I did the test... I don't know how I did it but I did and it was great. Unfortunately, my husband didn't give up and so by the time my son was five months I was smoking again, although never around my son, only when he was in bed asleep. I assumed that when I got pregnant a second time I would give up easily again... WRONG! I just couldn't do it and even after a positive test I tried to pretend that I wasn't pregnant and that it didn't count because I hadn't seen a doctor yet, etc. I have now finally managed to go without for two weeks and I am really pleased but at nine weeks pregnant I was still sneaking outside when my husband went to work (my morning sickness made no difference).

**Mumsnet fact**
Almost one in three women who already smoke continue to do so during pregnancy.
Health Development Association survey

What finally worked for me was that I saw this cartoon picture of a pregnant woman smoking and you could see into her tummy. The umbilical cord was grey and the baby inside was blue in the face and coughing with a thought bubble coming out saying, 'Please mummy... for me?' It really made me think and I have done it but it was really hard. Whenever I want a cigarette I do something with my hands – phone a friend, do a puzzle with my son, do some housework, etc.

*Ghosty*

**I am only six weeks' pregnant** but have 'almost' stopped smoking – I am finding it really difficult even though I was a very light smoker (four or five a day). It's because I was only smoking in the evening and no one at work thinks I smoke. I am shocked at how difficult it is.

I know this sounds really selfish but I actually feel as if I am depriving myself of a treat and the guilt is only increased because it is not something that is talked about openly. I try and tell myself that if I don't stop now I never will and I hate to see someone pushing a buggy with a fag in their mouth.

*Colette*

**I was really lucky as I got pregnant** more or less just after I gave up. Don't think too harshly of yourself for still wanting to smoke – you're still an individual with your own needs and problems, not just a pregnant woman. Every time you manage to go without, you should praise yourself, and every time you give in at least know that you tried. Maybe take up yoga (with an instructor trained to teach pregnant women) to learn other methods of stress management. I took up chewing gum – I'm totally obsessed with it, keep it in pockets, in my bag, all over the house. Just try, try, try – that's the best anyone can do in this life, and that's hard enough as it is!

*Music*

---

**What the experts say**
Cigarette smoking stunts the growth of the foetus and inhibits the growth of the placenta. So the baby is more likely to be born early, have complications during labour and additional breathing problems at birth. Smoking is also believed to be linked to miscarriage, sudden infant death syndrome, childhood asthma and other respiratory traumas for babies and children.

Kaz Cooke (*The Rough Guide to Pregnancy and Birth*).

Some studies show that women who quit smoking early in pregnancy – no later than the third month – can reduce the risk of damage to the foetus to the level of a non-smoker.

Murkoff, Eisenberg & Hathaway (*What to Expect When You're Expecting*)

---

**As a non-smoker** I've got a slightly different perspective. My mum was a smoker and I loathed it, even as a small child. I often had bad throats and bronchitis and the smoke made me feel even worse. I can still recall the effect of my mum lighting up, as my throat constricted and it affected my breathing, and it isn't nice.

Maybe seeing it from your baby's point of view and wanting to be around to see your baby grow up will give you the incentive to kick the habit.

*Baabaa*

**Allen Carr's *Easy Way to Stop Smoking*** worked for me when I was pregnant. I am intending to use it again!

*Wickedwaterwitch*

**There is an NHS Pregnancy Quitline** – they really have good stuff to tell you. It takes three weeks minimum to get the addiction (at least the acute bit) out of your system so slowly cutting down doesn't work.

*Pupuce*

**Do speak to your midwife.** There is a lot of information out there to help pregnant women stop smoking, as it is high on the government agenda.

*Mears*

**I am six weeks' pregnant** and have just given up. If you call the NHS Pregnancy **Quitline** you can get patches. Also, there is a pill you can take if you are in the middle of an intense craving. You just let this pill dissolve in your mouth and apparently that helps. I have a Satsuma every time I want a roll-up. My main problem though is my temper – I'm sure it's the hormones plus lack of alcohol and nicotine. The NHS guy's advice was to have a big glass of water whenever you get stressed. He said water is very calming and also obviously good for you too. I must confess that I didn't tell my doctor when I saw her that I smoked, I knew I was going to give up so didn't bother talking about it.

*Jessi*

**I smoked whilst pregnant with my third child.** I had given up smoking for nine years and in that time had my first two children. I had started smoking again about 12 months before I became pregnant with my third baby and always thought when that pregnancy test came back positive I would be able to stop. Needless to stay I smoked all through the pregnancy and am still smoking now.

My daughter is now one and not walking and she also failed her eight-month development check (although after subsequent hospital visits they are not too concerned – just basically a lazy baby). She also has synostosis, where the plates in the brain fuse too early but her brain is not affected although she is still being referred to Great Ormond Street Hospital as a precaution. My Health Visitor has reassured me that none of what my daughter is going through was caused by my smoking but you can't help feeling guilty.

*Bumblelion*

**My mother-in-law smoked 60+** a day whilst pregnant with her two children and they are still hail and hearty (non-smokers) in their mid 40s – but don't ask about the mother-in-law.

*Lindy*

# Diet – what did you stop eating?

**When I was pregnant with my first child** I was absolutely neurotic about food-poisoning, to the extent that I wouldn't eat meat unless prepared in my own house, I never bought processed meats (even vacuum packed ones), avoided sausages, pre-prepared salads, ice-cream, cream cakes and milk-shakes, just in case they weren't prepared in a sterile environment. If I ate a dish that could contain uncooked egg I would worry.

I am now 26 weeks' pregnant with my second child and, having seen how relaxed most of my friends are in comparison, have been a little more adventurous – I will now eat a ham sandwich if bought from a reputable outlet.

*Subrina*

**I was concerned about toxoplasmosis** because we have two cats and they used a litter tray. So when I had my routine blood tests I asked to be tested for it. The test confirmed that I'd had it before my pregnancy. If it had turned out to be during the pregnancy, then they could have treated it. I don't know when/where/how I caught it, but a lot of people catch it in childhood apparently. The symptoms are hard to spot – many people don't get any and if they do, they are meant to be like flu. My understanding is that once you've had it, you can't get it again – so if you're worried, have a blood test – at least it might put your mind at rest.

*Pamela1*

**I've just done a research project** on toxoplasmosis and it's worth remembering that it is very rare really and even if you did catch it while you were pregnant it wouldn't necessarily cause problems for your baby. You can ask to be tested but there might not be much point if you are well into your pregnancy. It might only make you worry more if you're positive on the first test (which quite a few people are, having caught it when young) as you'll have to wait whilst they do another test to try and work out whether it is an old or a new infection. You can treat it but it seems doubtful as to whether the treatment actually does anything.

*Sunflower*

**My worry is listeria,** especially since eating some lovely lamb chump (pink in the middle but delicious) and a plate of smoked salmon. The stats are in my favour but would you ever know you'd had it with no symptoms? A dietician told me that just to avoid the obvious (blue cheeses, etc.) and to eat a balanced diet.

*TigerFeet*

**The advice** (from the Food Standards Agency) is to avoid eating ripened soft cheeses of the Brie, Camembert and blue-veined types, whether pasteurized or unpasteurized. Feta, sadly, also counts as a ripened soft cheese.

Apparently a pregnant woman has a far higher chance of becoming ill from listeriosis than a non-pregnant person. Listeriosis can cause miscarriage, premature labour and stillbirth. However, just because you eat these cheeses it doesn't mean that you WILL get listeriosis – and even if you do, it doesn't mean you will necessarily suffer extreme consequences. But there is a risk.

*Oakmaiden*

---

**What the experts say**
Whilst there is evidence to suggest that getting your get-up-and-go from caffeine isn't the best idea when you're pregnant, light coffee drinking doesn't seem to be a problem.

Murkoff, Eisenberg Hathaway (*What to Expect When You're Expecting*)

---

**To suggest 'two cups of coffee'** a day to a confirmed coffee-drinker is ridiculous. I drank at least six mugs of strong (I am not talking puny instant muck) coffee during pregnancy and breastfeeding – I now have a very lively and active toddler!

*Lindy*

**Mumsnet fact**
Pregnant women who consume more than four average-sized cups of coffee a day could be putting themselves at risk of miscarriage or delivering babies of low birth weight.

Food Standards Agency

**The advice from my midwife** was that if I had ever had a reaction to shellfish (I have been very sick after eating mussels), then I should avoid them. I think for a most people a prawn sandwich would be fine. I guess some of the problems didn't exist for our mothers because listeria and salmonella were just not as common as they sadly are today.

*Clary*

**You can eat shellfish** safely if it is thoroughly cooked and piping hot all the way through. The same goes for everything really. No piping hot food can contain listeria. And hard cheeses are all safe too.

*Aloha*

**Well, I was really unknowingly evil** and ate about a million raw oysters when about five months' pregnant with my boys and on holiday in France. I'd read the dos and don'ts religiously but somehow missed the shellfish embargo. Good grief but they were tasty though!

*ScummyMummy*

**I'm really not sure about all these things** that they say you shouldn't eat. I can't imagine in France they take a blind bit of notice and keep eating whatever they want. What do Mediterraneans, who live by the coast and whose diet is mainly seafood, eat?

*Megg*

**I was told not to eat either smoked salmon** or Parma ham. I'm afraid I ignored the advice on salmon but did not eat Parma ham or any uncooked cured meats because, rightly or wrongly, I thought they were potentially riskier than uncooked smoked fish. A friend living in France reports that the French don't give a monkey's about unpasteurized dairy products (cheese, etc.) but that they are completely paranoid about le toxoplasmosis and recommend getting rid of the family cat for the duration of the pregnancy.

*Clare2*

**Mumsnet fact**
Vegetarians give birth to 85 boys to every 100 girls, while the national average ration is 106 boys to every 100 girls.
*Nottingham University study*

**All this makes you realize** that once you're pregnant you should stay at home, in bed, in a dark room and not leave it for the full nine months. My view, while I was pregnant, was to eat and drink what I liked in moderation, as I figured that's what people have done since the beginning of time and before we had doctors who told us what we couldn't do.

*Meanmum*

**I do worry about all this 'eat this,** don't eat that' stuff. Surely common sense prevails? When not pregnant you wouldn't eat anything that looked a bit iffy, so why would you when pregnant? I ate all soft cheeses, my neighbour's free-range eggs, and had mussels abroad. Pregnancy can be full of worries – just try and enjoy eating what you normally eat!

*Misspastry*

**One of my best friends lives in France.** Throughout both her pregnancies she ate shellfish, pâté, soft and blue cheeses and drank a glass of wine most days, as do most French women. I was at a wedding in Italy in October and was chatting to an Italian mum about food and she couldn't believe all the things we are told to avoid – she had a craving for Gorgonzola whilst pregnant so ate loads of it. I ate shellfish in both pregnancies. We live on a very clean shoreline with mussels and scallops available to pick if you want.

*Susanmt*

**I've just come back from a weekend in Italy** where I indulged in a bit of 'when in Rome...' (though I was in Bologna). Over there, nothing is banned except smoking and raw meat – even then, I was advised that I could have Parma ham if it was young – under two years. I asked if it was okay to have ice-cream (raw egg) and they said, 'As long as you don't think it's too cold for the baby'! They actively recommend liver twice a week and have no worries about wine. They were all laughing at my 'no-no' list.

Things have certainly changed between this pregnancy and the last. Last time round all shellfish was banned – now prawns are okay from reputable sources but I'm not allowed shark or swordfish.

*Bruntwig*

**There are fairly clear guidelines** about what to eat from the Food Standards Agency. Cold meats and smoked salmon aren't on the list of no-nos in the UK although they may be in other countries. The FSA also says that hard cheeses, even those made from unpasteurized milk, are all right as the risk of listeria is extremely small.

Many women all over the world carry on eating things they like in pregnancy and others deny themselves everything. These are only guidelines after all.

*SueW*

---

**What the experts say**
You've got nine months of meals and snacks with which to give your baby the best possible start in life. Try to make them count.

Murkoff, Eisenberg & Hathaway (*What to Expect When You're Expecting*)

---

**I am pregnant for the second time** and I eat soft cheeses, Feta, prawns, mussels, clams, peanut butter and even drink the odd glass of wine. I figure if you buy stuff from reputable supermarkets then the chances of getting listeria are near to nil. Everything in moderation is my pregnancy motto.

*Cha PM*

**I think it's always worth understanding** the reasons behind not eating something, as this helps you make a judgement. It's those first three months that are the most critical – this is when the foetus is at most risk. Pâtés and soft cheeses, raw eggs and seafood are a no-no because of food poisoning, but remember that most EC rules state these products must be cooked, pasteurized, etc., so they remain safe. Supermarkets don't want the litigation from dodgy foods.

*Snickers*

**Don't believe that anything** you buy in a supermarket is fine to eat. I managed to get food poisoning and ended up in hospital after a sandwich made from fresh bread, a new packet of butter and an unopened pack of smoked salmon that had a Best Before date a week later. The only other thing I'd eaten that day was Weetabix for breakfast, so the doc firmly pointed the finger at the smoked salmon. They gave me a huge anti-emetic injection to stop the vomiting and kept me on a monitor for a few hours as apparently bad tummy upsets and especially diarrhoea can set off labour, which wouldn't have been ideal at 34 weeks.

*Anto*

**The most violent bouts of food poisoning** I have suffered haven't been from any of the supposed danger foods. Instead, they would seem to have been caused by poor food hygiene and storage. In Japan, pregnant women eat sushi, although not in summer. I have a friend who ate sushi throughout two pregnancies as she had no idea she wasn't supposed to. I'm not sure that I would risk it, although I would say that people rarely get ill from sushi because the standards of food hygiene are so high.

*Ringer*

**I eat sushi.** There, I've said it. I did in my first pregnancy and I've eaten it about four times this time around – I find it's the only thing guaranteed not to come back up. I'm very careful about where I get it from, only proper, ridiculously-priced Japanese restaurants. But there, I'm living dangerously.

*Pie*

**My mum ate peanut butter** all the time whilst pregnant with me and my brother and we are both fine but it is so hard to know what to do for the best.

*Scarpetta*

**It is very easy to say,** 'Oh my mum ate that, and I was fine', but we have more knowledge now and it seems silly to ignore the advice. I doubt very much that my parents ate goat's cheese and pâté, as those foods were not so common as they are now. I know that I would never have forgiven myself if I had eaten anything that had subsequently caused my baby to miscarry.

*Chinchilla*

**When I was pregnant** we didn't have the same warnings – and I have a nut-allergic child, which is certainly worth a bit of pain to avoid. Nut allergy is increasing. As far as I know, no one is too sure why, but they think it may be because peanuts and peanut oil are widely used in foods now and hence more people are exposed to them during pregnancy or shortly after birth.

Women with any family history of allergy – including asthma – are advised to avoid nuts. This is actually much more difficult than you realize until it becomes a matter of life or death. Then you check every label and realize that it's in a lot of chocolate and ice-cream, and even when it isn't listed, nuts are likely to have been used in the factory so there is still a risk of contamination. You also get food like sausages cooked in groundnut oil and textured vegetable protein is often contaminated with peanuts so we've been advised to avoid that too.

If you have a nut-allergic child, anytime they eat anything away from home you worry about whether it's been checked properly. Other parents are reluctant to invite them around because they don't want the responsibility. Insurance is more expensive – so is food because special offers are often ruled out. Some children die from nut allergy. Despite that, your GP will try not to give you epipens because they cost £30 each and you need two each year. Your child's school will be difficult over keeping the pens. Your child may have nightmares about dying. I could go on – but that's enough to make you see why it's worth avoiding.

*Robinw*


**My take on all of this is** 'moan like mad if you want' as it is a pain in the bum missing out on so many of life's pleasures. However, when you have finished moaning, do everything in your power to stay safe in the knowledge that it isn't forever (and chocolate is not on the list).

*StripyMouse*


**I think the quality of information** given on food risks in pregnancy is appalling – most of it doesn't even explain what the risk is (i.e. what problem you're trying to avoid), let alone how common the problem is.

A lot of things are forbidden (shellfish, eggs, cooked meat, unpasteurized cheese, etc.) because of worries about basic food hygiene and are an attempt to avoid common or garden food poisoning (salmonella, campylobacter, e coli etc). These can be nastier in pregnancy and make you quite ill but otherwise there's no specific risk to the foetus.

Listeria is a specific problem (associated with certain foods like soft cheese, cooked chilled meals, etc.), which can cause miscarriage, but it is very, very rare (much rarer than 'normal' food poisoning). Then there's toxoplasmosis, which can be acquired from poorly cooked meat or from cat faeces and can cause foetal abnormalities. So there are quite different potential consequences, and likelihoods of them occurring, which might well affect your behaviour.

And then, some risks are not highlighted at all – like the risks if you catch chicken pox in pregnancy – likely to be much more serious than eggs with a runny middle!

*Elliott*

# Cravings – what were yours?

**I ate prawns** throughout my pregnancy even though it was officially a no-no. I wouldn't eat them in restaurants because you don't know how long they have been out but I would buy them fresh and clean them myself. I know I probably shouldn't have, but I'm afraid the cravings got the better of me!

*Scarpetta*

**I crave, but avoid, peanut butter** because my daughter has asthma. I'm still undecided on prawns but if I do eat them I'll probably end up worrying about it afterwards. I do have the odd glass of red wine, cup of coffee and I love choco-late more than ever. But I've completely gone off brown bread and crave stodge instead.

*Colette*

**During my first pregnancy** I avoided meat as much as possible, simply because it made me feel ill (and supermarket chickens reminded me of foetuses).

During this pregnancy, even though I have been sicker, I crave the most dis-gusting junk food, especially cheap meat – basically, all the stuff that is likely to make you ill. I have driven around for hours looking for doner kebabs and have just polished off some frankfurters.

*Clucks*

**When pregnant with my twins** I gorged on Chinese party food – spring rolls, sesame toast – the more fried and fatty the better. With my third I was much healthier… just ate chocolate.

*Roberta*

---

**What the experts say**
As you raise fork to mouth consider: 'Is this a bite that will benefit my baby.'
Murkoff, Eisenberg & Hathaway (*What to Expect When You're Expecting*)

There are two important things to remember: you need only eat to satisfy your hunger, and you and your baby are what you eat.
Adriana Hunter (*The Queen Charlotte's Hospital Guide to Pregnancy & Birth*)

---

**I craved ice lollies** when pregnant with my daughter – loads of them – and chicken with my son (not so good as I am a veggie). To compensate, I went around sniffing other people's dinners and eating chicken-flavoured food.

*Dreamer*

**At 31 weeks** I seem to have become addicted to sparkling water. It's not a thirst thing but I just can't seem to get enough of the stuff (about 3 litres a day).

*Detta*

**With my first pregnancy** I also drank a lot of sparkling mineral water – I never really drank it before and have not had an awful lot since. This time round I can't stop drinking milk. I also had loads of fruit lollies and started eating fish despite being a veggie with my first. This time I've eaten chicken and fish but will be going back to a veggie diet when number two is born. I think chicken must contain something the body needs.

*Peanuts1*

> **Mumsnet fact**
> Three-quarters of mums admitted to food cravings during pregnancy, including such delights as strawberries covered in Marmite and Coca-cola on Weetabix for breakfast.
> Cow and Gate survey

**I ate loads of ice** throughout my pregnancies. It helped with the very bad vomiting I had all the way with both. Two years on, I still crunch ice cubes on a regular basis, as do both my sons.

*Batey*

**My big craving was gravy** – I remember rushing home at lunch and my mum would have a cup ready. Weird!

*Alley22*

**When expecting my first,** my craving was for Cadbury's Creme eggs – loads of them. With number two I didn't have any cravings – I just threw up for the first three or four months every time I smelt food cooking.

*Ailsa*

**I have been craving Mini Chedders** dipped in the fondant bit of Creme Eggs – everybody thinks it's disgusting especially the father-to-be, who turned green when I ate it in front of him!

*Rachael17*

**Mini Chedders and Creme Eggs** sound gorgeous and I'm not pregnant!

*Badjelly*

**Food...**

*Ghosty*

**I crave** alcohol!

*Rhubarb*

**Pickled onion** sandwiches for me.

*Eidsvold*

**Fruit juice** – but it gives me serious indigestion so I am trying to ignore it. I am also desperately craving Haribo wine gums. Any wine gums will do really but Haribo are the juiciest and the best.

*StripyMouse*

**Milk** – and that for me is a really strange craving since I hate drinking milk and never do. In the last two months of my second pregnancy I suddenly thought 'milk' and had pint after pint, adding milkshake mix to take the nasty milk taste away. Strangely enough, my second son (the one I was pregnant with) is milk-obsessed. He was a very long and boney baby and now aged three years and eight months he still is very big-boned. All that calcium I suppose. Perhaps he was sending me 'must have more milk' messages from the womb.

*Frank1*

**Mumsnet fact**
Pregnant mums who added the fatty acid DHA to their diets had children who scored higher in intelligence tests at four years than those who didn't. DHA is found in oily fish and cod liver oil supplements.
*Practical Parenting* magazine

**My thing at the moment** is iceberg lettuce, which I think is a tragic waste of a 'craving opportunity' during pregnancy. With my first I had a chocolate/sweet craving. Iceberg lettuce... I'm almost embarrassed to admit it.

*EmmaTMG*

**First time, I would have not thought twice** about wrenching a Babybel cheese from a toddler! I ate about 12 a day. This time I have a thing for Double Gloucester, Red Leicester and Cheddar plus a really bizarre Wine Gum thing that came and went in six weeks but during that time I ate more wine gums than I've ever eaten in my whole life.

*Bruntwig*

**Mumsnet fact**
Chocolate and ice-cream are the favourite cravings during pregnancy, closely followed by fish-based products, pickled onions and cheese.
Cow and Gate survey

**I had my hair done the other day** and was desperate to stick my finger in the bowl of hair colour and eat it. The craving got so bad I had to sit on my hands and look the other way. Very unnerving.

*Dahlia*

**Good job** you're not a hairdresser.

*Frank1*

**With my daughter** it was jam sponge and custard, so I put on rather a lot of weight. With my son it was Extra Strong Mints but I felt a bit odd if I had too many in a short space of time so had to limit myself to a packet a day.

*Lollypop*

**My friend got a craving for sand.** She used to sit in her partner's pub waiting for him to close up. Meanwhile, she would be casually picking away at the stone fireplace. She loved the feeling of the grit on her teeth and gums.

*M2T*

**Prawns, lobster, scampi,** Stilton, goat's cheese, white wine, mayonnaise.... AGGGHHHHHH!

*Grommit*

**I started longing for a rare steak,** spaghetti carbonara and a large glass of red wine. It seems you go off all your favourite things (chocolate/coffee/Diet Coke/roast dinners) and aren't supposed to eat all the things you do fancy... at least it is only for nine months!

*Chinchilla*

**My only craving was chunky Kit-Kat** bars and I still crave them now my youngest is nearly 18 months old. But I did manage to convince a guy I worked with (single, naive) that I had a craving for bacon sandwiches. He used to go and buy them for me from the staff restaurant.

*SoupDragon*

# Weight – how much should you put on and how easily does it come off?

**There is evidence that not putting** on enough is bad for the baby. I'm a large lady and was a bit concerned – I'd put on close to a stone by 20 weeks and another 4 lb by 30 weeks. But I have not been weighed at any appointments and if the professionals aren't worried about me, I'm not going to get hung up on it.

*AliP*

**I've put on at least 2 1/2 stones** with both pregnancies and am expecting to do the same again this time. Every pregnancy book I ever read has said 20–35 lb is normal. Hope I'm not wrong.

*EmmaTMG*

**What the experts say**
The general recommendation is to eat about 300 extra calories a day. You'll need to gain 25 to 35 pounds (11.5 to 16kg) during your pregnancy.

Dr Peter J. D'Adamo (*Eat Right For Your Baby*)

**I put on 4 stones.** I got the most horrible stretch marks everywhere and was so big I could barely waddle. On the plus side I lost all the extra weight fairly effortlessly and got major compliments for just getting to within a stone of my pre-baby weight. I'm desperately hoping the excessive weight gain doesn't happen again with this pregnancy although I had some trouser trouble this morning and I'm only seven weeks, which does not bode well.

*Eefs*

**I think there was widespread advice** in the 1960s that women should only gain 15 lb in pregnancy. Accordingly, new dads used to brag about their 'whopping great 6lb babies'! Of course, women were given the okay to smoke then, were not supposed to exercise under any circumstances and were told breastfeeding was no better than bottle-feeding, and all children should be toilet-trained by 18 months old. So whatever you do, don't listen to your mum if she tells you you're putting on too much weight!

**What the experts say**
This is no time to go on a weight-loss diet or a fast. Either could be very dangerous for your baby and you.

Kaz Cooke (*The Rough Guide to Pregnancy and Birth*)

**I put on about 30 lb** with each pregnancy. I had small babies (the biggest one was barely 7 lb). And within two to five months post-partum I was nearly underweight. I can't help but think that 30 lb should be a 'minimum' total weight gain for any-body that didn't start out overweight. I think a good rule of thumb is something like 1 lb per week from 10 weeks.

*Zebra*

**I'd put on half a stone by seven weeks** and was mortified! By 20 I was over a stone heavier but now at 36 weeks I'm only up to just over two stones overweight and everyone comments how neat I am. I've found the weight doesn't go on uni-formly like the charts suggest – it doesn't have to be 70 per cent in the second half of pregnancy. You'll know if you're eating well (and as far as I'm concerned that does include a compulsory cake each day).

I have to say I ate crap until about 14 weeks when I felt like eating normal food again. It seemed wrong that all the books were telling me to eat all these healthy veg when they just made me feel nauseous and cakes made me feel better. The good thing about getting bigger is that there is less space in your stomach so you can't eat as much anyway. For a sweet craving sometimes a drink will do. Chewing gum helps take that horrid taste out of your mouth as well. Remember a lot of that weight is in your breasts and certainly for me that was a bonus.

*Ninja*

**Judging by my jeans,** a lot of the weight is in my thighs! I went on a no-carbohydrate diet after Christmas and lost a stone. Then I got pregnant and felt I shouldn't give up a whole food group and now I'm eight weeks and have already put on half a stone. I find it especially demoralizing as I only just lost a stone, plus I can't go back on the diet, and I am a total sweet addict.

*Monkey*

> **Mumsnet tip**
> For sugar addicts who are trying not to put on weight try drinking a glass of water every time you have a sweet craving. It definitely works for some.
>
> *Pupuce*

**I am in my 34th week** and I have already put on three stones, but my cup size is merely a C, everything has gone around my hips, bum, and of course, bump. I feel quite depressed as I don't think I will ever be able to wear my size 12 clothes any-more, since if you are a pear shape like me, the weight is a lot harder to shift. I have been advised to cut out the junk food and the cakes and to walk more, as in the last few weeks it's okay not to gain much weight, so I am not too far off the mark. Expect your weight gain to slow down after the end of the 30th week.

*Caterina*

I am 21 weeks' pregnant with baby number two and have put on one stone and 4 lb, which for me is good. First time around I put on over three and a half stones, which I found a nightmare to lose (and I'm an aerobics instructor!). In the last four weeks of my first pregnancy my shopping trolley was as full of chocolate and cakes as it could be. But don't get too hung up on this. If you have a bad eating day, try and be good the next day and enjoy your pregnancy.

*Crazynow*

**Mumsnet tip**
Make sugar-free jelly using diet lemonade in place of cold water (it's best to chill first). I pour the jelly in plastic cups so I can just eat the portion I want. It's sparking and fat free, so has very few calories.

*Champs*

As far as I'm concerned, pregnancy is a license to scoff. I developed an enormous and previously undiscovered sweet tooth when pregnant and indulged it and cravings for fried food endlessly. If you can't do it when you're pregnant, when (let's face it) you're not too worried about squeezing yourself into your tight jeans, when can you do it? I'm a big believer in your body telling you what it needs in pregnancy – I went off cigarettes, caffeine and alcohol and went on chocolate, sweets and deep-fried anything, so by comparison I had a super-healthy nine months. Shame it didn't last.

*Nancy*

## Heartburn and indigestion – what helps?

**I had awful heartburn.** Gaviscon EXTRA is the only thing that works. You can also try a drink of milk before going to bed, although that usually results in 10 trips to the loo during the night. Still, I found that preferable to heartburn.

*SamboM*

**Gaviscon, definitely.** Get it on prescription when you see the midwife – the taste is foul whichever kind you have but it works a treat – you can swig it straight from the bottle. I went through about four big bottles with the last baby.

*Emmy*

**Not drinking red wine,** plus the aforementioned Gaviscon, although I had it in tablet form and yes, it's vile!

*Emmagee*

**I've been told to raise the bed** by four inches at the head end, which can help if the indigestion is bad in the morning. I've also been warned to avoid peppermint, tomatoes, chocolate and alcohol of any type.

*Robinw*

**I had terrible indigestion** when pregnant. If I let myself get hungry the indigestion seemed to get much worse so I used to carry digestive biscuits around with me. I couldn't drink my usual fruit teas or anything else for that matter, so had to stick to cold water and made it slightly more interesting with a small slice of lemon in it. Night-time was a problem as well – it was best to sleep propped up on a pillow. The worst news was that it lasted all my pregnancy.

*Daffy*

**My pharmacist said that Gaviscon** was 'positively recommended' in pregnancy. I've been swigging the aniseed stuff and it seems to help. There's no chance of an overdose of it with that taste, I must say. Perhaps trying to get rid of the taste with Toblerone wasn't such a good idea, if chocolate is meant to be avoided.

*Pamela1*

**Other things to avoid are carbohydrates,** high-fat foods like cheese, and spicy foods. Also eat only very small amounts of food, perhaps having six meals per day rather than three and allowing time for each one to be mostly digested before eating the next one so that your stomach doesn't get overfull.

*Suew*

**What the experts say**
It's nearly impossible to have an indigestion-free nine months; it's just one of the less pleasant facts of pregnancy.

Murkoff, Eisenberg & Hathaway (*What to Expect When You're Expecting*)

**I had terrible problems** towards the end of my pregnancy and used Remegel 'sweets'. They come in a tube. I kept them in various coat pockets and different bags (always nearby!) and I still find them in strange places a year later.

*Maisy1*

**I had horrible, horrible heartburn** from the day I conceived almost until the day I gave birth. I resisted the Gaviscon option (foolishly) for months. My GP persuaded me otherwise when she told me that she had a bottle under her desk the whole time she was pregnant. However, before I gave in to the delights (aniseed is VILE, I recommend the peppermint), the only natural thing I found that cured it for a while was fresh pineapple. They are hard to come by and expensive but it certainly did the trick with me. Apparently, tinned or pineapple juice doesn't work – it has to be fresh. Also avoiding fatty food, eating well before you go to bed and 'sleeping' upright (ha, ha) supported by lots of pillows, helps.

*Cha*

**I've recently started getting chronic indigestion** and it's awful. I'm lucky in that I've not suffered from it everyday but oh boy when I do... I'm crap at taking medicines, as I hate having something in my mouth so even the Gaviscon suckables make me want to heave! I've now resorted to breaking them up into small pieces and swallowing them with water. Hot drinks sometimes soothe it a little.

*Wills*

**Try a yoga exercise** where you stretch your arms above your head thus elongating your upper body.

*Beetroot*

**Eating small amounts** all the time will also help. Leaving your stomach empty will not. Giving birth is the only real solution – rest assured then all your indigestion problems will disappear.

*SofiaAmes*

**I used to keep a cup of milk** by the bed (in warmer weather I kept it in a thermos) and took small sips.

*Bubbly*

**I tried everything** but got no relief until my consultant prescribed Zantac (Ranitidine). Some doctors are reluctant to prescribe it but my dear consultant said there was no evidence it was in any way harmful. It worked like a charm. I took it in the last few weeks of my first pregnancy and practically from the start of my other two.

*Jasper*

**Acupuncture works for me.** Mind you, I already have acupuncture for other things (horrible sinusitis, mainly) so it may be that my system's used to it – but my acupuncturist said helpfully she'd 'try something for the heartburn' last Wednesday and very much to my surprise it seems to have done the trick.

*Motherinferior*

**I have had fairly minor pregnancy indigestion** with both pregnancies. I noticed that it was only certain foods that caused it so it might be worth seeing if you can isolate the main culprits. Gaviscon tablets worked for me but I agree they taste terrible. I think the lemon ones are slightly more palatable that the mint.

*MrsS*

**Sipping hot liquid helped** – you could try peppermint tea. I also found that ginger was good. Take some fresh ginger, chop it in bits, put it into the teapot and pour boiling water on it (of course you have to like ginger for this to help).

*Isbee*

**I have noticed my indigestion flaring up** if I eat after about 6.30 pm in the evening or eat something rich. I had a hideous week last week where the heartburn seemed constant. Although I am only drinking (caffeine-free, low tannin) redbush tea, I found cutting this out for a few days and switching to peppermint tea did help. And a few nights of eating ridiculously early cleared it up (for now).

*Clare2*

**Whilst pregnant with my daughter** I used to eat my evening meal either standing up at the kitchen worktop or kneeling high against a coffee table – basically, elongating yourself to make the most room for your stomach. I then didn't sit down for at least an hour after eating – I took nice evening walks with my son and left my partner with the clearing away. I also drank lots of fruit teas.

*Jaybee*

**Try TUMS.** I used to buy them in huge bottles. They are just a simple antacid but worked well for me. And they taste like Refreshers so are nice to take!!

*Spanna*

**Try ice-cream** – it's cold, soothing and alkaline. I had it every night in the latter stages of my pregnancy. It really helped with indigestion, but I did put on a fair amount of weight!

*Lolasmum*

# Backache blues – what can you do to help?

**I am 35 weeks** and am like the biggest old crock imaginable. I feel about 70 and am shuffling round wincing at every twinge like an old granny. My husband thinks I'm laying it on with a trowel and keeps raising his eyes to heaven whenever I hove into view. But honestly, everything aches, particularly my pelvis and my lower back. This is my second pregnancy and it's so different from number one when I was smugly skipping round and doing yoga until the very end, being complimented on how 'neat' I was (I am a complete heffalump this time round). By the evening, a hot water bottle in the small of my back is the only thing that works for me.

*Anto*

**I have always suffered from back pain** but about 16 weeks into pregnancy I found it unbearable. My GP referred me to an NHS physio, who said it was my ligaments slackening early – all the loosening up that normally happens towards the end of pregnancy. I had to see the physio fortnightly and at about 28 weeks started wearing a back support (which was bliss, believe it or not). It was like a giant bandage that was worn like a girdle and helped to support my bump. I honestly don't think I could have made it to term without the help.

*Snugs*

**You could try swimming and osteopathy** but the best thing I found for immediate relief was a lavender wheat cushion. It could be heated in the microwave or oven and was fantastic throughout my pregnancy and labour. I would sleep in the foetal position with big knickers holding it in place. (Maybe too much information!) Now my partner, who also suffers from a bad back, has stolen it.

*Winnie*

---

**What the experts say**
The hormonal and joint changes of pregnancy cause the pain, and the way you sit, walk and sleep can make it worse.

Dr Yehudi Gordon (*Birth and Beyond*)

---

**I put my back out really badly** when six weeks' pregnant with my second son. Although I gained movement back, the pain was constant. At eight weeks I went to an osteopath and about six trips later the pain was gone completely. It was sore after each visit but the actual manipulation didn't hurt at all. I was completely pain free for a whole year – something I'd not had for ages as I've suffered from back pain for about 10 years now. The pain came back through general misuse, e.g. leaning out of bed to pick a hefty newborn out of the Moses basket. Again, the osteopath worked wonders.

A couple of other things to try are a hot water bottle or a little electric blanket. I also used my electric blanket to keep the Moses basket warm when I took my baby out to feed in the night, so I got a lot of use out of it. Another thing to remember is that if you swim, you shouldn't do breaststroke with your head out of the water as this puts strain on your lower back.

*SoupDragon*

**What tends to cause back pain** in pregnancy is that the curved bit at the small of your back gets more pronounced when you are upright to countereffect the weight of the bump in front. When you lie down, the muscles and ligaments start to stretch out, which can be painful.

Exercise is the best treatment. Ask to be referred to a physiotherapist by your GP for NHS treatment or pay privately for a manipulative physio/osteopath or chiropractor. Sadly, although treatment will help with pain relief, you may find that the problem doesn't completely resolve until after your baby is born as your bump is still growing. That's why a good exercise programme is invaluable to self-treat on a daily basis.

My top exercises are:

- Lie on the floor with knees bent, feet flat. Gently roll your knees from side to side. You should feel a stretch in your lower back as your knees drop a little further each time. Repeat 10–20 times.
- In the same starting position, clench your tummy muscles to push the small of your back down in to the floor so that you are eliminating the curve in your lower back. Hold for five seconds and release. Repeat 10–20 times. (These are called pelvic tilts.)
- On all fours, allow your tummy to sag so that your lumbar curve is exaggerated (not into pain) and then clench your tummy muscles and push your back up to the ceiling so you are rounding your back. This is called 'The Cat' in yoga. Repeat slowly 5–10 times.
- Finally, sit facing backwards on a kitchen chair, resting your arms and head forwards so that you are relaxed and get a partner or friend to rub the affected area to alleviate the muscle tension.

*Honeybunny*

**I had bad backache for months** when pregnant with my second. I found a good, hard pillow helped with the pain.

*Paige*

**I had dreadful backache during my pregnancy** and for six weeks after the birth too. The pain was so bad sometimes, particularly afterwards, that it would reduce me to tears. I finally found a physiotherapist who specialized in skeletal manipulation and the relief was immense. (The physios I was referred to on the NHS were frightened to do anything and had no experience of working on pregnant women.)

She showed me some very specific exercises to do. Here are some helpful tips she gave me:

- Do not carry a handbag on one shoulder.
- Whenever you can, get on all fours and let your bump hang down for a bit.
- To help relieve sciatic pain, get on the floor, lie on your back and press your bum up against a sofa or armchair. Raise your legs up so that your thighs are at right angles to your body and your lower leg rests on the seat of the sofa or chair. You need to stay in that position for at least 15 minutes.
- In bed place a cushion or pillow between your thighs.

*Molly1*

**I use a birthing ball** and it's fab. The real killer for my back is slouching on the sofa (which is exactly what you really feel like doing). Sitting on the ball keeps your pelvis tipped forward and your spine straight.

*Emmagee*

**Find out what position the baby's in.** My son was back to back and it was absolute agony for the last four weeks of my pregnancy. He was also quite large when born so I think that didn't help either. If your baby is in this position you can try spending some time on all fours to encourage him to move.

*Katierocket*

**As the bump gets bigger,** lying on your side means your leg has to twist over more to rest it on the bed. If you try and keep your back straighter by raising the leg it should stop the pain. V-shaped pillows are good to put between your legs, as you can rest most of the lower leg on it, and keep a straighter position.

*Lou33*

**You could try a TENS machine** – I had excruciating back pain in my first pregnancy and the TENS was a godsend. I used to spend the last hour before bedtime sitting in bed reading with the TENS on – bliss.

*Pamela1*

**For the last eight weeks** of my pregnancy my back pain got worse, to the point where I had to get up every hour during the night. You could try osteopathy (I did, and though it doesn't get rid of the pain entirely, it helped a tiny bit), otherwise, just look forward to the birth – my back pain went immediately. Of course, your little one will be waking you in the night then, but the quality of sleep improves straight away.

*Luluu*

# Migraines and headaches – what can you do to help?

**I'm currently 18 weeks pregnant** and for the last four weeks have suffered almost daily (with a blissful headache-free week in the middle) from the most appalling headaches. They're not migraines, I know what they feel like only too well, but start just under my skull on the left side, usually at about 6 pm each evening. Sleep and massage haven't helped, and taking paracetamol is about as effective as attacking an elephant with a fly swat. I'm at my wit's end.

*Slug*

**I had headaches at around 18 weeks** in my last pregnancy and they stopped when I got some iron tablets – my count was 9.2, which was horribly low for middle pregnancy and I didn't know it. I felt so much better after about three days on iron.

*Emmy*

**I'm twenty weeks and I have headaches** every day, usually in the afternoon. Luckily for me the paracetamol works well. My obstetrician also suggested I drink a lot of water, rest as much as possible and try not to be so stressed. Ha! Trying not to be stressed is very stressful but he did say that taking paracetamol every day is fine. The other thing he said is that a low dose of aspirin – i.e. less than 75mg – is fine too. So you could talk to your doctor/obstetrician about trying that.

*Jj*

**If you are drinking tea,** try to cut it out altogether (not a single cup). It really helps, I've found.

*Pupuce*

**In my experience** the headaches lasted until about 18–20 weeks. I just took paracetamol and went to bed but then it was my first pregnancy and I didn't have to look after any other kids (apart from my husband).

*Badjelly*

**I too suffer from migraines** that get worse during pregnancy. The unfortunate thing is you do pretty much have to stick it out – for me, paracetamol didn't help and I couldn't take the stronger painkillers. Mine stopped at about 17 weeks.

*Ejanes*

**I had terrible migraines** at least every week, from four weeks onwards. I tried acupuncture (in desperation) at 10 weeks and it worked brilliantly – after the first treatment the migraines disappeared totally. I can honestly say I haven't had so much as a headache since my first treatment and I'm 32 weeks now.

*Enid*

**I suffered with migraine** early on in my second pregnancy – I had the whole numbness/blurred vision thing, which was a bit scary, as I didn't have it first time round. My migraine was definitely dehydration-related. Although I did drink a lot, it was of the full-sugar squash variety (I tried to avoid artificial sweeteners) and apparently this was giving me high blood-sugar and increasing the headaches – so it's better to down lots of water.

*Subrina*

**Migraines** (especially with visual disturbances) can be a sign of pre-eclampsia. I had never had a migraine until my first pregnancy and then had a couple of whoppers with flashing disco lights before my eyes. Of course, I didn't think to tell the midwife or doctor but later on got pre-eclampsia and they were definitely related. However, I think headaches in general are quite common in pregnancy so don't leap to terrible conclusions, but it is worth mentioning to your midwife and getting your blood pressure checked as soon as you can.

*Bun*

---

**What the experts say**
If you experience for the first time what seems like a migraine, call your doctor immediately. The same symptoms could also be indicative of a pregnancy complication.

Murkoff, Eisenberg & Hathaway (*What to Expect When You're Expecting*)

---

**I had really bad migraines** in the early weeks when I had to simply lie in the dark and sleep. Now I'm 27 weeks they've subsided and I'm keeping my fingers crossed they don't come back. I found that drinking loads of water really helped with tiredness and headaches in the early weeks – even now I find a couple of glasses of water and a ten-minute sit-down refreshing.

*Loobie*

**I'm a migraine sufferer too** and they are very different from bad headaches – they're absolutely disabling. paracetamol may help with the after affects but, to my knowledge, it can't do a lot for the migraine – only prescription drugs, some of which you can't take during pregnancy, help. I think you have to suffer through it, though eye patches can be soothing. In my case pregnancy increased the frequency of migraines. I found I had more than usual in the first few weeks after my son was born, so even though I exclusively breastfed, I expressed some milk and kept it in the freezer for my husband, so that if it did happen when my baby needed feeding, he could do it while I vomited my way through a migraine.

*Emilys*

## Foetal movements – how do they feel, when do they start and do they mean anything?

**The first movements I felt** were at about 19 weeks, and were a bit like wind – sort of like someone blowing a wet raspberry on the inside of my stomach. Not a very romantic description, but that was what it felt like to me!

*Oakmaiden*

**I thought they felt like little muscle spasms** – it's so exciting, isn't it? I think this is the most fun part of pregnancy – enjoy it if you can.

*Ninja*

**I'd describe it as a butterfly** fluttering about in your lower abdomen. I felt my first quite early (certainly before 17 weeks) and then they just got stronger over the next few days and weeks.

*Princesspeahead*

**I remember the first ones** feeling like bubbles. Make the most of these ones, it'll soon be jumping on your bladder at the most awkward moments.

*Batey*

---

**What the experts say**
You are likely to feel your baby move at around the twentieth week of your pregnancy if this is your first pregnancy.
Adriana Hunter (*The Queen Charlotte's Hospital Guide to Pregnancy & Birth*)

---

**I didn't feel anything until 21 weeks** and the first movements felt like muscle spasms. Mine kicks under the ribs and in the pelvic/bladder region at the same time now. And I love every single kick!

*Bunnyrabbit*

**I didn't feel anything** until about 25 weeks – and was beginning to get worried, but in restrospect I think I just didn't know what it actually was and put early movements down to wind. He certainly made up for it by kicking the c\*\*p out of me for the last few months of pregnancy!

*Gini*

**I started feeling a sort of fluttering** at about 20 weeks, real kicks at about 23 weeks, I guess, and Muffin the Mule at about 30 weeks!

*SamboM*

**Mine felt like fluttery tummy** gurgles at first (17 weeks) and then turned into more definite shifting feelings at around 19 weeks – I wasn't sure last time that the fluttery ones were the baby but am more convinced second time round. It is a great feeling.

*StripyMouse*

**I remember feeling** as if I had a goldfish swimming around inside me!

*XAusted*

**With my first pregnancy** I felt movement quite early, at about 16 weeks, and by 20 weeks they were really quite frequent. I'm now 17 weeks in my second pregnancy and contrary to the general perception that you feel things earlier the second time round, I've not really felt anything yet. My theory is the thinner you are, the earlier you feel them. I've definitely got more padding this time.

*Quimble*

**My midwife pointed out to me** in the nicest possible way that I was too podgy to feel much movement second time around. First time I only felt gentle movements for ages and they said this was because the placenta was at the front (or were they just being nice?).

*Sobernow*

**I felt movement really early** second time around – about 12 weeks. I'm sure it's because I recognized the feeling from the first time.

*Paula1*

**I felt it much earlier second time** round and also put it down to the fact that my stomach muscles had gone to pot.

*SoupDragon*

**None of mine moved that much,** but when they did they were usually more active in the evenings than in the day. My three are the most lively, energetic, tireless children ever. So quiet bumps don't necessarily mean quiet babies and vice versa. When it does start to move it's an amazing feeling. My twins kept turning – a massive churning movement that could make me feel quite sick. They were still doing it at nearly 40 weeks.

*Kkgirl*

**The ONLY thing I miss about pregnancy is the baby kicking inside me – amazing feeling. My husband used to find it quite weird when he woke in the night and I was fast asleep but the baby obviously wasn't.

*Azzie*

**I am 25 weeks into my first pregnancy** and seem to have a very active bump, particularly first thing in the morning, at teatime and when I am hungry. There is rarely any movement in the afternoons. It seems to know exactly where my bladder is and to take delight in jumping on it in the middle of meetings. And all this whilst on the inside – I fear it does not bode well!

*Sam29*

**I had two non-stop** bumps and then got two non-stop boys.

*Hilary*

**I had a very active bump** (Bruce Lee, eat your heart out!) and now a very active 131/2–month–old.

*SnoobyKat*

**My bump always seemed to know** when to expect meals. Afternoons were definitely the quietest and the evenings were definitely riot time. After 'Duracel bunny' son was born the same sort of pattern applied – he's never conformed to the amount of sleep that babies are expected to need at any particular age. In particular the 'in bed at 7 and asleep for 12 hours, with a couple of naps in the day' pattern has been a total non-starter for us – he simply has too much energy/stamina. The up-side of all that activity is that he did hit all the physical developmental milestones really early (rolling at eight weeks, sitting up by five months, crawling before seven, etc.).

*GillW*

> **Mumsnet tip**
> Take a rest mid-morning and mid-afternoon in the last few months of pregnancy to help prepare the baby for daytime wakening as opposed to night-time.
>
> *Mamosa*

**My son never kept me awake** at night when he was a bump... wish I could say the same since he came out!

*Ghosty*

**In my first pregnancy** I had a very active bump and then a very active, very sporty child. During my second pregnancy my bump hardly moved. It was so quiet I even contacted the midwife a couple of times as I hadn't felt the baby move for a couple of days. The result was a placid, content baby.

*Jaybee*

**My bump was very active** and used to keep me awake all night and make me feel quite sick during the day. I was very active too, walking a mile or more to work each day until I was eight months gone. I was convinced I would have an active baby but, just like her father, she is very laid-back. She likes nothing more than to cuddle up on my knee and read a book. She won't walk more than she has to and would rather sit in the buggy.

*Rhubarb*

**Bump number one was the most active** of mine, especially in the evenings and at night but turned into an easy-going baby, who slept through from three weeks.

Bump number two was less active but turned out to be very highly-strung. (Thinking about it, he was 'nervy' in the womb, too, jumping at loud noises, etc.). Number three was fairly inactive compared to the first two and is a very calm person now. Bump number four was active. I felt movements from 14 weeks, but they almost never woke me at night, even when I got up to go to the loo. She must have been catching all the sleeping she wasn't going to do for the next two and a half years. She absolutely never stops, even now, and is exhausting. I even went to the hospital when 37 weeks with my fourth baby, as I hadn't felt her move all morning, not even during a relaxation class. The staff were lovely and didn't make me feel neurotic. As it was, my daughter was just taking a rest and she was fine but I was so glad I went.

I felt most movements with numbers one and four and I think this was because they were both OP. All the limbs seem to be at the front then and it's hard to ignore a foot or hand sticking out of your tum. The cat used to get annoyed at being booted in the backside or head by my stomach!

*Baabaa*

**I wasn't working when pregnant** with my first and it established a set pattern of movement, nearly always at the same times, but that was because I had a routine (lying on the sofa watching *Ready, Steady Cook!* half asleep at 4.30 pm). Second pregnancy I was so busy running around after big one, there was no routine and some days my second would be so quiet I would worry, but then he would make up for it and give me a big kick.

*Ems*

**Mine slept the whole day sometimes** or I didn't notice any movement due to rushing around all day. I remember a poster in my doctor's surgery with pictures and little rhymes telling you to count 10 movements a day. It had the mummy nicely at home waiting for her husband's return from work with apparently nothing to do but count baby's kicks and of course the obliging little baby was kicking regularly.

*Sml*

**I spent the last half of my pregnancy** worried because I couldn't count 10 kicks. The midwife kept scaring me at the check-ups, saying that I should rush to hospital if I couldn't feel 10 per day. The baby was totally laid-back during the birth as well, which also panicked the midwife. Suffice to say he is normal – it's just one more thing you don't really need to worry about in my view.

*Lil*

**I didn't feel movement** until 20+ weeks and when I did it was erratic. Nearing the end I was put on a monitor because of the lack of movement and lo and behold, baby put on a somersault show. It's so true about being busy and not noticing movements, although my baby had a daily bout of hiccups which was quite amusing.

*Mh*

**Mine always moved when his dad spoke to him** after not doing much all day. I thought he didn't move at night as he never woke me but my partner says he was often woken by being kicked in the back.

*Peanuts1*

**My daughter didn't move much at all** – a few kicks here and there, hiccups several times a day but nothing major. When I went into hospital to have her the midwives were so concerned about her lack of movement that I was hooked up to a foetal monitor almost constantly, which was a total pain. Everyone was really concerned about her not moving every 40 minutes and so there was real panic the whole way through my labour – they were so I worried I nearly had an emergency Caesarean. But out popped a very sleepy but healthy baby, ready to be fussed over by umpteen doctors. She was very sleepy for the first couple of weeks too but now I wish she would sleep more.

*Pamela1*

**Never ignore a slowing down** or absence of foetal movement even if late in pregnancy. Always get it checked out by a midwife or at the hospital. It's easy to assume the baby may be sleeping or have less room to move but if you haven't felt movement for a day or just feel things are not right then, check it out immediately – no one will mind you asking to be checked and if they do, then ignore them. I had a late loss (37 weeks) and wish I had gone to the hospital sooner to be checked out. I feel I was far too blasé about lack of movement but my baby had been really quiet and inactive throughout the pregnancy. It's very rare for a baby to die that late in pregnancy without obvious warning signs but it can happen.

*Mimmi*

**What the experts say**

If you are at all anxious and feel that there's been a definite change in the pattern of your baby's movements, call your doctor, midwife or the hospital and seek advice.

Mary Nolan (*Being Pregnant, Giving Birth*)

Foetuses are only human. Just like us, they have 'up' days, when they feel like kicking up their heels... and 'down' days, when they'd rather lie back and take it easy.

Murkoff, Eisenberg & Hathaway (*What to Expect When You're Expecting*)

**From around 32 weeks** my baby sometimes would literally not move for days on end from. At first, I kept going into the foetal monitoring unit to be checked but after doing this countless times I got embarrassed about wasting their time. Towards the end of my pregnancy, I started to lie to the midwives about movement as it was getting to the point where I would have been permanently hooked up. In the last week of pregnancy I maybe felt a total of two movements.

My daughter is a complete pudding, who is the archetypal 'thrilled to be watching mummy peel potatoes' baby and at 10 months shows zero interest in crawling or anything else requiring any exertion.

*Ringer*

**All babies are different,** some very active, some very quiet. It can depend on their position, you and what you are doing, their routine...oh so many things. It is quite common for movements to change in pattern and for there to be quiet periods. You can't help but panic even though loads of people tell you it's normal. But if the only thing that will convince you things are okay is to see some proof, don't be scared to ask your midwife to check the heart beat or have a scan or whatever you need for reassurance. They are used to neurotic mums and they'd rather catch something than take any chances. So don't be afraid to pester but rest assured that just about anything is normal.

*Hopeful*

# Insomnia – what can you do?

**I am 28 weeks' pregnant** and for the past three weeks or so have been having terrible problems sleeping. I try to go to bed around 11 pm and take a little time to nod off but I am waking again at least once and am finding it harder and harder to get back to sleep at night. I lay there for two hours last night, listening to my partner snore and wanting to belt him, before giving up. Nothing in particular wakes me. I usually don't need the loo, I just seem to wake from being a little uncomfortable with my growing bump and then I can't get back to sleep.

*Janus*

**Towards the end of my pregnancy** I found it easier not to go to bed until midnight or 1 am, and I would usually have hot chocolate late in the evening to help me to feel sleepy, though it didn't always work. Try and catch up a bit during the day. I suppose it gets you into the routine in advance of the new baby.

*Demented*

**I found that listening to the radio** helped. I've got a speaker that plugs into the earphone socket and slips under your pillow, so only you can hear it. If you can't get back to sleep, there's usually something interesting on the World Service.

*Bashful*

**I'm 27 weeks' pregnant and can't sleep** very well. With me it's partly because I'm uncomfortable and partly because my mind is racing. One thing I have found quite helpful is wedging an extra pillow between my knees. I read somewhere that it helps keep the spine in the correct alignment. I find that reading just before I go to sleep helps as well, but not factual stuff, something light or amusing.

*Melly*

**I'm 28 weeks and suffer from insomnia** every now and then (not continuously, thank goodness). I usually get up but don't do anything too active – e.g. I watch News 24 or listen to the World Service until it gets tedious enough to send me off to sleep on the sofa. I don't try going to bed later because I genuinely feel tired around 9.30–10 pm. I try and catch up with a nap in the day on the two days a week I'm not out at work. I think it's the hormones and baby activity that's responsible, but it's a real pain.

*Bundle*

---

**What the experts say**
Many people expect to sleep 8–9 hours but neurological research suggests that 5–6 hours of restful sleep is all that is required each day.

Dr Yehudi Gordon (*Birth and Beyond*)

---

**Give birth!** Seriously though, I had terrible insomnia all through both my pregnancies. I kept a book by the bed (make sure it's light reading) and just read with
a very dim nightlight until I fell asleep again. It's important not to get too agitated
about not sleeping, because it just makes you more awake. Also, try not to eat
dinner within four hours or so of going to bed. I found the acid indigestion kept
me awake too. Towards the end I had a little liqueur just before going to bed to
help take the edge off my insomnia. If your partner snores, as mine does terribly,
you can try giving him an antihistamine or alternatively, try ear plugs – I found the
yellow squishy ones are the only ones comfortable enough for sleeping.

*SofiaAmes*


**I had a pregnancy insomnia problem** and now I have a five-month-old problem
which is just as effective at keeping me awake. Try a few drops of lavender oil in
a warm bath every night. It really is relaxing and calming.

*Mo2*


**I'm on my second pregnancy** and seem to have woken up every night during it for
varying lengths of time. I'm now at 36 weeks and was up for an hour last night –
there is no obvious reason for it but I've become resigned to it and almost always
put the hall light on (so as not to wake my partner) and stay in bed and read until
I drop off again. I could almost say I've begun to enjoy this time and am getting
through so many books. I've suddenly noticed how much my partner snores.
Perhaps he's always done this but when I'm lying awake he seems determined to
get louder as the night progresses. I normally resort to belting him so he turns
over and stops for a while.

*Mog*


**Late pregnancy insomnia** is a really cruel trick of nature. I had it in both my pregnancies and found it very difficult to cope with. I think a healthy dose of fresh air
in the afternoon helps, particularly in winter when it is tempting to stay indoors
with the central heating on. With my second pregnancy, not trying to fight it was
what kept me sane in the end. I bought some really good books and when I woke
up, instead of tossing and turning I went downstairs and read. Sometimes I slept
better on the sofa than I did in the bed. I also think if you can avoid taking a nap
during the day, you will sleep better at night. Put your feet up for a bit but try not
to go to sleep.

*Molly1*

## Stretch marks – is there anything you can do to prevent them and get rid of them?

**I was absolutely fine** until the day I gave birth, then I got stretch marks right across the bottom of my belly. I did all the moisturizing, etc. but I was told that stretch marks are hereditary, so if your mother or sisters had them, chances are you will too. They did look awful to begin with, very purple, but now they are fading and don't look too bad. I was never into bikinis anyway and my partner doesn't mind them. I see them as scars of childbirth that remind us what a bloody painful time it was and helps stop us from thinking of having any more!

*Rhubarb*

**I have had three children** and started to stretch on the first. Now my youngest is two and a half and my body is returning back to my normal size. I can really see where all my stretch marks are. A tan helps and with age they do not look so purple, though to be frank as my skin does look a bit more like a pensioner's than a 28-year-old's.

*SAB*

**My tip is to use loads of Vitamin E cream** to try and prevent them and if that doesn't work, get a tan to cover them up!

*Emmagee*

**For some reason** I got no stretch marks anywhere except on my boobs.

*Callie*

**Whilst pregnant with my first baby** I did all the right moisturizing things and avoided stretch marks until the last five days. However, with my second baby they got much worse, sadly, especially around my tummy button.

*Suzie*

**I ended up with stretch marks** all over my lower belly after delivery. I guess that bit hadn't been too stretched during pregnancy but as my son made his way into the world he filled up spaces he hadn't before. According to a dermatologist friend, nothing you put on topically has any effect on whether you get stretch marks or not. Stretch marks happen many layers below the surface. Unfortunately, you either get them or you don't... I got them (lower belly, hips and boobs). Sigh!

*Chelle*

**I cringe when I think about** how long into my pregnancy I congratulated myself that I had no stretch marks, only to find when undressing in the presence of a low-level light that they were all hiding under my bump where I couldn't see them. It looked like someone had painted a roadmap on my stomach.

*SueW*

**I was pretty huge with number one** but got no stretch marks, smaller with number two but got them on my lower belly. They were at their most red and angry-looking in the weeks following the birth but did fade a lot by about six months. Third time around I seem to have the same ones again. I don't think there's much you can do. The rest of me is falling apart anyway!

*Jasper*

**Be proud of them.** There are so many women who can't have children and would love to. Wear them as a reminder of your beautiful children.

*Alycen*

**I wish I could wear mine proudly,** but they are quite bad and have had a seriously negative effect on my self-confidence. I know it's vain and silly, but I can't help feeling hideously ugly when I see myself in the mirror. My belly is absolutely repulsive, and I would have abdominoplasty and skin grafts if I had the dosh!

*Spacemonkey*

**My belly never stood a chance** – I'm prone to dry skin and my twins weighed in at 16 lb put together – that's before placentas, etc. I'm so, so grateful to have had healthy babies and I know babies are more important than bellies but I do feel utterly despairing when I inspect it too closely.

*ScummyMummy*

**I reached 5 ft 9 in by the time I was 12** and have stretch marks everywhere from growing so quickly, and having babies has added a nice set to my stomach. I only really bare my skin on holiday as the sun helps fade the marks, but I don't think I'm especially aware of them. I wouldn't be showing my belly à la Britney if I was!

*Pie*

**There is a hormonal connection** – the hormones that loosen your ligaments do so by softening collagen. They also soften skin collagen, so it is more vulnerable to tearing when the skin is stretched by pregnancy. Retin A cream and lasers have been shown to be effective at reducing stretch marks, but work best when they are still red.

*Aloha*

**I've got them on my thighs** and boobs from puberty but none from pregnancy. It doesn't really make sense to me that my stomach, which feels like it is fit to burst, hasn't got any, but my thighs and boobs managed to get them. My theory is that you have to drink lots of water to prevent them, to keep the skin nice and hydrated. I know I hardly drank anything when I was at school, mainly to avoid using the school loos.

*KeepingMum*

**When I was pregnant** I religiously applied cocoa butter cream to my stomach and got very few stretch marks there. However, I got loads on my upper thighs, from getting so big, where I didn't apply any cream.

*Mammya*

---

**What the experts say**
There's no scientific evidence that any of the creams which you can buy over the counter will help you avoid getting stretch marks if that is the way your body responds to pregnancy.

Mary Nolan (*Being Pregnant, Giving Birth*)

---

**I got them in puberty,** which considering the less than ample size of my breasts is surprising. I didn't get any during pregnancy but I thought that was because I was 'older' i.e. starting to stretch a little anyway. I always believed that younger mothers suffered from them more.

*Tinker*

**I remember reading** that you were less likely to get them the older you were, and also that zinc intake could help to prevent them. I know I didn't get any even with my twin pregnancy at age 35, so maybe there's some truth in it?

*Josiejump*

**I told my husband that** it was his legal obligation to oil my belly every night seeing as he was responsible for what was growing inside it. It didn't work and throughout the later half of the pregnancy it looked like there were flames rising from my pants. They did fade to shiny silver threads but have re-opened again with a vengeance second time. There really is nothing you can do to prevent them. It all depends on the skin you're in.

*Bruntwig*

**There's only one** sure-fire way to prevent stretch marks – don't get pregnant!

*TheOldDragon*

**I've just accepted** that I'm never going to reveal my tum in public ever again and will never be able to get my belly button pierced, but it's a small price to pay for three lovely kids.

*ChanelNo5*

## Braxton Hicks or early contractions – when do they start and what do they feel like?

**I have been having them since 16 weeks.** At 33 weeks I started having them very frequently – sometimes 20 and sometimes five minutes apart. They seem to always come if I go to the toilet or exercise but as they weren't sore, I didn't think I was in labour. As they are practice contractions, I'm hoping that practice makes perfect and I'm in for an easy labour!

*Ninja*

**My Braxton Hicks pains started** at about 16 weeks too. They used to wake me up every morning and later in the pregnancy they used to take my breath away, they were so strong.

*Mum2toby*

**I had a lot of Braxton Hicks** contractions from quite early – around 25 weeks. They would be strong enough to make me stop and catch my breath, prodding my tummy in the process and marvelling at how hard it went. They were completely different to the contractions that I got when labour started, which were low down in the uterus and were more like bad period pains. They didn't really get more frequent as labour approached, just stayed about the same until labour kicked off.

*Quimble*

**I started to get very mild** Braxton Hicks pains as early as 28 weeks. I'm now 39 weeks and they are getting quite strong, not painful really, but enough to make me stop what I'm doing and catch my breath.

*Melly*

**I am 32 weeks' pregnant** and have been suffering fairly uncomfortable contractions for the past week. I went into hospital and they confirmed that I was having moderate contractions but that I was not dilating. I have had a baby before and never had painful contractions until the real thing. I keep wondering if this is it and if one day they are going to get worse and worse, or whether I could be having these for weeks yet.

*Pop*

**I had contractions from about 34 weeks** with numbers two and three – I kept getting all excited, especially as I didn't go into labour naturally first time. Sadly, the pains didn't come to anything until 38 weeks when I had tightenings across the bump rather than down the sides.

*Angharad*

**I didn't have any Braxton Hicks** contractions with my first pregnancy, but I am having them now (I am coming up to 27 weeks). There is a definite tightening sensation with a dull ache and when I touch my tummy, it is rock hard. It lasts about a minute and I usually have two or three at a time. They seem to happen after I have been rushing around or doing a lot.

*Enid*

**I found my Braxton Hicks** pains got stronger with every pregnancy. With my fourth I was sometimes unable to walk the five minutes to school to fetch my daughter because of the pain. Having said that, they were nothing compared to the after-pains!

*Lou33*

**This is my second pregnancy** and I've been getting pains since 29 weeks. I am now 35 weeks and they have been getting progressively worse – so bad I've not been sleeping at all some nights. I'm assuming I'll know that they are the real thing when the timing becomes regular. My midwife has confirmed that the Braxton Hicks can get more painful with each pregnancy.

*Dixie*

> **Mumsnet tip**
> When Braxton Hicks contractions are really uncomfortable, take a couple of paracetamol and soak in the bath. Also, rest as much as possible.
> *Mears*

**I had contractions for the last four months** of my second pregnancy. The doctor said not to worry as long as they went away after a while. It helped me to change whatever I was doing, e.g. to walk around if I had been sitting and rest if I had been walking. If all else failed and I thought that it was the real thing, I took a long warm bath. That always stopped them. The contractions were painful and very annoying after a while. In the end I was induced, but that was a week before my due date.

*JJ*

**I never had a Braxton Hicks** with this or the last pregnancy – so it all kind of mystifies me.

*Percy*

**What the experts say**
Pregnancy contractions are called Braxton Hicks contractions. Not every woman feels them and it doesn't matter if you don't.

Mary Nolan (*Being Pregnant, Giving Birth*)

**Braxton Hicks contractions** are a normal part of pregnancy. Women who think that they don't have them probably are just unaware of them. We all have different pain levels therefore will react differently to them. Some may be so mild they are not noticeable whereas others may be pretty strong and painful. You will know when it is the real thing because you will notice a difference in intensity. The pain of a Braxton Hicks is usually fairly short-term whereas contractions are painful for much longer. If you find you are sitting wondering if these are contractions then they probably are not! The bad news is Braxton Hicks contractions can go on for weeks.

When experiencing a painful contraction for the first time, it is not always wise to assume that it is a Braxton Hicks. It can be undiagnosed labour or infection. If you are at all worried, do not hesitate to see your midwife or doctor.

*Mears*

**My Braxton Hicks pains** almost always happened at 1 am and were painful enough to wake me. I'd get out of bed and walk around, they'd eventually fade, and I could go back to sleep. One night they didn't fade and my son was born 48 hours later.

*Wmf*

**I had lot of strong Braxton Hicks** contractions when pregnant with my son. In fact one Sunday night when I was just 29 weeks pregnant we ended up in a labour ward, as I'd had contractions lasting from 2–20 minutes continuously all weekend. They registered on the monitors and were just as strong as the ones at the end but they never progressed beyond that. The more active I was (and the baby was) the more I had them. But not every activity had this effect; so try cutting things out one by one so you can identify which is the culprit.

The bad news is that once I started getting them, they came regularly until the birth, so much so that by three weeks before I'd had to give up swimming and my daily walk. I suppose it's the body's way of forcing you to rest.

*Carrieboo*

**I am 35 weeks'** pregnant and have been suffering painful Braxton Hicks contractions for the last five weeks or so. I was in hospital on a monitor at about 27 weeks and it showed that I was having a Braxton Hicks every half an hour or so but it wasn't labour and they sent me home. I do think it's worth getting checked out though.

*Hughsie*

**I thought I was having painful Braxton Hicks** contractions at 27 weeks and it turned out I was in labour – very scary. Luckily my GP sent me to the hospital 'just in case' and by the time we got there the contractions were about seven minutes apart!

*Mollipops*

**3**

# Tests and Scans

# Introduction

There can be few things more amazing than coming face to face with your unborn child for the first time. Your tummy's hardly protruded through the waistband of your jeans and there's certainly been no discernible movement, but within moments of the icy gel being squirted on your abdomen, there it is – a tiny alien-featured creature, sucking its thumb, turning somersaults and bringing tears to your eyes. It's all real, it's a baby and it's yours.

But while this miracle of modern science provides you with the first fuzzy photo for the album, scans and the tests that can go with them can also bring a bundle of anxieties and sometimes heartbreaking decisions. Medical advances mean that there is now a choice of tests that can either give you a mind-numbing mathematical probability or an element of certainty as to whether the baby you are carrying is healthy or not. But should you have the tests and, if so, which ones?

Is it best to opt for the non-invasive procedures, routine blood tests or the nuchal fold measurement that can bring you probabilities and an element of reassurance but no certainties? Or should you go the invasive test route and choose CVS or amnio, risking the tragedy of miscarrying a perfectly healthy baby but knowing for sure that your child is free of some of the more common defects?

What of the routine antenatal appointments – are the endless waits for five minutes of the doctor or midwife's time really worth it and is there anything you can do to maximize their value? And are you one of the 45 per cent of UK mothers-to-be who want to know the sex of their baby or one of the 55 per cent (*Practical Parenting* magazine) who try desperately not to notice whether the crucial bits of the anatomy are dangly or otherwise during the scan. Does finding out the sex in advance prepare you, or is it a bad idea that can bring mixed emotions?

The availability of tests and scans, whilst bringing joy to many also brings the potential for some extremely difficult personal and moral dilemmas. No one can offer any answers, no one can make the difficult decisions for you, but the experiences and opinions of those who've had to find the answers and make the decisions for themselves can help prepare and equip you for whatever the tests and scans show up.

# Antenatal appointments – how important are they?

**They're very important,** if only for reassurance. Having said this, they were also the source of major stress for me when I was pregnant. I went to one when various people had told me I looked small for my dates and I was worried whether the baby was okay, only to be told by a locum doctor that he couldn't hear the baby's heartbeat but that he was 'sure that everything was okay' – just what a concerned pregnant woman wants to hear!

Then towards the end of the pregnancy the midwife kept telling me that the baby was breech – I got very stressed about how I was going to cope with a C-section, until my sympathetic GP sent me up to the hospital to discuss turning the baby. They did a scan and we found out that she was head-down (and had been all along, because I would have felt if she'd turned). The midwife had obviously been confusing the bottom and the head.

*Azzie*

> **Mumsnet tip**
> Ask your consultant/midwife for a late scan to check the baby's position. If you say you're really worried about it being breech they are unlikely to refuse. I had one at 39 weeks and it put my mind at rest.
> *Roberta*

**I think antenatal visits** are very important – in fact, in my case, had I not been to them I would have lost both my son and my daughter.

*MABS*

**I had to keep an eye on my blood pressure,** which was up and down throughout my pregnancy, as was my weight. These are just the some of the smaller problems that can happen unexpectedly in between appointments, so I think it's best not to skip any of them.

*Nick*

**I had an ovarian cyst** and had regular scans, which I loved, as did my husband. I also went regularly to have my daughter's heart monitored as she didn't move very much during the day (but made up for it all night) and I'd rather have made a total fool of myself worrying and asking for help than risk anything going wrong.

*Ionesmum*

**I'm a midwife** and it has long been suggested that we see women too much during the ante-natal period, and that they could safely reduce the number of appointments without compromising maternal or foetal well-being. The directive now is really to try and be 'woman-led', so if you want to be seen you are, but if you're happy not to be seen (and all is well), then you can go a little longer between appointments.

The trouble is that all the women we don't worry about too much (i.e. those who attend regularly and have no problems) like the assurance of midwife appointments, so see a lot of us. Those we do worry about (those who don't attend any clinics/appointments and are out when we visit) would choose never to be seen, so we end up having to chase them.

Suffice to say, antenatal care is extremely important. However, there is a balance between being seen too much, and not at all. As a general guide, we like to see women at the following times:

- The 'booking' appointment – first midwife appointment
- 15 weeks
- Scan at 20 weeks
- 24 weeks
- 28 weeks
- 32 weeks
- 34 weeks
- 36 weeks
- Every week from then until delivery

This is only a rough guide. Some women will need/want to be seen more. The dates of the scan, etc. also vary from place to place.

*Leese*

**I didn't feel I got a lot** from my appointments but the antenatal care in my area was noted for being poor. I benefited more from the aqua natal sessions I went to, where I saw the same midwives each time and they were happy to be asked questions about anything. I was worried unnecessarily by being told in the last four weeks my baby would be small – she turned out to be well over average weight and with a head circumference in the top 5 per cent. She was also lying badly and I didn't get advice that might have helped turn her. I had a lot of appointments but not a lot of care.

*Robinw*

**I would recommend** you have at least some of your antenatal appointments at the hospital rather than all with midwives at your GP's surgery. I think it is important to see a doctor. In my case my twins had twin-to-twin transfusion syndrome (TTS) – a condition which can be fatal if left untreated, and which affects roughly one fifth of identical twins. The key symptom is polyhydramnios – i.e. you swell up with amniotic fluid. This happened to me and at my 24-week appointment I was enormous.

The midwife, who clearly knew nothing about TTS, asked me whether the father of the babies was tall! I went untreated and as a result went into labour at

25 weeks. Thankfully the hospital I ended up at had an expert in the field and through his interventions I managed to hang on until 30 weeks and the babies were fine. I do think, though, that a doctor would have been more likely to pick up the problem at 24 weeks. So, in my view, not only are antenatal appointments essential, but also I'd have them at the hospital, where you are more likely to be seen by obstetricians.

*Berta*

**Mumsnet tip**
If you have a toddler in tow take plenty of activities/treats for them plus nappies etc. – the waits can seem endless to a two-year-old. And don't (as I did – twice) get all the way there and realize you've left your notes at home...

*Haley*

**I think they're vital,** especially for first-time mothers. However, I think it's also important to be aware of potential health risks and the symptoms to look out for and not always to rely on stressed-out midwives and doctors to spot everything. One thing I only discovered during my second pregnancy, for example, was the danger to the baby of an infection called Group B Streptococcus (GBS), which lots of women carry without being aware of it, but which can kill a baby if left untreated during labour.

My hospital didn't offer the tests routinely, or even mention it to me, but when I asked (demanded!) the test they did it and I was, fortunately, fine. I'd urge any pregnant woman to get herself tested (it's very easy, just a vaginal swab) and not to panic if she is a carrier, but just to make sure the hospital staff are aware of it so they can treat her accordingly.

*Bon*

**Mumsnet fact**
Group B Streptococcus (GBS) is the most common cause of life-threatening infection in newborn babies in the UK, infecting around 700 babies a year (1 in 1,000) of whom, sadly, 100 die and others are left with long term physical and/or mental problems... Once you know you are a carrier, risks to the baby can be drastically reduced by intravenous antibiotics given at intervals from the start of labour until delivery. There is also a new, more reliable GBS test (enriched culture method, ECM), which has recently become available in the UK.

gbss.org.uk

**I went religiously to all appointments** first time round and quite enjoyed it, despite the absolutely endless waits. I knew what 'midwife team' I was in, went to the extra water birth sessions and was full of confidence in the whole system.

Sadly, this proved a bit unfounded. No one had spotted that the baby was breech and I had a rather disastrous birth experience ending in an emergency C-section. Plus none of the midwives I'd seen at antenatal sessions were around.

Second time around I found the waits a nightmare with a two-year-old to entertain and I left a couple without being seen, having waited for two hours or more. However, I think I made better use of the few I went to by knowing what to ask, having my questions written down and making notes to tell my husband, who had long since stopped coming with me! Also I felt I knew a bit more about what to look out for health-wise and if I had any anxieties I just went to my GP.

*Biza*

## Non-invasive tests (nuchal scans, triple tests) – what are they, how do you get them and are they worth having?

**I had a nuchal fold test** at my 12-week scan. It gives you a probability of Down's, which you can then use to decide if you want any further tests (e.g. amnio, CVS). This probability is based on your age and then the size of the nuchal fold (which is at the back of the baby's neck and is thicker in Down's babies).

It is purely based on probabilities, i.e. they tested about 3,000 women and compared the size of the nuchal fold and whether or not their babies were born with Down's. It also depends on what you feel is a tolerable risk and what you would do if the risk was higher than you wanted.

For my age my risk should be 1 in 700, following the nuchal fold test the risk was brought down to 1 in 2000 – but I wouldn't have considered doing anything about it unless the risk was more than 1 in 100 and even then I'm not sure what I would have done.

*Pamela1*

**With my first child** I hadn't even heard of nuchal scans until a colleague asked if I was having one. My hospital had a policy of only giving it routinely to over 37s or those who asked for it. I was told I had a low risk of Down's and combined the nuchal scan with the triple test. However, somewhere between my two pregnancies I got paranoid about being the 'one' in the 1:2,000 risk assessments they talk about. So, with my second pregnancy, aged 36, even though I still had a relatively low risk and I wasn't sure I'd terminate if there were a problem, I chose to have CVS.

*Hayley*

**I had both tests** although we decided that whatever the outcome, we would keep the child – it was just a question of preparing ourselves. I went to a private clinic where they do a blood test and combine that with the nuchal fold to give you a probability. Obviously it's not foolproof but the only tests that are (amnio and CVS) both carry a risk of miscarriage.

*Ringer*

**The nuchal fold test** is a good one to have as it is non-invasive and early. Same for the blood tests. I only had these two tests even though I gave birth at 40. We had decided not to terminate for Down's anyway and did not want to risk miscarriage. I'm aware though that there are a lot of false positives and false negatives associated with the triple test.

The problem with all antenatal tests is that we then have to make choices. It's great if we get the result we want (although nothing's guaranteed) and not so great when we don't. Pregnancy is a very worrying time and I don't think we realize how much we worry until we feel the relief of seeing our newborns.

*Cam*

**Mumsnet tip**
Don't forget to take a bottle of water with you for your scan. Then you don't have to drink it at home and be desperate for the loo if they are behind.

*Miranda2*

**My hospital only offers a scan** at 20 weeks unless you are unsure of your dates so I paid for a nuchal scan. I found it reassuring just to know that the baby was developing, to be given a good Down's risk was a bonus. I had an amnio during my first pregnancy and although I was convinced it was the right thing for me at the time, there was no way I could do that again.

*Late30smom*

**I would recommend the nuchal fold scan,** but be aware that you have to have it at a very specific time, so if you want it, hassle your midwife/doctor. Due to a cock -up I actually missed it, and then at my blood test a few weeks later I found out (again after chasing people up) that my chances of having a baby with a disability were actually very high for my age, so I had an amniocentesis. Fortunately, everything was fine, but if the problem had shown in the nuchal scan I could have had CVS, which can be done much earlier than amnio.

*Batters*

**I had a nuchal fold scan** and afterwards was given a revised risk figure for Down's – it went from 1:350 to 1:3,500. I found this reassuring and had no other tests. I have a friend whose daughter has Down's – this was initially picked up by a nuchal fold scan and confirmed by amniocentesis. Although she never considered terminating the pregnancy, this gave my friend time to plan for her daughter's arrival and it also meant that she had the baby at a teaching hospital with loads of specialists on hand. In the event they weren't needed as the birth was completely normal and the baby didn't require any special treatment.

*Sweetie*

**If you really want to find out** if your child is affected with Down's syndrome, having considered it fully, then a nuchal scan is a good idea. In my area it is not offered under the NHS, but has to be financed privately. The AFP (or triple test) offered routinely at around 15–17 weeks of pregnancy – has an approximate detection rate of 60 per cent. The nuchal scan on its own is supposed to be about 70–80 per cent accurate. Some areas also offer the 'OSCAR' test, which is basically a nuchal scan and blood test combined, which reports an accuracy rate of 90 per cent.

It's important not to assume that just because you're younger, you'll be fine, and therefore decline all tests. Of all the babies born with Down's Syndrome in our area in the last three years, a high proportion were born to younger girls – simply because they assumed they would be fine, based on age-related risk. Older women had less incidence of giving birth to a baby with Down's primarily because the majority chose antenatal screening and they may well have gone on to terminate a pregnancy.

*Leese*

> **Mumsnet fact**
> The average risk for a 25-year-old of giving birth to a Down's syndrome child is 1 in 1,400, for a 45-year-old the risk increases to 1 in 30.
> Down's Syndrome Association

**I was not offered a nuchal scan** but had read up about it and chose to have it done privately as I was 42 when I became pregnant. I was told my 'risk' was low at 1 in 250 but then went on to have a baby with a rare medical condition (now resolved) of 1 in 4,500! My point is that we tend to think everything can be tested/screened etc when the reality is that these tests can't check for every single possible 'abnormality'.

*Lindy*

**I wasn't asked if I wanted a nuchal scan,** my doctor just assumed I would have it. I was given a really low risk factor (something like 1 in 4,000) which made us happy but then the radiographer said, 'Of course this doesn't mean that your baby isn't the 'one'. It really upset me – but she was probably only trying to be helpful.

*Ghosty*

**Even as a midwife** I breathed a sigh of relief when my AFP came back normal. That was the only test available then. These tests do not, however, tell you if your baby is 'normal'. They tell you the risk factor of your baby having a neural tube defect or Down's. Abnormal results can fill women with dread as they then go through a battery of other tests to often find that their baby is, after all, 'normal'.

There are more and more people speaking out about the hurdles women face in being offered so many screening tests. As a result of this the joy of pregnancy can be tarnished.

*Mears*

**They don't offer nuchal testing** at my hospital and at my 19-week triple blood test the result came back that I was high risk 1:172 of having a Down's baby. After deciding not to go through with an amnio (having miscarried at the beginning of the year), they did a thorough scan and couldn't find any of the classic symptoms of Down's, i.e. smaller head, smaller limbs, thick neck or just lying sluggish in the womb and not moving much. Plus the heart was completely formed with all the blood pumping so if it were Down's it wouldn't have been so badly affected anyway. Getting the amnio at 19 weeks would have meant that by the time my results came back, aborting the baby would have meant injecting it to kill it, then being induced and giving birth to a dead baby, then registering it and burying it. I decided to take what I was given.

*Mima*

**My hospital** (and I think most hospitals) has a genetic counsellor, who can go through everything explaining risks, etc. either before or after a scan. They are generally much more informed about the latest research than GPs or consultants and better at explaining it.

*SofiaAmes*

**I had a 1:250 risk of Downs** (after Bart's blood test, nuchal measurement) and still decided to have an amnio. I guess we all need to ask ourselves what we'd do if we had a positive result from an invasive test, and if the answer is 'nothing', then there's not much point in going ahead with it, given the risk of miscarriage. One friend had a 1:33 result and didn't opt for invasive tests (both of us had fine, healthy babies).

*Bundle*

**I had a risk of 1:80** and decided not to have an amnio because I would not have wanted to terminate the pregnancy, even if the amnio showed an abnormality. My obstetrician was very understanding, and commented that there are far worse things than Down's syndrome/spina bifida that can't be tested for, and we usually don't spend the whole pregnancy worrying about those!

A risk of 1:80 sounds bad, but in fact, 79 babies will be 'normal'. A risk of 1:500 sounds good, but one of those babies will not be 'normal'. There are plenty of mothers out there who would have been classed 'low-risk', but still had a child with a problem, but the vast majority, tested or un-tested, are entirely 'normal'.

*Funkygibbon*

## Invasive tests (CVS, amnio) – why would you have them and what are they like?

**With my first child** I had a nuchal scan and the triple tests and felt satisfied. But I then came across someone who, aged 34 and having had a 'good' nuchal scan, had gone on to have a child with Down's syndrome. It occurred to me that even if you're given a risk assessment of one in a million, someone is going to be that one. I wasn't convinced that I could abort a child – ever – and I certainly knew that there was no way I could abort a child at 18–20 weeks – which was around the time a friend of mine had finally got her amnio results. So I went for CVS. You have it early and get some results straight away – before 12 weeks.

I was told by the receptionist (at a private clinic) that the doctor had a 100 per cent record of success (i.e. no miscarriages). When I turned up, the doctor was furious and said she had no way of knowing how many women had suffered miscarriage, but that the average was around 2 per cent. She evidently thought I was crazy going through the procedure and we had a horrendous time after she'd 'counselled' us, when we were left to decide whether we still wanted to go ahead.

By this time we had seen our baby on the scan and the risk of losing it was so much more real. My husband was at a loss and in the end it was my decision to go ahead. The actual test was over very quickly and was more uncomfortable than painful. They numb a part of your tummy then stick a big needle in and seemed to pump away for a moment and take some liquid out. They are scanning all the time and won't do the test unless the baby's in the right position.

The danger time is the next 48 hours and that was horrendous. You get some slight cramping as a result of the procedure, but you keep wondering if this is it and you're going to miscarry and somehow it'll be all your fault. Fortunately I didn't miscarry and the results, which were phoned through two days later, were good and I went on to have a healthy boy.

I still wonder what I would have done if the results had shown some abnormality – certainly immediately afterwards I decided I wanted to keep my baby no matter what, but perhaps that was my guilt at putting it at risk. I later read some horrendous statistic that for every 'damaged' foetus aborted something like four healthy foetuses are miscarried. It was good to know that the baby was free of some of the more common disabilities, but I can't say I'd recommend the procedure and actually admire those who choose not to take it.

One small thing to beware of: they can tell the sex of the child at this stage so if you don't want to know, make sure you tell them.

*Shy*

**I had an amnio,** because of a one in 30 risk of the baby having Edward's syndrome, which showed up on a Bart's blood test. The amnio itself was fine. The scan she did before/during the amnio was very detailed – Edward's babies usually have crossed-over fingers and she kept saying what lovely hands my baby had and it was fine size-wise (Edward's babies are small for the dates). The amnio results confirmed what she'd seen at the scan and all was well.

*Bundle*

**There is a way of speeding up amnio results** (with an amnio there is slightly less risk of miscarriage than CVS but it has to be done later). You have the test done at your local hospital and ask for a second sample for a quick private analysis. You can't get the test done earlier but at least you don't have to wait two or three weeks for the result. My hospital didn't tell me about this until I asked but it turned out that for £75 I could get a basic result (ruling out Down's Syndrome and other major chromosome abnormalities) in three days.

*Lizp*

**What the experts say**
Some women are happy to accept the outcome of the pregnancy no matter what, others want the reassurance of screening tests and some who might be at high risk want a diagnostic test. This is a very personal issue and your views should determine what tests, if any, are carried out.
Professor Ian Greer (*Pregnancy: The Inside Guide*)

... there still remains a chance that amniocentesis causes miscarriage. Because of this small but definite risk, there is no point having it unless there is a well-above-average chance of your baby being born abnormal.
Sheila Kitzinger (*The New Pregnancy and Childbirth*)

**We felt we wanted to proceed straight** to amnio because I was 36 and we knew we wouldn't be reassured by blood tests alone. We knew that amnio, whilst detecting certain syndromes, doesn't guarantee that you will have a healthy baby, but we felt that we needed to have the information. Second time round we did the same, but I was even more scared, even though I knew what to expect. Apart from the obvious anxiety about the result, the thing that worried me was coping with my daughter after the procedure, but in the end I got help and it was fine.

I think the decision is always a tough one and especially so if you have had problems earlier on in the pregnancy (I had continual heavy spotting from 6–12 weeks), so putting yourself at risk, albeit very small, of having a miscarriage is hard. I was a nervous wreck, and viewed myself as a race-horse with three big hurdles to get over: the test itself, the risk of miscarriage and then getting the result. I just wished I could have fast-forwarded to the following week!

*Melly*

**I had two amnio tests at ages 36 and 41** and dreaded the result more the second time around. Having experienced motherhood, the idea of losing a baby through me choosing an amnio test really got to me. I think the hospital advised me to take two days to recover physically. You're given some fact sheets with information but I would definitely ask what to do post-amnio face-to-face so the consultant can talk to you as an individual.

I felt fine after the amnio, but think it's a good idea to have time away from your toddler if you have one, at least initially. If you're with them, it's difficult to avoid all the lifting and cuddling.

*Frank1*

**I had an amnio when expecting my fourth** at 41. It was done in the morning and then I set off on a 1,000-mile-round car trip for the weekend after the hospital okayed it. When I mentioned it to a doctor friend she nearly passed out and said I should have rested for between 24–48 hrs. However, nothing untoward happened and the result was fine too.

*BaaBaa*

**I felt a little 'odd'** post amnio, but had no pain. I took in headphones and a portable CD to play to calm me down during the procedure. We also paid extra to have the early result, which was a huge relief. For this they use a different technique – PCA rather than tissue culture – and it doesn't give you the full results. For those you still have to wait the standard two weeks.

*Hmb*

**I had an amnio** when an early scan/blood test brought up a higher than expected chance of problems. The consultant said that it was obvious from the scan that everything was okay and that we shouldn't have been so silly as to have had an amnio. Although that sounds harsh, at the time when we had to wait for the results his comments were actually reassuring. I was told to rest for 24 hours, so I came home, went straight to bed and stayed there until the next morning.

*Allatsea*

**I had an amnio with my second pregnancy.** I stayed at home afterwards and didn't do anything strenuous, but I don't remember worrying about whether or not to lift my son. The risk of miscarriage with an amnio comes from the hole where they poke through not sealing up and infection getting through to the baby. The risk of this is highest in the first 24 hours and decreases after that.

My understanding is that there are pretty clear signs of infection (fever, bleeding, pain, leaking) so if you don't have them in the first 24 hours I wouldn't worry too much. I paid for the amnio PCR, which was nice to have in advance, but probably not worth the money – it took a week (not two days) for the results and two weeks for the normal results so the difference wasn't that great. Also, the woman who did the amnio was so positive about what she could see from the scan whilst doing it, that I really wasn't worried.

*SofiaAmes*


**I've had two amnio tests,** and after both I felt some discomfort, a bit like period pain, during that day, but nothing else. Then I stayed at home for the rest of the day and took it easy. I think if you are going to miscarry, it will happen whatever you do – the advice to rest afterwards is just for your comfort.

I had the preliminary results back after about 36 hours, but I understood this was a relatively new technique they were using, just looking at three pairs of chromosomes. Then the full results were confirmed a couple of weeks later.

*Rosy*


**If you would keep the baby regardless of the result,** surely it's not worth putting yourself through all of this, especially with the risk of miscarriage. It sounds a scary procedure and I'm not sure that I would elect to have one, but then I would probably keep the baby no matter what.

*Rhubarb*

## Finding out the sex – should you find out and how does it feel if you do?

**We found out the sex** at the 20-week scan. We already have a gorgeous little boy and it looks like we're expecting another. I'm almost ashamed to admit that when we were told my initial feelings were of disappointment instead of all the things I should have felt (i.e. relief that baby is fine, happiness at having a healthy pregnancy when so many people have problems, etc.).

I'd convinced myself I was having a girl as the pregnancy was so different from the last. Initially all I could think about was a future filled with noise and dirty sports kits, feeling alienated by my husband and sons as they disappear to football matches and not having anyone to shop and gossip with. But now I'm just so excited about meeting this little person! I am glad I found out the sex before the birth because it means I can concentrate on the most important thing – looking forward to my new beautiful baby in 18 weeks' time.

*BoysMum*

**I was also a bit disappointed** when I found out that I was expecting another boy, technically my third. We lost our first baby (a boy) when I was six months pregnant because of severe foetal abnormalities so I felt doubly guilty about feeling like I did. I love my son to bits and now that I've had 18 weeks to get used to the idea of another healthy baby boy, I'm getting more and more excited about meeting him. I still have moments when I secretly wonder whether the hospital got it wrong as the pregnancy has been so different, and I would be ecstatic if they had, but if he's anything like as cute as my son he'll be adorable.

On the plus side I've saved a packet on not having to buy in a load of pink and flowery things for a girl, we might never need to go in for the more girlie toys, they'll hopefully be great playmates, keep an eye on each other at school/in later life, and perhaps have more in common than if I'd had one of each.

*Honeybunny*

> **Mumsnet fact**
> Sixty-one per cent of mums, given the choice, would choose to give birth to a baby girl.
> *Practical Parenting*

**I have no less than five boys!** Although I would have liked a girl last time round, I purposely didn't ask the sex during the scans. In the event, I had problems with the pregnancy during the final months and was just very happy to have a healthy baby at the end of it. I think once the baby arrives, it is the personality that becomes important, not the sex.

*AnnieG*

**I must admit when my second son** was born, we initially felt very disappointed that he wasn't a girl. We had a host of girls' names lined up but only a couple of boys' names! But I can honestly say three years on that I hardly ever think 'if only'. My two are very different and far from feeling outnumbered in an all-male household, I feel like the queen bee!

*Xanthe*

**I, too, was initially disappointed** when my scan revealed a boy. I had a daughter sitting on the bed at the time and really wanted another girl. I think they thought that I would be delighted to know it was a boy but I burst into tears when they told me! However, I was glad I knew I needed that time to get used to the fact he was a boy, though I still hoped he'd be another girl when he was born. He's 14 now and I don't know what I'd do without him.

*Alibubbles*

**When I was pregnant** I desperately wanted a girl, as my husband already had two teenage boys from a previous marriage and I knew that this would be my only child. He didn't want another child and my baby wasn't planned, but I thought 'if it's a girl he'll be delighted'. I had always pictured myself with a daughter.

I didn't find out the sex, I waited until the baby was born and prayed that it would be a girl – I think I was actually convinced it was. I had a Caesarean and when the doctor lifted the baby out, the first thing I saw were the testicles! I can't explain the shock and disappointment. My husband was sitting right there and luckily he seemed happy with the baby, no matter what the sex was. It took me a while to get over the disappointment.

*LiamsMum*

> **Mumsnet fact**
> In American surveys, 25 per cent of parents said they would use 'MicroSort', a technique of choosing the sex of their child, if it were available.
> *The Times*

**If you do have a child of the same sex** think how good it will be to get all the little togs out from first time round and see another little fellow filling them out. You will get a chance to revisit those favourite plush dungarees, that first silly hat, etc. If we ever have another, I would find out the sex, and if it were a girl I'd probably be a bit disappointed at first even though we already have a boy.

*Clare2*

**I was sure I was having a girl** throughout my first pregnancy but wasn't at all bothered to have a boy. I was just so glad to have the baby that I didn't even think about what sex he was towards the end. I am due another in a couple of week's time and have no idea what it will be. I am quite surprised at how many people are bothered by the sex. In my experience kids are all very different regardless of sex and I really don't like the 'Barbie-pink-girly thing' vs the 'Bob-the-Builder-plain-functional macho thing' but realize that there is not a lot we can do about it.

*Eulalia*

**When number three boy was born** I had a lot of 'I'm so sorry type' behaviour, someone even said 'never mind!' and whilst I was pregnant again everyone kept saying 'I bet you're hoping for a girl'. When I found out he was a boy at 20 weeks I made sure I told people before they could say it! When I was pregnant with number four I had the same all over again. When SHE was born, the world went mad and I felt very guilty and protective of my three wonderful boys. They, on the other hand, joined in the celebrations and were so proud of her and still vie for her attention.

*Countrybumpkin*

> **Mumsnet fact**
> Assertive women have an 80 per cent chance of having a son because they have higher levels of testosterone.
> *Journal of Biological Psychology*

**I think these scans are a bad thing.** They just allow people to feel disappointed and then guilty and then as soon as they see the child, they fall in love anyway. My husband wanted a boy, as most men do, and we had a little girl. As soon as he saw her and ever since he's been spellbound. I wouldn't find out next time because I would hate to be disappointed.

*Tillysmummy*

**Although massively nosey by nature** I didn't want to find out the sex of my children. There are so few genuine surprises in life and you've got to have something to look forward to after all that hard labour. I have a friend who found out by accident the sex of her child. She didn't care either way but didn't want to be told and felt very strongly that she'd had some of the magic of childbirth taken away. On the other hand if it really matters to you I think it's best to be forewarned and have time to get used to the idea, one way or the other.

*Shy*

**We discovered that we** were having twins at the 13-week scan and decided to find out the sex – the shock of twins was quite enough excitement and I felt I needed to be prepared. When I got pregnant again it seemed only natural to find out again, so we asked at the first dating scan and were told by the scanner that though he couldn't be 100 per cent certain at that stage, he thought it was another girl (our twins are identical girls). We were mildly disappointed only to find out at the 20-week scan that our girl was in fact a boy! Bizarrely I had slightly mixed feelings, as I'd quite come round to three girls, which just goes to show how capricious it all is and that really you come round to whatever you get.

*Roberta*

**I've now got two boys and a girl,** so I don't know what it is like to be faced with the 'only boys in the family' thing. I did however spend my pregnant months worrying about whether the last son would be healthy. I think you just have to repeat to yourself: 'the only thing that really counts is to have a healthy baby'. Think how difficult it is for those who don't and be thankful.

*Minchen*

**I have rationalised it this way:**
1. I want to have another healthy baby.
2. I don't want my son to be an only child.
Of course it would be great to have one of each, but the above two factors far outweigh that preference. I have found that by thinking of it in this way, it releases the pressure that I put on myself to have a girl. I think it's a great idea to find out the sex as by the time you have your second son, you are going to be so looking forward to meeting him and there's no chance of hanging on until the birth to have any feelings of disappointment. Also, aren't babies designed brilliantly? So scrumptious, all those podgy bits and cute little smiles – ultimately who cares what the sex is? It's made by you and it's marvellous!

*Jessi*

**4**

# Twins and Multiples

# Introduction

Despite the rise in fertility treatment, the vast majority (around three-quarters) of twins are still conceived naturally, so unless you come from one of those families in which every granny, cousin and even the pet hamster is a twin, the chances are that the news you're carrying two or more will come as more than a teeny bit of a shock. In my case (and as I write this my pair are nearing five), it's one I'm still getting over.

So whilst the rest of the world – partners, prospective grandmas, work colleagues, even the postman – thinks it's a great hoot, all you can focus on is how on earth your body is going to survive the ordeal. As Dr Carol Cooper, author of the best-selling *Twins & Multiple Births*, bluntly puts it: 'The human species is really only geared to producing one offspring at a time.' You know what next door looked like at full-term and she was carrying a modest one. Just how will your meagre frame weather the transformation to full-blown whale? And crucially, given those women who are carrying half as many children as you complain of swollen ankles the size of Japan, what are yours going to look like?

These bodily concerns are swiftly followed by a lament for the labour you're now most unlikely to have. Bye-bye water birth in your front room, burning incense and a solitary midwife, hello bright lights of the operating theatre, the whirr of the electronic foetal monitor and a squadron of medical staff. But does a twin birth really require the attention of more doctors than appear in the average episode of *ER*? Do you really have to be monitored at all times and what are your chances of getting away with a natural birth, even if it's likely to be in a distinctly unnatural setting?

And then there are all the terrifying prospective complications of premature birth and special care units that are statistically more likely with twins – no wonder 92 per cent of women say they'd rather have one child at a time.

In fact there's so much to worry about with the pregnancy and birth you may not even have time to dwell on what comes afterwards – the small matter of two newborn babies to look after. Read on to find out what to expect and how to prepare from those who've dealt with double the trouble. And if all this leaves you filled with more than a little trepidation, don't despair: you can look forward to double all the good stuff too.

## Finding out – how did you feel and what should you consider?

**I think I spent most of my pregnancy in shock** – I really thought one at a time was quite enough. It didn't help that everyone I talked to gave a chuckle followed by something like, 'you'll have your work cut out for you then'. But it's so magical watching them interact, grow and play together, I actually feel incredibly privileged now (they're three) – which is a long way from what I felt at the 13-week scan, believe me. Remember, you have the perfect excuse to take every short cut – think maternity nurses (finances permitting), dummies and jars of ready-made baby food, and consign the ironing board to the loft for the foreseeable future. Everyone will think you're 'supermum' anyway and sooner than you know they'll be best friends (most of the time) and amusing each other in the mornings.

*Berta*

**I have two-and-a-half-year-old boy/girl twins** who are lovely but oh yes, what hard work. I was blissfully unaware for the first four months of my pregnancy that there were two babies, as it wasn't picked up until my second scan – a shock to say the least, but I wouldn't change it for the world, even though my boy has slept through the night three times in his life and my girl is not much better!)

*Cassius*

> **Mumsnet fact**
> In 1980 one in 50 children born was a twin, in 2000 the ratio had risen to one in every 35.
> *The Mail on Sunday*

**I initially felt both shocked and euphoric.** Then relief at having a reason for being sooooooo sick. But now I'm feeling quite scared about what is in store, especially about both my health during pregnancy and the health of the babies.

*Pop*

**I went through the whole gamut of emotions** when I found out – from total panic to super smugness. I remember they wouldn't let me go home without having a cup of tea first because I was so shocked. TAMBA (The Twins and Multiple Birth Association) produce some good leaflets on various subjects, from breastfeeding to buggies. They can also advise you on how to find your nearest twins club.

Take as much help as you can from whoever offers. Ask at the local colleges if any of their students need work experience. Twins do attract lots of attention – shopping used to take three times as long once people discovered I had two in the pram, and if you have an older child they'll require lots of attention to compensate. Also, as I'm sure you can imagine, two small babies are a lot of work.

You'll probably need to have some strategies in place for making sure that an older child isn't overlooked. For example, that you and/or your partner spend some time with him alone, if at all possible.

It's worth reminding all the adults in your children's lives to make a special fuss of any older siblings – they won't need reminding to make a fuss of your twins!

*Ted*


**There are so many positive things** about having twins – the pleasure and fun they derive from one another, the double levels of excitement and entertainment they afford us, my partner and I each having a baby to cuddle, the list is endless.

Try and get as much help as possible – my mother came for the first two weeks, and then my husband had a week off. I got a cleaner for two hours a week, which I really valued, as I didn't have time to do any housework.

*China1*


**I remember feeling apprehensive** during pregnancy (complete panic actually!). I already had three children, who were four, three and 20 months when my boys were born. I was able to afford a cleaner for four hours a week and also had help from social services (the Crisis Team!), which was organized by my midwife. I also had a student nursery nurse for a few hours a week.

Many twins do have to go into special care for at least a few days, so it's worth looking round your hospital's unit before the birth. It reassured me after they were taken there when they were born.

*Cfr*


**I didn't have a clue** that I might conceive twins as there are none on either side for as far back as anyone can remember. Since finding out we're having twins, we've been reading anything we can get our hands on, which is pretty terrifying. There seems to be so much that can be difficult with a twin pregnancy.

*Tinkerbell*

**Mumsnet fact**

Ninety-two per cent of women would prefer one child at a time, with only 7 per cent preferring twins.

National Birth and Motherhood survey

**I have eight-month-old twin girls** and would advise anyone expecting multiples to be careful what they read on the subject. I found many publications were keen to point out the hard work and the expense and had quite a negative feel to them.

I think that twins are a blessing. My girls are extra-special little people who have brought me nothing but joy. As every mother of multiples has a different experience it's far better to join a twins club and get real life experiences.

*Janet*

**I was 21 weeks and had an 18-month-old girl** when I found out and it was the biggest shock of my life! Try to look after yourself and keep fit, as it will help you towards the end of your pregnancy when you look like Mr Greedy!

I found the early weeks incredibly tiring and stressful, until I got them into a Gina Ford-type routine. By eight weeks they were having two naps a day; five feeds a day; bath at 6 pm; bed by 7 pm (i.e. peaceful evenings); one more feed at 10.30 pm (before our bedtime) and then they were only waking up once a night between 10.30 pm and 6.45 am, which was comparative bliss. You do have to be quite strict with the feeding – 3–31/2 hours between feeds – or you'll find yourself feeding the whole time.

I recommend you get as much help as possible in the early weeks and join your local twins club (TAMBA will give you details or look at tamba.org.uk) and they will put you into touch with other twin mothers and other people expecting twins so you can go through similar experiences together – I didn't get this opportunity and I wished I had. Also the Multiple Births Foundation runs information evenings in London and have lots of literature which you can order from their website.

If you want to breastfeed, make sure you get plenty of support in hospital. I found it better to breastfeed them together but I introduced bottles early so that other people could help feed if they were around – the twins were happy with whatever they were given – breast or bottle.

*FifiDella*

**When I went for my first scan** they told me it was twins. Then three weeks later I started to bleed heavily and was sent for another scan, convinced I had lost them. The woman who was doing the scan asked me if she was looking for two embryos. I said yes. 'Why then do I have three heart beats?', she asked. Stunned wasn't the word!

*Triplets*

**Mumsnet fact**
The number of triplets born has quadrupled in the past 15 years.
*The Mail on Sunday*

**I was 20 weeks when I found out** and I remember feelings of sheer panic. The main thing is to look after yourself and stay calm. I had a straightforward pregnancy and went to nearly 40 weeks but twins usually come earlier. If anyone offers help in any way, take it – it is a big step to two babies and the first months can be very demanding, but there is life after twins. Mine are six now and are very rewarding.

The first time my husband and I took them out to Tesco we were mobbed by old ladies cooing over them and asking us all sorts of questions. It took about 20 minutes to get down the first aisle. It was amazing but something you can do without when you're worried about feeding, crying and nappies.

*Kkgirl*

'**Ooooooh, Double Trouble.**', 'Which one is your favourite?', 'Who's the eldest? He can't be! He's smaller.', 'They're identical, aren't they? No? Are you sure? I'm sorry, love, but I think you're wrong. They look EXACTLY the same to me!', 'Hey, Twins! I'm a twin!' Or 'My mother/brothers/sisters/sibling/granddad/thirteenth cousins twelve times removed are twins!', 'You've got your hands full there, love,', 'Rather you than me!', 'Twins! You are SOOOOOOOOO lucky.'

I think I heard each of these about a million times for the first 18 months or so of my twin boys' lives! However, I have to admit I was proud as a peacock of my beautiful babies and often nodded sagely at these sort of comments and tried to look worthy of the honour/burden. Try not to worry too much – despite having heard it so many times, I genuinely agree with the last comment listed above.

Do look into childcare and finances as soon as possible if you want to return to work. I had no choice but to stay at home full-time with my twin boys for well over two years because I could not find affordable childcare until they were nursery age. I must admit that twins were a huge financial shock for us!

*ScummyMummy*

**We have twin boys** and I felt totally panicked as well as totally elated when I found out. First of all, EAT – you want big babies that feed well and sleep well from the start, so you are aiming to grow them in-utero as big as you can. That takes massive amounts of food, so now is not the time to be worrying about your figure.

Secondly, arrange for lots of help now. You will definitely need extra support and encouragement, especially if you want to breastfeed, as you will have no time for shopping, cooking, washing, hoovering, etc.

I think routines are definitely a must with twins. My boys were born in the US, but I put them on Gina Ford when they were about 12 weeks as I was exhausted, and not coping with constant feeding – of course my US friends thought I was a cruel, heartless, chilly British cow – but it was the best thing I ever did. They went almost immediately to four-hourly feeds and started dropping the night-time ones, and within weeks were sleeping through the night. Bliss!

The wonderful thing about twins is you are let off any guilt about using bottles, dummies, disposables and paid help. Everyone considers you a heroine for even delivering two – let alone caring for them – so take advantage of your new-found status as a supermum and take all the liberties/short-cuts in the book.

Finally don't let anyone say to you: 'Oh you poor thing, twins, what a lot of work.' It's so negative and doesn't begin to cover the fantastic thrill of two first smiles and two first steps. And when they start interacting with each other, it's fascinating. My two are best mates, and the fact that they share a room means they don't need us in the morning for entertainment, or in fact at anytime for entertainment, they have each other. So there are many, many situations where having two works to your advantage. Only listen to the positive comments about twins, they are a total joy – yes, hard work, but worth it, worth it, worth it.

*Suzeg*

# Being pregnant with twins – how bad is it?

**I've been pregnant with twins** as well as with a singleton and I reckon it's much the same but the chances are you'll get everything a bit more severely with twins. Actually I was sicker with the singleton (boy) pregnancy than with the twin girls but my backache, indigestion, constipation and general aches and pains were worse when carrying two. On the plus side, you have an even bigger excuse for taking it easy and letting everyone else run around after you when you're expecting two and the chances are they might come a bit early. Oh, and of course twins are great (at least from about a year old, they are).

*Roberta*

**I did get very tired towards the end** of the pregnancy, but worked up to 35 weeks (they arrived at just over 38). I also felt very sick, and had horrible heartburn, but otherwise no health worries.

*China1*

**I am 31 weeks' pregnant** with identical twin boys and have severe SPD. I have a support belt and crutches. I have now been given a prescription for Clexane (a blood-thinning drug), which I have to inject daily, because I am apparently more at risk of blood clots due to my limited mobility. I asked if the babies could be delivered early (i.e. at 35/36 weeks) due to these problems, but my consultant has refused – saying I have to go to 38 weeks. It is looking like a C-section as twin one has always been breech and twin two is still transverse. I am so upset at having to take these drugs and being so immobile – I just can't see why they can't deliver a bit earlier.

*Hen*

> **Mumsnet fact**
> Women who take folic acid are nearly twice as likely to give birth to twins as women who do not.
>
> Twins Research

**I have 20-month-old twins** and had quite a tricky pregnancy. In general I would say take it as easy as possible – lots of rest, lots of protein – and don't worry. Twins are hard work in the beginning but very special and when they start playing with each other (from about one year on) – it's magic.

*Justine*

**I've felt pretty awful** from about 20 weeks. I think that having had one pregnancy already you think you will know what to expect but this has been so different. I've had scans every two weeks already so I am being well looked after but we've been told that one twin is not growing and to prepare for being delivered (I'm 31 weeks' pregnant). I had steroid injections to mature the lungs (I think I have a very padded bottom because I seem to be the only person who didn't find it too bad – I knew there was a reason for my ample buttocks!) and have been in twice more for scans and Doppler tests, as well as being in twice overnight with strong contractions.

Yesterday's scan showed some growth of the little one so we won't have another week until the next scan. I am finding it really hard as I do not know whether I am coming or going and everyone keeps telling me to rest, which is easier said than done with a bouncy two-and-a-half-year old!

*Pop*

---

**What the experts say**
Scientific studies show that at term the inner volume of the uterus is five litres with singletons and nearly 10 litres with twins!
Dr Carol Cooper (*Twins & Multiple Births*)

---

**I'm 27 weeks' pregnant with twins** and also have a 20-month-old with tantrums. I am getting to the point of being permanently uncomfortable whether I'm eating, sitting down to work or sleeping. I'm going to hang in there until at least until 36 weeks and will then start jumping up and down with vigour to encourage the delivery!

*Barnzee*

**I think the pregnancy experience** and the eventual health of the babies is mostly down to luck, unfortunately. I loved being pregnant up until the last month or so. My pregnancy went to 41 weeks and both boys were very healthy but all I did was to regularly tell the babies not to come out early and to eat lots and lots and lots, which perhaps provides a clue as to why I liked pregnancy.

There can be a big difference in the size of twins with no ill effects – my own had a weight difference of a full 2 lb at birth and seeing them at three years it's clear that they are just built very differently.

*ScummyMummy*

**Mine came out at 30 weeks,** having first tried to appear at 25. They had twin-to-twin transfusion syndrome – a condition with identical twins whereby connections in the placenta mean one twin gets too much from the mother and one too little (mine were very different weights at 25 weeks).

I went into labour at 25 weeks because the twin that gets too much basically pees so much that the amniotic fluid swells (polyhydramnios) and the pressure triggers labour. They stopped it by draining fluid from me using a needle, much like an amniocentesis (they took out six litres in all). I had steroid injections and basically had to take it easy from then on but my waters broke at 30 1/2 weeks.

Both twins came out at roughly the same weight (miraculously) – 2 lb 12 oz and 2lb 14 oz – and the lungs were sufficiently mature that they didn't need a ventilator. They had five weeks in special care but were basically fine, just small and in need of fattening up. It's not easy coping with premmie babies but it's also not as bad as you might think.

*Berta*

**My friend delivered identical twins at 32 weeks** after they developed twin-to-twin transfusion syndrome, and she developed pre-eclampsia at the same time. They weighed in at 4lb 6 oz and 5 lb and were fine, coming home from special care after only three weeks. They are 18 months old now and seemingly very advanced for their ages. She had to have regular check-ups for them but has never had any problems.

*Lou33*

**A friend who had twins** was absolutely fine through her pregnancy apart from the usual early morning sickness. However, I had a really awful pregnancy. I fainted on an hourly basis through most of it. I ate very little during the nine months and as soon as I gave birth I actually weighed a stone and a half less than before I got pregnant.

My only advice is to get plenty of rest and to treat yourself whenever possible. After the nightmare of the pregnancy the first few weeks were a bit of a fog for all concerned but it really is worth it. My two fight like mad but they love each other so much. To see them discovering life together is just magical. If one of them is upset, the other goes across and gives them a big sticky kiss and cuddle. My favourite times are when they play hide and seek together and collapse in a fit of giggles when they find each other.

*Twinsmum*

## Birth stories – how was it for you?

**Due to the higher risks** associated with giving birth to twins there is pressure on the mother to accept far more intervention during labour. I was made to feel quite guilty for asking to try for a vaginal delivery as opposed to a Caesarean, despite both my babies being head down. I accepted the higher risk of the second baby turning at the last minute, so had an epidural sited in case this should happen. It didn't and both my babies were born naturally as I had wanted.

*Thea*

**I had a talk with my obstetrician** some time before the birth of my twins. He warned me that whoever was on duty would persuade me to have an epidural, which I really didn't want (I'd had three children already, without epidurals), and he also said that this was for their convenience so that a C-section could be done immediately if necessary. So I asked him to write in my notes that I wanted to have a general anaesthetic if an emergency arose.

Having said that, they did try to persuade me to have an epidural, and the registrar on duty was furious with me for refusing. He couldn't understand why anyone would want to suffer pain when they don't have to!

I actually believe that I may have lost at least one of my twins if I'd had an epidural, as they were in fairly poor condition when they were born (which took the medical staff by surprise), and if my labour had lasted any longer, they may not have survived. I also asked to be mobile (upright) for as long as possible, as I'd found in my other labours that this was the only way for me to keep the contractions going. Funny how the midwives listened to me, but the registrar thought he knew better.

*Cfr*

**I've only just found out that I'm expecting** twins and it's completely scuppered my plans for a lovely home water-birth. I was booked for a home birth with my first child, but ended up in hospital on the midwife's advice for an epidural after 23 hours of labour. This time I was determined to have a home birth. Now I'm really fed up with people implying that I'll end up with a C-section. I'm blowed if I'm going to let 'em cut me open unless there's a very good reason!

*BrightSide*

**What the experts say**
Given the risks twins face, there are persuasive medical reasons which make home births totally unsuitable.

Dr Carol Cooper (*Twins & Multiple Births*)

I had my own twins at home... I am glad that I weighed the risks and benefits of going to hospital and made the decision to stay at home, though I remained flexible about switching to hospital if labour was not going well, or if the babies were not in good condition.

Sheila Kitzinger (*Homebirth*)

**You can give birth naturally** but it hinges on having a good team with you. I too had a home birth planned (and booked) but it's a no-no with twins.

However I told the midwives that we wanted as little intervention as possible – whilst allowing for the fact that we might end up having a C-section. They were fantastic and let us do our own thing – music, oils, massage, the lot – and five hours later they popped out. I was on all fours for the boy, then as I was rolled over onto my side so they could check where his sister was lying, she popped into the midwife's hands. One word of warning is that a twin birth is often seen as a teaching opportunity by many hospitals, so if you don't want loads of student midwives, doctors and nurses watching, make sure you say so.

*JoeR*

**I too had hoped for a home birth** until I found out it was twins. Actually I ended up having a C-section at 30 weeks as they had twin-to-twin transfusion syndrome and my waters broke. I had an 'elective' (like I had a choice!) Caesarean the next morning. All I can say, though, is that it was a wonderful birth. All very relaxed with music playing in the background. All the hospital staff were lovely and the babies were put onto my chest before they took them off to special care. What was most important was that they were given the best chance they could be given as they were so small (2lb 12 oz and 2lb 14 oz).

*Berta*

**I had my twins six weeks early.** After four weeks of daily scans the doctor decided it was time to bail out as one was not growing. I opted to be induced rather than go for a C-section but unfortunately got to the bitter end and was pushing when they discovered one twin was face first, so I had a section anyway.

*Pop*

**I had an elective caesarean** at 38 weeks as the first twin was breech (after having had a natural birth with my first child). It was absolutely fine although you do take longer to recover than from a natural birth.

*FifiDella*

**I had a wonderful birth with my boy twins.** In fact I am worried about doing it again in case it's not as great. I gave birth in the US as we were living there at the time and the key thing that I think contributed to my excellent experience was that my expectations were correctly managed from day one.

I was advised to keep all options open, and not to get too wedded to any one scenario. Happily for me, both babies were head down. I was in active labour for nine hours and had an epidural about halfway through (standard procedure in the US in case they need to intervene in a hurry about halfway through). The babies arrived safely, naturally and in very good shape (one 6 lb 8 oz and the other 6 lb 13 oz).

I had time to rest up between the births, and the second one was a walk in the park as the doors were open and all I needed to do was push a couple of times and he was out. There were a lot of people in the room, but music was playing and I had a fantastic epidural, which meant I could feel enough to push with the contractions, and not simply be numb. All in all, I can say that it was the best thing I have ever done, and I was wheeled out, saying that I'd do it all over again.

---

**What the experts say**
Labour with twins is not twice as painful or twice as long as with singletons. In fact, it can even be less uncomfortable because the babies tend to be a bit smaller.

Dr Carol Cooper (*Twins & Multiple Births*)

---

**Of course there are many scenarios** when it makes sense to go for the C-section, and your doctor should talk you through all that, but if the babes are in the right place, and you are in good shape then there is no reason not to proceed with a natural, but with all the back-up, should things change at the last moment. Just keep your mind open – in the end all that matters is that your babies come out and in one piece. If you don't build your birth experience up to be something that is about you, and concentrate on the fact that it is about the safe delivery of your child, then it won't matter how that happens, just that it happens. And rest assured, having twins is an absolute joy!

*Suzeg*

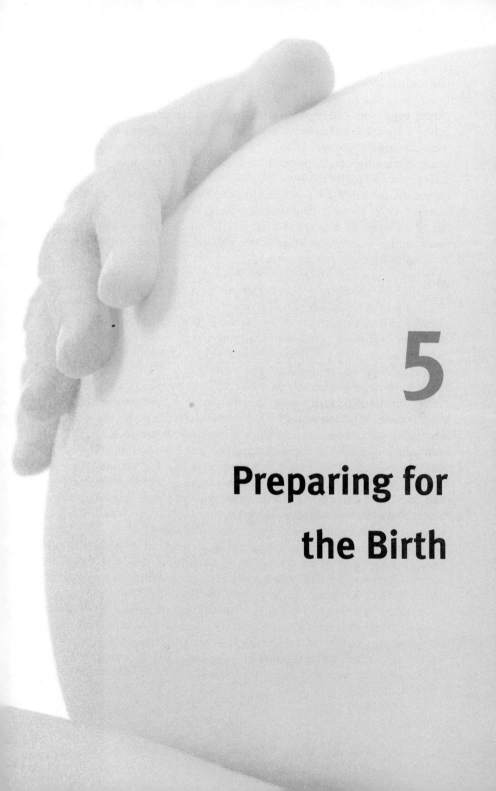

# 5

# Preparing for the Birth

# Introduction

Never before has the expectant mother been faced with so many choices when it comes to giving birth. For our own mothers it was a pretty much a case of lying back and thinking of England. Nowadays, we are able to pick and choose where and how we have our babies in the same way we would mastermind a family holiday.

Yet the debate about home versus hospital birth is not a new one. Way back in 1871, Florence Nightingale was an influential advocate of home birth: 'As a general rule the mortality is far, far greater in lying-in hospitals than among women lying-in at home.' By the end of the 1950s over a third of women were still having their babies at home, but by 1987 the rate had fallen to a record low of under 1 per cent.

Planned home births are on the rise again, accounting for 2.6 per cent in 2001. If you're considering joining the rising trend, what are the pros and cons? And if you do decide to stay at home, is it worth turning your living room into a birthing paradise and erecting a pool, or do you simply prepare your bedroom with newspapers, plastic sheets and a bowl of hot water? Should you warn your neighbours and, if you already have kids, should you allow them to be spectators?

Of course, opting for a hospital birth doesn't mean any fewer decisions to make. First of all you need to choose which hospital to go to. Do you choose the one closest to home or travel further afield to a venue that you feel more comfortable with? What about birthing centres? How do they stack up?

These days your partner will be welcomed in the delivery suite (by everyone else at least!) but whether or not he's there, you have other options as well. You could hire a doula to accompany you into motherhood or even an independent midwife to ensure you get the birth you want. What exactly can you expect from them and are they worth the money?

Then there are birth plans in which you can map out your route to delivery to avoid congestion, pile-ups and right-hand turns. But do they engender unrealistic expectations? Should we be planning something as unpredictable as childbirth or is it better just to go with the flow?

Of course however much you plan in advance, there's no getting away from it: childbirth is unpredictable. But it's worth at least being aware of all the options so you can be comfortable that whatever hazards you encounter you can be confident that you'll reach your final destination with your sanity preserved and without too many accidents.

# Birth Plans – should you bother making one?

**I recently told a friend** who'd spent a lot of time on her birth plan to read it over a few times and then tear it up and chuck it in the bin. Cynical I know, but I just cannot see why anyone should be encouraged to 'plan' their birth It's just not realistic to plan anything unless you have an elective C-section.

*Ghosty*

**My birth plan didn't even** come out of my bag. My husband was well briefed and my labour was not complicated. It is important to know your options and understand what can happen so that you feel in control if interventions become necessary.

*Lalaa*

**I think that if you have a plan** you are setting yourself up to be disappointed. Go with the flow is my advice.

*SamboM*

**My plans for a wonderful water birth** didn't happen purely because if anyone had laid a finger on me or asked me to move to get into a pool I would have knocked them out! I found a position that I was happy in and I wasn't giving it up. Nor did I deck out my room in lavender candles, put the CDs I'd picked out on the stereo, or any of the lovely things I thought I'd do. I did, however, have a relatively easy delivery and wouldn't have changed a thing about it. The downside of writing out a birth plan is that when it doesn't go that way it could lead to disappointment.

*ThomCat*

**For my daughter's birth** I didn't really put a birth plan together because I didn't know what to expect. For my next birth, there are certainly some things I would like to ensure happen/don't happen; things like, I was given pethidine – I wasn't even asked – and it didn't work so I would like to avoid having it again as it's pointless. Also I would like (if possible) to put the baby straight to the breast. It was at least half an hour last time before I even held her.

*Wills*

**The first time I wrote a birth plan** and it all went out of the window as things went quite wrong. The second time, I felt so much more in control of what was happening and the midwife took into account everything that I had written.

*Lara2*

**I think birth plans are a good idea** especially if you are likely to be delivered by someone you've never met before. It will help them to know something of your attitudes and hopes for the labour. My first one was quite vague and hedged with 'ifs' and 'buts' as I didn't want to make myself a hostage to fortune with categorical statements about no pain relief! Next time I will be much more dogmatic, though the content will be very similar.

*Elliott*

**I didn't have a birth plan** when I had my daughter, I just thought I'd go with the flow and see what happened. We're now trying for baby number two and I'm not even pregnant yet but I have a piece of paper where I am jotting things down that I will eventually turn into a birth plan when I'm pregnant. Because I've been through labour and birth before I have very definite ideas of how I want things NOT to happen (if possible), given the circumstances of my last labour. I know every birth is different but this time I hope to be more in control and will ask a lot more questions about what is going on.

*Linnet*

**I wrote a plan** that outlined my basic philosophy (based on as little intervention as possible, promoting my own endorphins, etc.) and included some specifics. I requested that if there was any need to change from the plan, it should be explained along the lines of what were the risks, side effects, and what would be the risk in 'doing nothing'. I also included details for the midwives, telling them to make themselves at home, help themselves to tea, coffee and food from the fridge. My midwives were great, and really took account of my beliefs and personality. When things went drastically 'off plan', and we did need to go to hospital for a complete catalogue of interventions in the last 15 minutes, they were still asking my permission about every minor detail. This helped me enormously, and made me feel as if I was still a person, despite the difficult ventouse and episiotomy.

*Blu*

**I still stand by everything I wrote** in my birth plan. Everything I wrote may not have happened but my choices were clear and, where possible, we followed them. I think they're extremely worthwhile if you accept that they are only a plan (or wish list if you prefer) and not set in stone. Mine covered pretty much every eventuality up to emergency C-section and SCBU. My midwives referred to it, which meant that my wishes were clear and also that my husband had some idea of my wishes.

*SoupDragon*

---

**What the experts say**
It's not a contract but a written understanding between doctor and/or hospital and patient, with the goal of bringing childbirth as close as possible to the patient's ideal while heading off unrealistic expectations, minimizing disappointment and avoiding major conflict or miscommunication during labour and delivery.
Murkoff, Eisenberg & Hathaway (*What to Expect When You're Expecting*)

---

**I know I'm lucky,** but everything I put in my birth plan happened. It said things like I wanted my husband to cut the cord, I wanted the lights kept low, etc. I included provisions for ending up in hospital too, such as not having students present. When you write a birth plan, make sure your partner (or anyone who is going to be there with you) knows your wishes too, since you might want them to speak up for you. Ideally you should discuss it with your midwife before the birth too.

*Wickedwaterwitch*

**The main thing is to ensure** your birthing partner knows the score. We had planned for my husband to cut the cord, but as it was, my son didn't breathe when he came out so the midwife had to work very quickly and clamped the cord herself so that our son could be revived. That sort of flexibility is crucial. I have to say that I had very good midwives and was asked when I got into the labour room if I had any specific requests. I trusted the midwives I had implicitly and when it came to me having an epidural as my contractions were going nowhere, they made the decision with my partner as I was not on this planet by then!

*LucieB*

**As a midwife, I really like it** when women come in with birth plans so that you get some idea of what their thoughts were prior to going into labour. Sometimes I have seen birth plans that are written in such a way as to infer that midwives do not know the reasoning behind requests, and have no knowledge of natural childbirth. In the main though, I think they are really positive.

*Mears*

**Mumsnet tip**
Keep your birth plan to one side of A4 in bullet points, so it can be read quickly and understood very easily in case of a rush/emergency.
*Outofpractice*

**I think birth plans are useful** for after the birth. For example, if you want your baby to receive the Vitamin K orally instead of by injection or if you want them to check your baby for certain conditions that may run in your family. These are things that you might not remember at the time because you are so overwhelmed by the birth. I also used my birth plan to remind the staff that I'm allergic to certain drugs even though this is all over my notes as well.

*Princesspeahead*

**Mumsnet tip**
Try to make your birth plan focus on the positive, instead of giving a list of what you don't want. Use words like, 'we hope to' or 'we plan to', rather than, 'we don't want' or 'we want to avoid'.
*Monty*

**I think it depends on the midwife** who attends you in labour as to whether a birth plan is of any use. Some are brilliant and will go out of their way to try to keep things the way you would prefer them, even to the point of arguing on your behalf with doctors. Most will read the birth plan and stick to the bits that seem practical in the situation. Of course, we all write birth plans with the understanding they cannot be set in stone. Sadly I have seen a few midwives laughing about the things in people's birth plans. I think, therefore, that you should write your plan, but be realistic and be aware that circumstances may cause a deviation from it. Legally nothing can be done to you or to your baby without your permission. Everything, from taking your blood pressure to injecting you with something, should only be done if you allow it, although holding out your arm if someone waves a blood pressure cuff at you is taken as implied consent – and there is a bit of leeway in a true emergency!

*Oakmaiden*

**I think that it's a good idea** to write a plan as it will help you think through the options and what matters to you. I included in my birth plan that I wanted my husband with me as long as he was comfortable (he was very nervous and I didn't want him forced into a situation where he was distressed – for example, if I had a Caesarean). Also, I added that we wanted to be consulted, advised and given all options. It turned out this was the most important part for us and was brilliantly followed by our doctor and midwives, who explained everything throughout. In the end, I had an emergency C-section – but even that was presented as an option. This meant that although I had a C-section I never felt like I'd lost control.

*Sjs*

**As a midwife, I really appreciate birth plans.** These days it is unlikely that you'll know the midwife looking after you in labour, and given that you meet her when in considerable pain and not feeling up to much discussion, it is useful for her to get an idea of your preferences. Naturally, if she feels something won't be possible, she should raise the issue. Unless there is a complete emergency situation, there is no excuse for not reading them. It is important to realize that no birth plan should be set in stone. Things can change, either by choice or necessity. However, nothing should be done without your full informed consent.

*CheekyGirl*

# Home or hospital birth – what are the pros and cons?

**Having experienced both,** if I were to have another child I would choose a home birth. At home I had a hundred distractions, which I could choose to use or ignore. I decided when to bath, when to eat and when to run up and down stairs naked. No strangers were able to walk into the room when I was facing the door with my legs in the air. The food was considerably better and on demand and, despite my partner's fears, no mess went beyond the pads and sheets we had prepared. My other children could meet the new baby when we chose and not according to visiting times. Finally, I was able to practise feeding in privacy rather than in the presence of all the relatives of the person in the next bed.

*Bubbly*

**Mumsnet tip**
Collect plenty of newspapers on the run-up to your due date. They're handy to lie on the floor of your birthing room and bathroom. Newsprint inhibits the growth of germs and so is considered hygienic.

*Monty*

**My experience of home birth** was brilliant. When my waters went I had a quick bath whilst waiting for the midwife. It was totally relaxed. I moved around a lot and gave birth on the edge of the sofa with a beanbag behind me, which was very comfortable. Gas and air kept the edge off the pain and the midwife was wildly excited as I 'breathed the head out'. After the birth I snuggled down on the sofa whilst my daughter had a feed and the midwives tidied up and made tea. An hour later we were all tucked up in bed. My son slept through the whole thing and wandered in the next morning to find a baby in the bed. I'm sure it all went so well because I was relaxed and comfortable. There was no rushing into the car or bouncing down the lane – just calm pottering about. Compared to my first delivery in hospital it was heavenly.

*Hopeful*

**What the experts say**
In your own home you are the centre around which everything else revolves, rather than a patient, dependent on the routines of an institution. Your attendants come into your home as guests.

Janet Balaskas (*New Active Birth*)

Childbirth is as messy as a pig slaughter. Why in the world would you want to sacrifice your beautiful sheets, not to mention your mattress, to such a thing?

Vicki Iovine (*The Best friend's guide to Pregnancy*)

**I spent most of my time** wandering around the lounge. I find walking the most comfortable way to pass labour and it seemed to speed things up considerably. I didn't bother with any pain relief in the end. I was so relaxed and felt so much more in control. The last few pushes merely seemed like an interruption to the conversation we were all having! I think it very much depends on which midwife you get, and how she helps you through it.

*Sc*

**I had my daughter at home.** My labour proceeded very slowly and my first stage was nearly 42 hours. However, I had a very experienced midwife, who was confident that the baby and I were fine, which was the key point in making it such a success. If I had been in hospital, I would have ended up with a lot of intervention and the outcome could have been very different, possibly even a Caesarean.

*Pimpernel*

> **Mumsnet fact**
> Two per cent of babies are born at home, but up to 20 per cent of mothers would prefer this type of delivery if they had the choice.
> The Commons Health Committee

**At home, a midwife will come** as soon as you call her and she will call for a second midwife when she feels you are getting close to delivery. After the birth one takes care of the baby and the other of you (to deliver the placenta, take your blood pressure, etc.). At my house it was all very friendly. After the birth we drank champagne together and they ran me a bath. Then they went to see my son, who they had delivered 20 months earlier. They left my house, past midnight, completely tidy. We had to empty the pool but everything else was perfect.

*Pupuce*

**My second baby was born at home.** It was a planned home birth with an independent midwife. My labour was astonishingly fast – I ended up delivering the baby all by myself, my midwife was still on her way and my husband was watching videos with our toddler. My midwife arrived 15 minutes after the birth. She sorted me and the baby out, cleaned the bathroom, put the dirty towels in the washing machine and made tea and toast.

*2under2*

**I was dreading my second birth.** I'd been induced with the first and went from nothing to full-on labour in the space of one hour. I didn't cope at all well with the pain until the bliss of the epidural. When I thought I was starting labour with my second child, I phoned the midwife to come and check me out. Imagine my amazement when she told me I was already 9 cm dilated and that I should forget about going to hospital unless I wanted to give birth in the back of a car.

I won't say there was no pain, but it was certainly manageable, and I was so calm that my eldest (then 29 months) stayed in the room and was there when her sister was born. It really was magical. Of course, it's not the sort of thing you can really plan, as you never know how it's going to go, but for me, having my older daughter there made the whole thing perfect. She is now absolutely obsessed with watching any TV programme about birth and babies.

*Emsiewill*

**If things are progressing** quickly, let your midwife know ASAP, or ring the local delivery suite, who will contact the 'on-call' midwife for your area. You should also contact the ambulance service – paramedics are trained to deal with anything until the midwife arrives. If things go this quickly there really should not be much for anyone else to do – so just get on with it but don't cut the cord! Just wrap your baby snugly against yourself (skin to skin). Babies born quickly can look a bit 'blue' or congested – this is normal – a quick firm rub down with a towel helps.

I've been called to quite a few BBAs as we term them (Born Before Arrival at hospital), and most of the time it's just a quick clean up before leaving the happy family at home. In some instances babies have had to be transferred into hospital for observation because their body temperature has been allowed to drop – remember, don't worry about anything else but keeping that baby warm.

*Leese*

**Mumsnet fact**

A baby born at home is likely to have a higher Apgar score, is less likely to need resuscitation and is less likely to suffer birth injuries.

National Birthday Trust Fund

**I had many sleepless nights** worrying about my son and where he would go at various stages of the day and got lots of friends and neighbours involved as emergency fall back. People told me it would all fall into place and sure enough, my son slept through the whole thing only two rooms away – my second son was born at 6.55 am and my first son woke at 7.10 am!

*Hughsie*

**From my experience of home birth**, I believe that if you are a fairly scream-free labourer, it would be lovely to have your other children around. Unfortunately I'm not and so my children came over an hour or so after the birth and were so pleased to see me in my bed with their new sister.

*Emmy*

**I had all four of my children** at home. I shouted the house down but none of the others woke up. They were not actually there at the birth as they were asleep but I have known people who have had their toddler in the pool playing with ducks!

Having the babies at home was the most wonderful experience.

*Countrybumkin*

---

**What the experts say**
It is sensible not to restrict the child [from being present at their sibling's birth] and if he has followed your pregnancy through, the experience will be an enlightening one... Someone responsible must be there besides your partner to take care of him during labour. Run through everything with him, especially the birth of the placenta as this may be the bloodiest part. Warn him that you won't be able to answer his questions because you'll be busy and that if the midwife says he must leave the room, he must do exactly as she says.

Dr Miriam Stoppard (*Pregnancy and Labour Book*)

---

**I had a home birth** with my daughter (aged 20 months) upstairs playing in her bedroom with the two aunties. She was fine, not at all stressed by the experience, but just a little shocked when her daddy walked in with a baby in his arms. She had a few hours of labour to listen to but she was not fazed at all. What was lovely about being at home was that her routine was not changed at all. It was perfect; could not have been better.

*Gingersj*

**I had half a home birth.** I started labour at home with a water pool and very supportive midwives. I was at home for the whole of the first stage and found it fantastic. Just as I was about to start pushing, the midwives discovered that my daughter was breech so I went to hospital, quickly and with little fuss. Labour is always going to be unpredictable and I would definitely try for a home birth again, but I don't feel I failed by ending up with the full surgical procedure.

*Emmagee*

**My main reasons for opting** for a home birth are really to avoid the things that I didn't like about my previous hospital birth – for example, the awful ride in the back of the car in advanced labour, the delivery by complete strangers, being expected to lie down on the bed and the hideous post-natal stay. I think it would be great not to have to be away from home at all. I also think the midwives will have a much clearer idea of the kind of approach you want at home. I like the idea that I can decide at any stage to go to hospital – it's only about 20 minutes away – so if things are going slowly I can always change my mind.

*Elliott*

**The main thing to remember** is that pregnancy and labour are normal physiological events. If you are fit and healthy and your pregnancy progresses well, why should anything go wrong? I think it is imperative that if you decide on a home birth you are 100 per cent confident in your own ability. If you are concerned then you might run into difficulties because anxiety can inhibit labour.

*Mears*

**My son was born with a severe infection** and had to be whisked to an ITU within minutes, where he spent the next two or three days fighting for his life. This was completely unexpected as I'd had a textbook pregnancy and he was full-term. Giving birth isn't just about 'you' and which whale music you want to listen to, but also about your baby and the unforeseen things which can happen.

*Emmabee*

**I would have loved** to have a home birth, but decided with my first that I was too old to take the risk. I ended up having a C-section so a home birth wouldn't have been safe the second time around. As it turned out I had a post-partum haemorrhage, which had nothing to do with the previous C-section or being in hospital. But if I had been at home, I might have died from the blood loss.

*SofiaAmes*

**I never considered a home birth** with any of my three as it just didn't appeal to me. But when my second birth was quick and fairly uncomplicated, I thought the birth of number three would be a breeze. I was wrong. Out of all three, this was my worst birth. It was extremely painful from early on in labour, meconium was present in the waters when the membranes ruptured, my baby got distressed, had the cord around his neck and needed resuscitation at birth, and I haemorrhaged badly and needed a drip and IV antibiotics – and stitches for an episiotomy. Thankfully we were both okay, but it does worry me what may have happened if I had decided on a home birth.

*ChanelNo5*

**One of the downsides** to home births is the transfer by ambulance. It's easy to say, 'Oh, the hospital is only six miles away', but it is no fun being in the advanced stages of labour in an ambulance. I thought it took at least half an hour when in fact it was 15 minutes. The ambulance driver drove really carefully and was avoiding all the bumps in the road but I thought we were driving along pot-holed lanes. This was four hours into the second stage. Anyone considering a home birth should bear in mind that it is not pleasant if you do have to transfer.

*Gem13*

**I am not 'anti' home births,** they just wouldn't suit me. One of the joys of having my babies was bringing them home. If I'd had them at home, I would have been too aware of housework and the needs of my elder son. I felt so far from my normal life at home and that's what made it feel so special.

*Lil*

**In the hospital ward** post-birth, there were three other new mums and their new-borns (lustily crying), two pregnant women being continuously monitored (with beeps), one woman in labour, midwives bustling to and fro. Then there was the woman trying to persuade us to have the babies' photos taken at great expense, and all afternoon, huge numbers of partners, parents, friends and toddlers, all chatting in various different languages. But despite all this, I actually enjoyed my hospital visit even though I didn't get any sleep.

*Philippat*

**Mumsnet fact**
In about 5 per cent of home deliveries a transfer to hospital during labour is required.
Murkoff, Eisenberg & Hathaway (*What to Expect When You're Expecting*)

**I loved having a hospital birth.** Luckily at our hospital all women have their own room from arriving at hospital until they leave. It was also ensuite with a bath and shower and it was exceptionally clean. The midwives were fantastic; helpful and not intrusive and very determined that I would have no intervention. I was often left on my own with my husband just to get on with it, which suited me fine.

If I had any problems I just had to buzz and a midwife would arrive immediately to help me with positioning for a feed and nappy changes. My meals were delivered to me and I enjoyed having that time completely on my own with my daughter once she was born and only having to entertain visitors at visiting time. It was so enjoyable I am really looking forward to going back into hospital for my next birth. I feel I am getting all the benefits of a home birth plus the added bonus of not having to worry about cleaning my house or the dog sniffing around!

*Forest*

**I was very keen to have a home birth** with number two until I was present during the labour of a friend who was having one. I realized that I would not be able to relax properly with the midwives in the house. My home is a bit of a sanctuary to me and I'm not comfortable with strangers, even a midwife I'd seen throughout the pregnancy, being in it. In the end I had my second in hospital on a six-hour turnaround – I'm probably one of the few who have found NHS understaffing a benefit! We were pretty much left alone to get on with it, with one midwife turning up when called for the pushing and actual delivery. We had a lovely peaceful couple of hours alone with our new baby daughter before heading home to our rather high-maintenance toddler son!

*Azzie*

# Choosing a hospital – what criteria do you use and can you change hospitals during pregnancy?

**Your choice of hospital** depends on the type of birth you want. I chose the one I went to because I thought the care in labour would be more midwife-driven (as opposed to doctor-driven) as it is not a major teaching hospital. You can do a tour of both hospitals in my area and I would really recommend this as a good way of getting a feel for the sort of care you'll get.

*Lisac*

**I phoned up the hospitals** in my area and asked for any information they had. You can also make an appointment to visit a hospital or go on a tour for mums-to-be and see which you prefer.

*Wiltshire*

---

**What the experts say**
When you go around the hospital (on a tour) try not to be distracted by the surroundings or décor, and instead try and remember that what is important is the attitude of the obstetrician and midwives towards you and your baby's birth.
Murkoff, Eisenberg & Hathaway (*What to Expect When You're Expecting*)

---

**I had a choice of two hospitals** and asked which one the midwife team would prefer to send me to. I think it was the right question as they did have a preference because most of the midwives had closer links to one of the two hospitals. I found out from my post-natal group that those who had been to the other hospital had all had their babies delivered by midwives they didn't know, whereas of those who had been to the preferred hospital, some had known the midwife.

*Meid*

**You don't have to go** to the hospital 'in your area'. I wanted to go to a different hospital and asked my GP to refer me there. It helps if you have a reason. The first time I said it was because my gynaecologist worked there, and the second time because my first child had been born there). For me the main criteria, apart from wanting to be under my gynaecologist's care, were availability of a birthing pool, together with not having to be moved if the baby or I needed special care, and the attitude of the staff.

I'm not certain it matters all that much whether you know your midwife when you deliver; I'd much rather have continuity of care during the pregnancy, and an open-minded midwifery team during the birth. It could be a good idea to research things like intervention rates, c-section rates, breast-feeding at discharge rates, births per midwife per year etc., but it's important to view such things in context.

For example, the hospital I gave birth in has relatively high rates for certain interventions, but that is because complicated pregnancies/births are referred there nationally, so only a minority of births are uncomplicated.

*Boyandgirl*

**You might want to check** how many births per midwife per year each unit has. I believe there is a cut-off point of about 30, over which it suggests that the unit is struggling at busy times to provide optimum coverage for its clients. There is much more to it than that, of course.

We have chosen the local hospital whose figures do suggest overworked midwives, rather than the one which is less overrun, because the former has a good reputation locally, a brilliant Head of Midwifery Services, decent consultants, a 'can-do' approach to VBAC and a proper birthing pool. You can also find out whether there is an anaesthetist available 24/7 to do epidurals. Visiting, and asking the midwives themselves, is also well worthwhile. I also asked the local NCT branch and their views were unanimous, no matter what kind of birth you were likely to expect/want.

*Clare2*

**My advice would be to ask around.** Find out what kinds of experiences people have had at each. Weigh those personal experiences in with the statistics.

*Expatkat*

> **Mumsnet tip**
> Don't listen too hard to hospital horror stories. Every hospital or practice will have screwed up somewhere down the line, but I don't think that has to reflect on the overall standard.
>
> *Pie*

**There are now a number of NHS** midwife-led units that cater for low-risk, 'natural' births. The one I attended had a birthing pool, low-sensory room, showers and baths, gas and air and pethidine (or equivalent) on hand for pain relief. Epidurals are not available but the unit was on the floor below the STD maternity unit so I could have been transferred if necessary. I had my own room with ensuite bathroom. The small team of midwives were brilliant at helping me manage without an epidural and really supportive of my choices.

*NickiB*

**I had my daughter on** a birthing-centre floor. I wanted to have a VBAC (vaginal birth after caesarean) and did – and they were amazingly supportive. As it turned out, I had a haemorrhage after the birth and had to be whisked up to the theatre on the regular labour floor. This was done with no problems or communication gaps. I spent the night up there and then was allowed to come back down to the birthing centre for the next few days and I stayed there. During the last few months of my pregnancy I had all of my check-ups at the birthing centre. Every midwife I dealt with was friendly and helpful and the floor always seemed calm and not oversubscribed.

*SofiaAmes*

---

**What the experts say**
[Birth centres] are seen as the result of hospitals responding to public demand – a safer option than giving birth on a couch at home and a more pleasant and natural option than giving birth on trolley under bright lights in a room that smells of industrial-strength Dettol.

Kaz Cooke (*The Rough Guide to Pregnancy and Birth*)

---

**I had my son in a birthing centre.** It was fantastic; very clean and new and the care I got was great. As it is just around the corner from the labour ward, it is easy to be transferred there if you need to be. I stayed in my room in the birthing centre until I went home the next day, but if it is busy you may get put in the post-labour wards, which can be a bit grim.

I had my first two children in the labour ward, and the birthing centre was just a million miles better. If I were to have another baby, I would definitely go there again.

*TalkingTree*

**My partner went to a birthing centre.** It really was the best place to go to as we found it very relaxed with caring midwives and lovely big comfortable homey rooms. She started her labour there, but unfortunately, after about 21 hours the labour wasn't progressing and she was in a lot of pain. We decided (they left it to us but were very helpful) that my partner needed to go to hospital for an epidural.

As soon as we made the decision they were great. They called an ambulance and within 30 minutes we were on the way to hospital. A midwife went with us to hand over, and we got messages throughout the rest of the labour that they were phoning to see how my partner was doing. I know she really regrets not being able to give birth at the birthing centre, but at least we started off there, and it was the best thing in the end that she was transferred to hospital.

*Dot1*

**I switched hospitals midway through pregnancy.** In my case it was because I wanted to have a home birth, and only one of the three choices open to me offered these. I changed through my GP, but it wasn't a problem. Remember that as long as you're in the catchment area, it is your choice.

*Berta*

**A friend of mine switched** very late in pregnancy. After a 36-week scan her original hospital said that she had to book in for C-section the following week for low-lying placenta. She was none too happy and switched hospitals, telling the first she wanted a second opinion.

After talking to a consultant at the second hospital, she decided on a vaginal delivery but after a weekend of talking it over with her husband, elected for a C-section anyway at the second hospital. She felt more at ease with the staff there and felt they had supported her when she needed it. All she had to do was write a letter telling hospital one that she had decided to switch care to hospital two.

*Suew*


**I changed hospitals** whilst I was being transferred from home. I simply told the paramedics that this was the place I was going to! It was the same distance so they took me there.

*Cadi*


**It does depend on where you live.** Where I am, you have to fight to switch out of the main hospital into one in a neighbouring area. Yes, it's supposedly your 'right' to do so but that doesn't make it easy! You can, of course, simply turn up at the hospital of your choice in labour if you have any problems switching. This is what a friend was advised to do by her GP when the 'powers that be' were being difficult about allowing her to switch.

*SoupDragon*

# Independent midwives and doulas – what do they do and are they worth it?

**From the beginning,** I knew that I wanted my baby to be born at home. I knew I didn't want much in the way of antenatal testing, and I knew that I was likely to go overdue. I didn't want to spend my pregnancy having to justify my decisions or fight medical protocol, so we opted for an independent midwife very early on. As it turns out, it was a very good decision to make. My partner was able to make it to almost all of the antenatal appointments, so we all knew each other well by the time I went into labour, 13 days overdue.

I had a very long slow labour (44 hours) but my daughter was born in the gentlest circumstances – under NHS care, I would probably have ended up in hospital with a lot of unwanted intervention. It was well worth the money and we'll do the same again next time, even if we have to juggle the finances (it would certainly come ahead of a holiday).

*Pimpernel*

**I used an independent midwifery** practice and think it was the best money I ever spent. I decided to go private when I lost confidence in the NHS after a bungled nuchal fold scan. I was considering an elective C-section but my midwives patiently explained over and over again that my body had the power to give birth naturally and to go with it. I decided to go for a water birth and it was the most amazing experience of my life.

My waters broke on a Sunday but my contractions didn't start properly until the following Friday. If I'd been at hospital, I would most likely have been induced within 48 hours. My son was also in a posterior position but my midwife managed to turn him internally, which eased my pain 10-fold. I could go on and on – I feel really strongly that everyone should be able to give birth the way I did but sadly this isn't the case. It was worth every penny and I'll definitely do it again.

*Lamin*

**I definitely would have had an independent** midwife last time around if it hadn't been for the cost. A friend who had one subsequently made me realize it was just what I had been looking for. First you see the same person throughout your pregnancy and are able to develop a rapport and bond with them. On the day they provide you with a fantastic level of care and support based on a great deal of knowledge.

I think the second reason to hire one is that you are much more likely to have the birth you desire and you won't be treated as a commodity on a conveyor belt. You need to book someone as early as possible, because they limit their number of clients in order to give the best care.

*Emmagee*

**A friend of mine** tells me that some independent midwives will accept payment in installments, or are willing to negotiate around your requirements, to keep costs down. If you're really keen on the idea, you could always ask friends and relatives for cash to go towards a Midwife Fund, instead of the usual gifts for the newborn.

*Baabaa*

**I booked an independent midwife** for my pregnancy and birth and am now 37+ weeks' pregnant, so the next few weeks will prove whether I think I made a good decision. In my opinion, their real advantage is for people who want continuity of care and to see the same midwife throughout their pregnancy and birth. They are also good for people who have had previously traumatic experiences/or had Caesareans and want to try for a vaginal delivery second time (some hospitals aren't very supportive of this) or want to have a home/water birth.

You need to ask an independent midwife what her relationship is like with your local hospital as there is a 'grey area' surrounding what they can do once they enter a hospital. For example, she may not be registered to practice in your hospital, and although she should certainly go with you into hospital it may be that she then has no greater influence/status than that of a birth partner. A lot of this is to do with hospital insurance policies. Many independent midwives have left NHS practice because they strongly believe in the 'pure concept' of midwifery i.e. one-to-one woman-centred care, and they fundamentally disagree with the high levels of surgical intervention/obstetric practice that occurs in hospitals these days.

Hospitals are hierarchical places and in terms of seniority consultants and registrars rank way above midwives, so once you are in hospital a consultant may have a different view to your midwife on the need for intervention and have the ability to 'enforce' this, with your consent of course. I had assumed an independent midwife was just someone who took over the ante-natal stuff and then came with me to hospital, but the reality was a bit more complex.

*MotherofOne*

**I am a doula.** I spent four days training with Michel Odent, the water birth pioneer. A doula is someone who can support a mother before, during and after the birth of her baby. These days we all lead busy lives and no longer have extended family available. Mothers are leaving it later to have first babies and sometimes find their own mothers too old or out of touch with childrearing and childbirth.

A doula can be with a mother before the birth to help make a birth plan, be a supporter during labour and in addition to or instead of the woman's partner. They are not there to interfere or give medical advice but purely as a friend and helper.

We have lots of techniques to help us encourage a labouring mother to progress, go with her own instincts, etc. We are able to attend after the birth, help establish a routine, feeding, etc. Fees depend on times and hours, but you choose when and how often. There is a minimum number of hours payable, but all doulas are flexible.

*Alibubbles*

**Birth doulas usually meet pregnant mums** several times before their labour to discuss what choices they want and to help them prepare for labour. These are tasks which would be done by a midwife if they had the time but the ten-minute appointment you often have at each stage of pregnancy is not really enough time to establish any kind of relationship.

Doulas are present at the birth and usually visit you once after the delivery. They offer emotional and practical support and are cheaper than an independent midwife. A doula isn't there as a replacement (or competition) for your partner but as someone who has more experience and will stay with you during your entire labour to ensure continuity. They can also act as the liaison between you and the midwife. Birth doulas charge a flat fee rather than by the hour and this can be anything between £250 and £400 per birth. Therefore, if you have a five-hour labour, it might turn out to be expensive but if you have a 48-hour one then the doula will lose out. Birth doulas do this out of passion, not for money: trust me – you don't get rich by being a birth doula!

*Pupuce*

---

**Mumsnet fact**

68 per cent of expectant women fail to get the one-to-one midwifery care which doctors and the Government agree is best for them and their babies.

National Audit Office

---

**I had my first baby on the NHS.** It was a Caesarean birth caused by 'failure to progress', which I suspect was unnecessary and I was pretty upset about it later. I had my second baby in the US – terrified that I'd end up with another unnecessary Caesarean.

I hired a doula. It was without doubt the best thing I could ever have done for myself and for my son. She helped me find the right hospital (lower caesarean rate) and switch to a team of midwives instead of consultants (who'd be likely to put more restrictions and rules on my labour). She also took me through a huge process of emotional preparation – coming to terms with my fears, planning how I'd handle my 'worst case scenarios', etc.

By the time I was ready to give birth I'd regained confidence in my body. I'd come to terms with what happened before and wasn't scared. I knew that whatever happened I would be able to cope with it (even another caesarean) and that she'd be by my side. I also had a whole armoury of practical techniques for pain. In the event, I hardly needed her. I just got on with it in my own way and had an amazing drug-free five-hour birth supported by switched-on, flexible (but super-qualified) midwives.

*Sleeplessinseattle*

**Doulas are not substitutes** for midwives but an additional extra. It is illegal for anyone except a registered midwife or doctor to provide care for a woman in labour, unless it's in an emergency and it would be unfair to ask a doula to attend if you did not have a midwife there also.

*Oakmaiden*

---

**What the experts say**
Recent studies show women who are supported by doulas are much less likely to require Caesarean or forceps deliveries, induction and pain relief. Births attended by doulas may also be shorter with a lower rate of complications... Though an expectant father may fear that hiring a doula will regulate him to third wheel status, this isn't the case. A good doula is also there to help the father relax, so he can help his partner relax.

Murkoff, Eisenberg & Hathaway (*What to Expect When You're Expecting*)

---

**I used a doula** who came to my home to help me with the birth of my first child and it was fantastic and well worth the money. I first heard about doulas whilst in the US and when we came to the UK I decided I wanted a home birth, having done a bit of research and visited the London hospitals!

When I first started my contractions, I called my doula, who said she would come and stay the night 'just in case' – it was 9 pm. She called the midwife at 3 am when I was fully dilated and I gave birth at 6 am with no painkillers or stitches!

My husband and I had every confidence in our doula and so I had no anxiety or stress, which led to an almost pain-free labour. I would never have had the confidence to have a home birth without a doula and I would highly recommend it to anyone. It meant that my husband could be there for me without having to worry about whether to take me to hospital or not, whether to call the midwife, etc. I know that I would have ended up in hospital if I didn't have a doula as it happened so fast and I don't think the hospital would have sent a midwife. As it was, the midwife who came took an hour to get here and I had never met her before.

*Bozzy*

# Water birth – what's it like?

**I had a home water birth** with my second child. With my first child I had an epidural when I was about two centimetres dilated. With the water birth I managed without any pain relief at all. When it got to the stage where I asked for some, the midwife suggested getting in the pool and I found the effect of the water helped so much, I did not use the gas and air. I wasn't sure whether I actually wanted to give birth in the pool beforehand but once I was in the pool, I did not want to get out and my baby was born in the pool about one and a half hours after getting in. I also delivered the placenta under water with no injections, which I preferred. It was a really good experience, helped by having two lovely midwives who were experienced in home and water births.

*Janus*

**I had a water birth** in a hired pool at home and I would highly recommend it. I used a TENS machine in the early stages of labour (which went on for two days) and my midwife advised not to get into the pool until I was very near the end as getting in too early generally slows labour down. I waited until my waters broke. As soon as I was in I loved the feeling of being in my own separate environment, and the fact that the water took a lot of the weight away. I used some gas and air until I was ready to push, by which time I was so tired with the long labour and the warmth of the water that I nearly fell asleep. I don't think the water stops any pain, but it definitely helps you feel more relaxed. My daughter was born into the water, and I cut her umbilical cord. I also didn't tear, which I think is quite often the case for women who labour in water.

*Tiu*

**I had a water birth** two years ago in hospital and it was fantastic. I got in at 5 cm dilated and the pain virtually disappeared altogether. I stayed in for about four hours, then my midwife made me get out to check me as she thought the pool had slowed labour down because I was 'too happy'. I was then 9 cm and my son was born about an hour later. I also believe that the warmth of the pool limits damage to you. My son was over 9 lb and I had no tearing or stitching.

*MrsS*

> **Mumsnet fact**
> Just 1 per cent of mothers who spent time in a birth pool before or during delivery required an episiotomy compared to 11 per cent for low-risk births nationally.
> Department of Health funded study

**If you like water,** I would definitely recommend a water birth. I adore being in water, and simply love a long hot soak in the bath. Both my sons were born in water and both were fairly quick labours. On arrival at hospital it took about an hour to persuade the midwives to fill the pool and let me in, but then both boys were born within an hour of being in the pool, so the water certainly didn't slow anything down. Once I got in the water, it was bliss and really helped me relax, and 'work with my body', rather than being tense, stressed, and worried.

*Scally*

**I had a water labour** for my child. Because the water makes you weightless, it enabled me to squat without getting too tired, which was a really good position to labour in. Having a water birth also meant that I got the best room in the labour ward, with a great big double bed. If you don't like it, you can always get out, so the decision to have one isn't final.

*Gumsy*

---

**What the experts say**
When a woman in hard labour was expressing an imperative demand for painkillers, we had something else to offer than a shot of Demerol (the most popular painkiller of the 1970s). We could introduce the mother-to-be into the aquatic birthing room, so that she could watch the beautiful blue water and hear the noise of the water filling the pool. The room had been painted blue, with dolphins on the walls. From that time the question was not, 'when will you give me a painkiller?' It was more often than not: 'How long does it take to fill the pool?'

Michel Odent (*Lessons from the first hospital birthing pool*)

---

**Even if you are unsure** about actually giving birth in a birthing pool, it's worthwhile considering using it for labouring in. Generally it means you will get a great midwife, who will have trained specifically for this type of birth and so will often have a more caring approach to childbirth. My midwife was fantastic and really treated me as a person. It also means you have a room double the size of a normal delivery room as it has to accommodate the pool.

*Clogger*

**I had a round birthing pool,** which was about 5 ft in diameter. It was far bigger than it needed to be and I only really used half of it. I think an oval one would have been better because then you can stretch out one way, and brace yourself across it the other way. I used a pool with rigid sides, which made it easy to lean on the sides. This may not have been as easy in a pool with inflatable sides. It also had a thermostat and a filtration system, which meant that it was always ready for me to use towards the end of my pregnancy. I think it was worth spending the extra money and would have the same one again next time. I booked it about two months before I needed it, but there was no choice of pools by that stage, so next time I'll book as soon as possible. You also need to think about where in the house you are going to put it and whether the floors will stand the weight of the filled pool.

*Pimpernel*

**Mumsnet tip**
Take a little step to help you get in and out. (The type toddlers use to reach the loo), as they can be quite high, and you are not at your most adept. Also, a blow-up bath pillow is good for leaning on, as is a flannel to wipe your face with, as I found it quite hot.

*Melaniespeaking*

**I was in the pool for seven hours** and thought it was great. I used gas and air too. It gets VERY hot and humid in the pool room so if you have a birthing partner, he/she might want to take some shorts/T-shirt to change into. My other tips would be to take plenty to drink, and if you want to listen to music, take a battery-operated CD player with you. My hospital had CD players in the delivery rooms but not in the pool room as they come under bathroom regulations and there were no electrical sockets.

*Gingernut*

**I had opted for a water birth.** The only problem is that you have to take the TENS machine off and I found that without the TENS, I really felt the contractions. However, the period in between the contractions was far more relaxing. When I came out to be checked after a couple of hours my midwife discovered I'd stopped dilating and if anything, was going backwards. After that, it all became a bit of a nightmare so I didn't get a chance to go back in the water. It's possible the water could have slowed things down.

*Willow2*

**What the experts say**
The golden rule of water labour and birth – if progress is slow in water, try land; if slow on land, try water.

Janet Balaskas (*Active Birth Centre – Birth and Baby Diary*)

**I had a water birth at home** and would highly recommend it. Unfortunately I was only able to get in at the start of the second stage because the midwife asked me not to get in before she arrived. I don't think I realized how far along I was before I called her. You need to wait until you are in established labour (about 5 or 6 cm dilated) before you get in, otherwise it could slow your labour down. That's where I went wrong – I was waiting for established labour to start before I called the midwife when in fact I was actually starting the second stage. All that time I could have been in that water and I missed out.

When I finally did get in it was almost bliss (if you can describe anything about labour as bliss). It still hurts but takes the edge off. I tried standing up out of the water at one stage to see if gravity would speed things along and quickly plunged down again. My baby was born in the water and she was very calm but alert in the minutes following the birth. The whole experience was quite serene. I also delivered the placenta in the water, which I don't think most hospital midwives will let you do.

*Weezer*

**Mumsnet tip**
Make sure you give the hospital plenty of notice as it takes quite a while to fill up the pool.

*Sjc1*

**After having my waters broken for me,** I went into the pool. Up until then I had been reading my new book and thought that I would take it in the pool with me. I wondered why the midwife gave me a funny look. Needless to say, the pain kicked in and all thoughts of sitting serenely with book in hand and music in the background vanished. However, the pool was bliss, although I didn't fully appreciate it until I came out – rather like TENS machines. I don't know if the pool facilitated the dilation but I was in for about 50 minutes when I decided that I wanted pethidine, which necessitated getting out. It turned out that I was 10 cm dilated and couldn't have anything – I wanted to get back in the water because it really helps support everything but I wasn't allowed. Next time I would go straight to the pool and stay as long as possible, preferably to the end.

*Harrysmum*

# Should fathers be there?

**I had three very different experiences** with my births. With number one, I felt completely out of it and needed my husband there to 'fight on my behalf' with the rather over-aggressive midwife. With number two, I had a water birth, which was a much more pleasant experience for him to witness and for me to go through. With number three, I had an epidural and wondered why I hadn't done so with the other two. I could not have gone through any of these without his support (even though he says he felt like a spare part) and he would have missed out on something so unique if he hadn't been there. I can, however, appreciate that some men don't want to be there and some women don't want them there. I used to joke that 'if this is going to hurt as much as I think, then I want you to witness all my suffering'. I know that witnessing the birth has made my husband realize that I do have a lot of inner strength.

*Binza*

**What the experts say**
At the very time when the labouring woman needs to reduce the activity of her intellect, and to 'go to another planet', many men cannot stop being rational. Some look brave, but their release of high levels of adrenalin is contagious.

Michel Odent (*Is the father's participation at the birth dangerous?*)

This is the right place for the man to be. It is not only ludicrous but pathetic to leave him to stride up and down a hospital corridor, smoking cigarette after cigarette, whilst the woman 'gets on with it' alone.

Sheila Kitzinger (*The Experience of Childbirth*)

**Some husbands don't want to be there.** Mine definitely didn't but I didn't realize just how much he didn't want to until we were actually in the middle of it but everyone we knew who had children said he'd miss out if he wasn't there. There was a lot of pressure. In the end, he wasn't there for the C-section anyway.

*SueW*

**There was absolutely no doubt** in our minds that my husband would be present throughout, it wasn't even an issue. However, afterwards, from a purely selfish perspective I would have rather he hadn't been there, although I would have hated to deny him the joy of seeing the birth of his son.

I had gone into the birth with the completely wrong view. i.e. millions of women have done it, so it can't be that bad. I felt I didn't cope at all well with either the contractions or the pushing and I virtually fell to pieces. I spent much of the time announcing that I was going to die and that I simply couldn't do it.

Also, I slightly shudder at the view of me up on all fours screaming my head off, let alone the stitching up process, which took forever.

I felt that my husband was unable to do anything to help me through the labour (through no fault of his own). In the end it was a ventouse delivery and afterwards I felt a big fat failure for not having been able to maintain any degree of self control. Having said that, my abiding positive memory of the whole thing is of him racing around the delivery room with a tiny, very cross, bawling alien in his arms, crying and repeatedly saying, 'Look at him, look at him!' Next time, he will definitely be there but hopefully my expectations will be a little more realistic.

*Croppy*

**The thought of giving birth** alone filled me with fear. When my husband popped out of the delivery room I felt so alone and I was sure the pain intensified. I did get really 'fed up' when he tried to read the paper during the early stages and I think he felt a bit of a spare part, especially during transition when I hung onto the bed, bum in the air crying, but I just needed him there. I think I should have prepared him more for the volume of blood. Talking it over afterwards is important too.

*Kate71*

> **Mumsnet fact**
> Men often feel ostracised during birth and pregnancy. Around one third of those surveyed by the NCT felt medical staff largely ignored them during their partners' pregnancies.
>
> *NCT*

**My husband has very fond memories** of our children being born, although at the third birth he opted to leave the delivery room before the gore, as the placenta, etc. emerged. As for me, he was the familiarity I needed at those very scary moments and I don't think the actual arrival of each baby would have been quite so special without having him there to share it with. I can't say he did anything very heroic but his presence gave me strength.

*Jezzz*

**My husband is one of the most squeamish** people I know – he can't even watch *Casualty*, but even he went down to the 'business end' for a look. I think he surprised himself.

*SoupDragon*

> **Mumsnet fact**
> One in 10 British men fail to stay by their partner's side throughout labour because they find it too stressful.
>
> Survey conducted by Mothercare

**I cannot imagine** having gone through labour and childbirth without my husband. He was a source of immense support in the early stages at home and when 'dealing' with aggressive midwives. Then when I had to transfer to hospital with an undiagnosed breech he helped me to deal with the conflicting urge to push and the instructions from medical team not too. Finally, someone who could hardly look at a nosebleed, watched the Caesarean and gave me a 'commentary' of what was happening and told me that our baby was a little girl.

*Emmagee*

**Having my husband in the theatre** for an elective Caesarean was immensely reassuring and he was glad to be there too. Whilst they were performing the op, he was sitting with me holding my hand and we had a good chat with the anaesthetist. He was the first to see our son and hold him, and he values the hour or so he spent sitting with our son before I came out of recovery as the finest of his life. He was not allowed in when I had to go back to theatre, of course, and this was an incredibly lonely and stressful time for us both.

*Clare 2*

**There is no way** I would have coped without my husband. I had an emergency Caesarean after 50-odd hours. The only clear thing I remember about the whole thing was the fact that, as a result, my husband was the first to hold our daughter, and I will always treasure the memory of the look on his face.

*Viv*

**During birth I was totally involved** in what was going on inside my body, and the gas and pethidine I took made me not very aware of my surroundings and I lost my sense of time. My husband was constantly at my side and this had a real practical benefit. He reminded me of who was around and what was happening, especially when midwives changed duty. My very real fear of one midwife or nurse taking over and making a mistake through lack of information was drastically reduced.

*Frank1*

**My husband and I have always** viewed labour and birth as a joint thing and in some ways, when the labour is long, I think it is harder on the partner only being able to watch and support. My over-riding feeling is that 'It is OUR baby we are delivering and I don't see why I should do it on my own'. My husband has bathed all our babies and dressed them, straight after birth.

*Rmea*

> **Mumsnet fact**
> In 1970, only 15 per cent of fathers were present during labour in Britain, but by 1990, that figure had jumped to 92 per cent.
> Kate Figes (*Life After Birth*)

**I would have been devastated** if my husband had not been with me whilst I gave birth. He was the only person in the whole hospital that I had ever met before and the only person who was with me throughout my 20-hour labour. I had four mid-wives, plus a whole emergency team at the end. The pain and the drugs dimmed my ability to concentrate on anything outside my own body and my husband would often be the only person I could hear or understand. I found the pain so overwhelming that I couldn't stop being sick and he held those ridiculous tiny cardboard dishes whilst I puked endlessly. He also spoke for me when I was unable to master control of my own tongue and got stroppy when I had been pushing for three hours to no avail. He deserves a medal because I know I would have wanted to run away rather than watch anyone go through what I did.

*Molly1*

**After my wife gave birth to our son,** she was my total hero! She laboured for almost two days, and the boy got stuck in the birth canal. I asked the surgeon if my wife could have a spinal tap so that we could both be 'present' at the birth (us men are kicked out for Caesareans under general) and they tried without success for 45 minutes to get one in. My wife was in agony, and exhausted – she was falling asleep between contractions. It was one of the worst moments of my life. When they said they had to put her out, she screamed, 'Yes! make me sleep!' and I had to go into the corridor, leaving my family in the hands of the medical team – it was awful. After 10 minutes of sitting in the corridor (crying!), I was handed this beautiful little bundle covered in blood and pooh. I cleaned him up and we spent the next three hours together ('This is a corridor', 'That is a car park', 'Those are trees', 'That's the back of a midwife') – one of the most treasured times in my whole life. I went through an emotional rollercoaster that day – the best and worst times of my life all happening within minutes. When my wife came round from the operation, her first words were 'Can I sleep now?'. I showed her our son, helped get him latched on to her breast (he had been bemused by my lack of ability in this department) and she fell asleep as he suckled. I will never forget sitting, gazing at the two of them, as long as I live. She was gutted that she'd had to have a caesarean, but I told her she had done incredibly well, and that she would always have a big smile on her tummy to remind her of her son.

*Tom*

**6**

# Labour

# Introduction

The chances are that it won't be long after that thin blue line confirms that you're pregnant before you start wondering how on earth you're possibly going to get the baby out. You don't need to have actually given birth to wonder why labour isn't easier. Surely there's a design fault somewhere? How on earth can something so relatively large, fit through something so small?

The trouble is you're not quite sure whether you can trust your best friend's assurances that it will all be just fine. It's common knowledge that the pain and horror of childbirth is bizarrely erased once the baby makes its way into his mother's arms. But the more pregnancy books and magazines you read and the more antenatal classes you attend, the more you start to realize what a contentious issue childbirth really is.

First, there's the minefield of pain relief and which sort to go for. Do you opt to give birth through a hazy cloud of morphine or chuckling with gas and air? Should you bother hiring a TENS machine or rely on your partner's techniques of massage and a birthing ball? The idea of an epidural sounds too good to be true: childbirth without the pain. Yet so too does the notion of a drug-free labour to be enjoyed as a sensuous pleasure, as described by Shelia Kitzinger and her ilk. But how on earth do you know which to plump for when you've no idea what you're going to be experiencing?

The dilemmas of labour start well before you reach hospital. The 'rest' you are told to enjoy during the last couple of weeks of pregnancy is marred by constant fretting over whether you are about to go into labour. Every twinge is greeted with the thought, 'Is this it?'. So when it actually happens, how will you know? And once you do know, when should you go in to hospital? You don't want the disappointment and humiliation of being turned away, nor do you want to be in the local press for having given birth in the car on the way there. And what if you go beyond your due date – is a vindaloo followed by a night of passion really the only way to bring it on? Perhaps your doctor's planning an induction – what's involved and are they a good idea?

The most frustrating thing about giving birth is that it's up there with the biggest of life events and yet, unless you opt for an elective C-section, nature defies you from organizing it in advance. No decision can be set in stone because you just don't know exactly what's going to happen. It's a somewhat irritating cliché but no two births are ever really the same, but by reading about how other people have dealt with their circumstances, we hope you'll get a bit more of an idea of what can happen. With a bit of luck, armed with this knowledge along with your essential oils and your birthing ball, you can stride forth into your own unique labour with at least a modicum of confidence.

# Getting ready for birth – are there things you wish you'd known beforehand?

**Since giving birth** I have heard more horror stories than I would ever have thought possible. Had I been aware of some of these, I would have chosen different options during the course of my son's birth and would not have suffered anywhere near as much as a result. Additionally, I think if more fuss was made of the 'horror stories' they might not be as frighteningly commonplace as they are – because either I have a really unlucky circle of acquaintances, or standards are nowhere near as high as they should be out there. The view is that we should all sit quietly and not scare anyone. Surely the only way you can have an 'informed' birth is if you are aware of both sides of the coin? And surely, if you are aware of the bad, then you can take steps to limit it?

*Willow2*

**Mumsnet fact**
Eight out of ten mothers are scared while giving birth.
*Mother & Baby* magazine

**When I was pregnant with my first daughter,** I asked my friends and neighbours what giving birth was like and all of them smiled a kind of 'well, look, you'll survive' shrug before going into any detail. Afterwards I said to my neighbour, 'Why didn't you tell me what it was actually like?' and she answered, 'What could I have said that would have prepared you any better?' There will always be examples of bad medical practice and we can't really prepare ourselves for that. I don't think I'm perpetuating a myth when I try to reassure first-timers. I think the only way to approach it is to believe that it's going to be worth it in the end.

*Sobernow*

**I had fairly easy births** but there are some things that would have helped to make things easier. Feeling that you are in control of the situation makes a big difference and that, to some extent, means knowing what is happening. I too had the, 'Well I didn't want to tell you how much it would hurt' from a friend. It is silly to keep something like this secret. I feel antenatal classes should prepare you better.

*Eulalia*

**I was one of those people** who read every pregnancy book and magazine and positively encouraged women to scare the living daylights out of me before giving birth. Our antenatal classes focussed solely on the birth and I don't believe I could have been better informed.

*Ionesmum*

**I think the most important thing** to pass on is that you honestly can't plan how it's going to be. If you're the kind of person who takes control through knowledge that makes it very difficult. Being able to turn off your thinking brain and tune in to your body's requirements is a very tough thing to teach.

*Philippat*

**What the experts say**
The amount of pain actually felt almost always bears a strong relationship with what is expected. Of course you should be realistic but your expectations can be greatly modified by what you learn, the information you are given and how confident you feel when you go into labour.

Dr Miriam Stoppard (*Pregnancy and Birth*)

**I wish someone had told me** that there is something you can do about a baby that is positioned badly. Even if it hadn't worked, I'd have felt I'd tried. I regularly bless the person who told me about arnica and wish I'd met them before my first daughter's birth. I also wish I'd taken a hot water bottle to hospital and had hired a TENS machine.

*Robinw*

**I had hypnotherapy** before my second son in the hope that it would make me more relaxed – which it did – but it didn't lead to the pain-free birth I was hoping for. I certainly envy the women who say: 'You forget about the pain' and genuinely mean it. That's pretty much all I remember from either of mine!

*SoupDragon*

**I wish I had known** that it wouldn't hurt as much as I thought (each one getting easier and less painful).

*Bumblelion*

**What the experts say**
Most women must expect at least half an hour or so of pain or great discomfort at the end of the first stage.

Sheila Kitzinger (*The Experience of Childbirth*)

**I wish that someone could have told me** about the real possibility of labour 'not progressing'. I knew that it was possible to have a C-section if there is a problem with the baby, but it never occurred to me that I would not be able to give birth myself. I felt like the biggest failure on the planet after 40 hours of staying at 5 cm. I also wish that someone could have told me all about the possibility of not loving my baby the moment I saw him – that was a real shock to me. He could have been anyone's baby and he certainly didn't feel like the one that had been in my tummy.

*Ghosty*

**Because I was induced,** there was little time for pain relief, so I wish I had known that the feeling that I was getting to do a pooh was a sign that I was ready to push. When I told the midwives this, all hell broke loose. One good piece of advice I had been given was to keep upright and keep moving. This helped a lot.

*Queenie*

**I wish I'd been able to ask more** during the birth but I was too high on pethidine. I saw the scissors for the cord and thought they were going to be used to cut me and completely panicked.

*Lollypop*

**I wish I'd have known** not to have curry the night before I gave birth.

*Berries*

**I wish I'd known more** about what having sex could lead to...

*Rhubarb*

# What can you do to get labour started?

**I was 12 days late** and lobster finally did the trick for me. It was a choice of that or sex, as lobster and sperm have the same labour-inducing hormone, and believe me, at my size neither my husband nor I fancied the sex.

*Manna*

**I was induced with my first labour** and I wanted to avoid this with my second and so I tried everything. I believe that what really worked for me were three sessions of acupuncture on consecutive days when I was 10 days late. This seems to be a 'natural' way of getting things started and I went into labour just after the third session, despite my cervix being well and truly closed and posterior just before the session. I would recommend it to anyone.

*Micky*

**Mumsnet fact**
Prolonged pregnancies are more common in the summer.
*Practical Parenting* magazine

**Herbalists prescribe raspberry leaf tea** to help the birth go more quickly and smoothly and minimize the risk of tearing. It is also said to reduce the risk of haemorrhage, help with after pains and promote recovery after the birth.

*Windmill*

**I drank two boxes of the stuff** in the last four weeks of my pregnancy, and my daughter was still 12 days late. By that stage you'll try anything though.

*Elwar*

**I used raspberry leaf tea** for the last two months of my pregnancy. I was in labour for 36 hours, and my daughter ended up being a ventouse delivery and I did tear... not sure I will bother this time round.

*Pie*

**I drank raspberry leaf tea** whilst in hospital with high blood pressure. I drank three cups between 8 pm and 10 pm, my waters broke five hours later. I went into 'established' labour very quickly and within an hour of strong contractions I was 4 cm dilated! My son was born four hours later and five days early.

*Mum2toby*

**Mumsnet fact**
Only one in 20 babies arrives on their due date.
*Practical Parenting* magazine

**A few drops of clary sage** on a handkerchief is supposed to be good if your contractions stop and you want them to start again. It seemed to work for me when I was three days overdue.

*Lusardi*

**Manic cleaning of the kitchen floor** got my second daughter on the way. Being down on all fours helped the baby get into the right position.

*Batey*

**Walking helped bring my labour on.** The week before I gave birth I had done a 30-minute walk every day. The day I went into labour I had done this twice. I also bopped around the room like a crazed raver to MTV. It worked and I went into labour three hours later.

*Viksy*

**My midwife recommended** going up and down the stairs to accelerate labour. I had just been examined and told I was 3 cm dilated. I didn't particularly want to endure the hospital stairs but I was also not prepared to endure the agony for another seven hours. As soon as I finished this exercise, which I managed to do quite quickly, I was having urges to push. Thirty minutes later I was in the water and delivered 40 minutes after that. Needless to say, I wish I had done this during my first labour, which went on forever.

*Pupuce*

**I heard nipple tweaking** was a good way to get things started but that you need to do it for five or six hours a day! I wonder how they know that – surely it hasn't been tried and tested?

*Art*

**In Sweden, midwives** suggest nipple tweaking to get things going and the German contingent swear by castor oil.

*MalmoMum*

---

**What the experts say**
Gently massaging one nipple at a time (massaging both nipples at once has been shown to cause foetal distress), either by hand or with a warm, moist cloth, alternating nipples every 15 minutes for three periods of up to an hour each day, can stimulate uterine contractions and ripen the cervix.

Kaz Cooke (*The Rough Guide to Pregnancy and Birth*)

---

**My midwife hinted to me that castor oil** might work when I went over due. I got it over the counter at the chemist and went into labour within eight hours of taking it. I must admit that at the time I was not sure if the pains were because the baby was on the way or because I needed to make a dash for the loo. When I went to the hospital I told them what I had taken as I did not want to make a fool of myself, I don't think they were too impressed and wanted to know which midwife had suggested it.

*Sister*

**As far as I understand it,** the curry/castor oil theory works on irritating the bowel, which is (naturally, at this stage) fairly squashed up against your uterus. This can stimulate/trick the body into producing the hormones needed to start labour. I guess in the end, nothing is going to work unless your body is ready to go.

*SueW*

**As a midwife** I would not advise taking castor oil. It is bad enough having labour pains without the discomfort of having to go to the toilet every five minutes. Try not to hurry things along – enjoy these last few days of peace and quiet. Stock up on sleep instead – you'll need it.

*Mears*

**I thought I'd try pineapple,** so drove myself to the all-night supermarket and bought a pineapple and ate it all at 10.30 pm. At 7.30 the next morning I felt the first signs of labour by 10 am and was 9 cm dilated. My baby was born at 11.45 am. I don't even like pineapple but it seemed preferable to another night of being pregnant.

*Thomson*

**Pineapples, sex, blow jobs** (if you can face it, yes – apparently it is supposed to be more effective than sex because it goes into your digestive system), nipple tweaking, curries and don't forget the raspberry leaf tea. By the way, none of the above worked for me.

*Tillysmummy*

**Well, well, you learn something new** every day – blow jobs! Can't work out why sperm in the digestive system is more effective. Sounds like a cleverly devised male plan to me! The prostaglandins in sperm, although not that powerful, may have some effect on a cervix, which is already thinking about labouring/getting ready to labour. This is what we term a 'favourable' cervix and that is the point – they have a direct effect, as an irritant if you like, on the cervix. The aim should therefore be direct contact with sperm and cervix – all your stomach acids would destroy any prostaglandins.

*Leese*

**What the experts say**
Semen is rich in prostaglandins, which ripen the cervix – the easiest way to
'administer' it is by having sex with, ermm, a man... orgasm results in several
strong uterine contractions; it is thought that these, combined with sexual
arousal, can stimulate prostaglandin production.

Kaz Cooke (*The Rough Guide to Pregnancy and Birth*)

**Go to the hairdressers!** I don't know whether it was the head massage they gave
me whilst washing my hair but it worked for me and a friend of mine had been to
the hairdressers the day before both of her births. It means you look good in the
photos too.

*Bon*

**What worked for me** was going to a posh drinks party and staying on my feet for
fours hours whilst consuming several glasses of champagne – contractions
started in the early hours of the morning and I was five days early.

*Berta*

**I tried everything to start labour** off: cervical sweep, sex, bumpy car rides, jumping down stairs(!), hot curries, pineapple juice but none of it worked. I think you
just have to accept that, without severe medical intervention, the baby will come
in its own time. Not that this makes it any easier when you're waiting.

*Gillymac*

## How do you know when you are in labour and when should you go into hospital?

**Each time, I started labour** first thing in the morning and have known immediately. The pain feels different to the usual Braxton Hicks contractions – much more intense. With my first-born (who was four weeks early) I woke up with stomach pains, went to the toilet and had a show, then diarrhoea and then my waters went; not a gush but a trickle. Despite these being all the textbook signs of the onset of labour, because I was early, I was in denial and didn't really believe it was happening until I was examined at hospital and was 6 cm dilated. The second time, I woke up and recognized the pains immediately. This time my waters didn't go and were actually ruptured during labour. With my third, I woke up, went to the loo and when I got back into bed there was a 'ping' and mighty gush of water. My contractions didn't actually start until an hour later. Although you sit at home wondering how you know, when it actually happens there is no question about it.

*Ra*

> **Mumsnet fact**
> The rupture of membranes before labour begins is uncommon, occurring in less than 15 per cent of pregnancies.
> Murkoff, Elsenberg and Hathaway (*What to Expect When You're Expecting*)

**I had very painful Braxton Hicks** contractions about a week before I went into labour with my son. At one point they were a minute long and five minutes apart and went on for some time. They started suddenly and then stopped suddenly, whereas the first contractions of my labour were quite mild, but once they started they just never stopped. And the Braxton Hicks also felt different to the contractions of labour. The pain was associated with his head grinding in my pelvis, whereas the labour pains were muscular.

*Gingernut*

**I found that Braxton Hicks** were more all over my belly, whereas 'proper' contractions were distinctly lower down, especially at the beginning.

*Boyandgirl*

**I knew when labour started** that it was different. And of course established labour was a whole quantum leap different in terms of the pain... The Braxton Hicks were 'all over' tightenings and the real thing was more like period pain cramping.

*Elliott*

**When you think you are ready** to go in, you should ring the hospital, describe what is going on and they will advise. They usually prefer a warning that you are on your way. Of course that begs the question of when to phone. If you are comfortable and are happy at home, then fine. If it's a bit much and you'd just feel safer in hospital, then go on in.

*Hopeful*

**The time to go to the hospital** depends on how far away you live, to some extent. If it doesn't take too long to get there, I would suggest waiting till the contractions are regular – about 10 minutes apart and strong. You might feel regular contractions but not experience any discomfort. Try and ignore them. As your contractions get stronger they will make you stop what you are doing so you can breathe through them. You do not need to go in if you have a 'show' and nothing else. If you have any bleeding, with or without contractions, you should go in. If your waters break, with no contractions, most hospitals advise you to go in. Many women go in with false alarms but that is not a problem. That said, it is better to avoid going in too early if you can – pottering about at home is much better.

*Mears*

**Think about your journey to hospital.** During my first labour, we had to drive into central London in the middle of morning rush hour. As soon as my contractions started, they were coming every two minutes and so during the journey I was on all fours on the back seat howling through the window. I did feel a little self-conscious in the middle of a traffic jam. I couldn't believe it when second time round, my contractions began at exactly the same time in the morning. Once again, they came on thick and fast, and we had to go in pretty quickly. This time we took a different route, in an attempt to avoid heavy traffic but this meant I had to endure road after road of speed bumps – I don't know which was worse.

*Bon*

**Mumsnet tip**
Make sure you have a few cushions in the car and invest in some sunblinds for privacy on your journey into hospital.

*Monty*

**With my first baby I went in far too early** and was back and forth between home and the hospital for the next 48 hours before my daughter was born. With my second, I resolved to leave it until the last minute. I was sitting at home having contractions, thinking the pains were probably Braxton Hicks. Eventually my husband insisted on going to the hospital – and our son was born an hour later!

*Spacemonkey*

### What the experts say

For most mothers the best odds for a safe and satisfying birth come with labouring at home as long as possible.

William Sears MD and Martha Sears RN (*Everything You Need to Know to Have a Safe and Satisfying Birth*)

You can walk around your own house to help labour along or you can walk around the hospital. At least at the hospital you won't feel compelled to make all the beds and unload the dishwasher while you walk. And you won't have to rush to get there.

Vicki Iovine (*The Best Friends' Guide to Pregnancy*)

**I seem to remember a friend saying** that if you can talk lucidly on the phone to the hospital through a contraction then it's probably too early to go in. I went in when I thought they were getting to the point I could no longer cope.

*SoupDragon*

**The midwife told me** to wait until the pain starts to seem a bit 'toe-curling'. That was about the right point with both of mine.

*Zebra*

**With my son** I went to a hospital that was about an hour away from home. Obviously we didn't want to leave it too late. Labour started at around 9 pm, and by 3 am I thought it was time to get moving. We got into the car and drove up the motorway with contractions three minutes apart. My poor dad was driving. We made it to the hospital in a record 40 minutes. Of course, on reaching the hospital, my contractions stopped and I spent all night alone in the maternity ward in sheer agony. My son didn't arrive until the next morning.

*Anais*

### What the experts say

You are not a moron if you feel contractions, go to the hospital and then get sent home. It happens all the time. It simply means that these contractions you are feeling are not noticeably dilating and effacing your cervix, and you might have a few more hours or days before things start opening up in there.

Vicki Iovine (*The Best Friend's Guide To Pregnancy*)

**The problem is that with your first labour** you just don't know what to expect, no matter how many books you've read, and so if a midwife tells you you're not in labour it can be very difficult to argue.

*MBB*

**This is something you shouldn't worry** about too much beforehand. Just tell yourself you will go in if you are worrying and anxious – the hospital get so many 'false alarms', and would rather put your mind at rest for a few hours than have you panicking at home. You should certainly ring if your waters break (or if you think they may have broken), especially if they are not a clear/pinky colour (sometimes they look browny-green, in which case you should go in and be checked over straight away). The usual advice is to go to hospital if you are experiencing pains every five minutes, lasting 30–40 seconds. These pains should take your breath away – if they don't, and you're still thinking 'should I/shouldn't I?', you're probably okay at home a while longer – but do ring and ask.

*Leese*

---

**What the experts say**
If you feel you're ready but the hospital doesn't seem to think so, don't take no for an answer. Ask if you can come in and have your progress checked. You can take your suitcase along 'just in case', but be ready to turn around and go home if you've only just begun to dilate.

Murkoff, Elsenberg and Hathaway (*What to Expect When You're Expecting*)

---

**The best thing you can do** is not worry about it. The signs vary so much from woman to woman (and pregnancy to pregnancy) that it's hard to follow anyone else's guidelines. First time around I waited to go in until I was having contractions three to five minutes apart and in screaming pain but I didn't have the baby for another 30 hours. Second time around I had the baby several hours after my contractions were 3–5 minutes apart. My neighbour had her first baby two and a half hours after she felt her very first contraction. They never got to the point where they took her breath away and she almost didn't get to the hospital in time. None of this is meant to scare you. Just to say go to the hospital when you find that you are no longer comfortable (mentally) with being at home.

*SofiaAmes*

# Being induced – what's it like and is it a good idea?

**I was induced with both my births** and the downside was going straight into full-on labour pains rather than experiencing a gradual build-up. On the plus side, it was fairly quick and therefore not completely exhausting, plus it all took place during the day and so I had a good night's sleep the night before. It was also really nice to be able to prepare my elder child for the birth and sort out her childcare. I'd say it was much less frightening all round.

*Zaria*

**All three of my children were late.** With my first child I managed to delay induction by five days and went into labour naturally the day before I was to be induced. With my third child, there were discrepancies over the due date. When I went 14 days past what the doctors believed was my due date they insisted I was induced. They tried twice with prostaglandin pessaries but nothing happened. After that I was scanned and monitored, and told to come back to the Foetal Assessment Unit every two days. Eight days after the failed induction attempt I went into labour naturally and my son was fine.

*Gillymac*

**If your waters have broken,** there is no need to be induced as long as the water draining is clear, the baby is active and you are monitoring your temperature. You should have a swab done to exclude Group B Streptococcus (GBS), which can cause serious infection where the waters have been broken for a long time. I would expect you should have a scan to see how much water is remaining around the baby. Research says that in an uncomplicated pregnancy, often labour will start spontaneously within 92 hours of the waters breaking. If you do end up needing to be induced, you could ask about oral prostin. This is a tablet that is given every hour for a certain number of doses that acts in the same way as the drip. It works better in women who have laboured before. That means you could stay mobile and have a more 'natural' induced labour.

*Mears*

---

**What the experts say**
If oxytocin is given in a drip, ask for it to be inserted in the arm you use least and check that you have a long tube connecting you to the drip. You should then have more room to move around even if it's just on the bed.
Dr Miriam Stoppard (*New Pregnancy and Birth Book*)

---

**You could request a cervical sweep** to speed things along. This is where the midwife sweeps her finger across your cervix. Usually it is done anyway once your contractions start, just to check how far open your cervix is. It can speed up contractions or bring them on if they haven't started yet.

*Eulalia*

**I went to hospital** at 41 weeks and a cervical sweep was performed at about 10.30 am. I felt mild contractions at about 5 pm and my baby was born at 5 am next morning. I found the sweep painful, but then compared to the pain of the actual childbirth, it was more like stubbing your toe!

*ChanelNo5*

**I had a sweep** with both my babies and it didn't hurt at all – you have to relax as much as possible. If you've been learning how to breath, this is the time to put it to good use. In both cases it seems to have done the trick and it sure is a lot less interventionist than drugs.

*Emmagee*

> **Mumsnet fact**
> 25 per cent of natural births are induced.
> National Birth and Motherhood Survey 2002 (*Mother & Baby* magazine)

**I was induced** when I was four days overdue. I was given a sweep at the same time as the Prostin gel but the contractions that resulted were rather sporadic and six hours later I had to be induced using a drip. This certainly got things going; my labour was only two hours and 40 minutes, which is pretty quick for a first baby. My advice is not to expect it to happen straight away. I thought it would be a simple matter and that full labour would start immediately but this is often not the case. You should make sure you have plenty of things to keep you occupied – music, food, TENS, etc. Someone I know went round a museum in between pessaries!

*Pamela1*

**I was induced at 40 weeks** and 10 days and I have to say that it wasn't a particularly pleasant experience. The prostaglandin gel didn't have any effect at first and I spent five days climbing stairs in the hospital, walking around the grounds, reading books, the papers and playing board games with my husband. Next time I will try my utmost to avoid induction unless they can actually find some way of showing me that it is necessary. I've been told that prostaglandin gel rarely works the first time and several doses are often needed.

*Alison222*

**With my first baby** I was two weeks late and was keen to be induced as I didn't think it would be much different to going into labour naturally. However, after two failed prostaglandin internals, I was given oxytocin, which I found awful. I was unable to cope very well with the pain. It felt unnatural and I couldn't have an active labour because I was strapped to a monitor. Next time I'd hold out until the last minute for induction.

*Lizzer*

---

**What the experts say**
Studies have shown that there is no evidence of any natural advantage in routinely inducing births that are 'overdue' and a failed induction frequently ends up as a Caesarean section.

Janet Balaskas (*New Active Birth*)

---

**I was induced with number two** when I was only five days overdue (I think the doctor wanted to go away for Easter!) and actually found it preferable to my first birth experience, which seemed to go on forever and during which I'd felt horribly out of control. I had the drip in the morning and nothing much happened until they turned it up. Then suddenly I was in labour. It was fast and strong. Before I knew it, I was pushing and my son was born just after midday.

*Mollipops*

**I've been induced twice.** The first time I had my waters ruptured and was given oral prostaglandin. My baby arrived four hours later after an easy labour. The second time was at my request at 41 weeks. I had one dose of prostaglandin gel, started labour six hours later and gave birth nine hours after that with no problems, although it was more painful.

*Baabaa*

**I have been induced** and it was less problematic than I was expecting. I had a gel pessary in the morning and when they examined me a few hours later I was 4 cm dilated. They broke my waters and I delivered in 22 minutes. My son and I were fine, I had no stitches and I was up and about as usual.

*Lou33*

**My daughter was ten days late.** I was due to go in for induction on the Wednesday evening and she came naturally on the Tuesday evening. I think it was because I had finally resigned myself to being induced, whereas before I was constantly thinking about when it might happen. As soon as I relaxed and thought there's nothing I can do about the whole thing, out she came. It was then that I regretted having wished away my last few days of peace and quiet – not to mention sleep.

*Tillysmummy*

**At our hospital, women are usually** induced between 12 and 14 days post dates. However, if all is well, there really is no immediate rush, and they can be left a bit longer, with some monitoring of both mother and baby. You should not be afraid to ask for what you want and remember that it's your body and your baby.

*Leese*

**I was induced after 42 weeks.** It was not a very nice experience and felt very clinical. I almost felt as if I'd been 'robbed' of the experience of my waters breaking naturally and rushing to the hospital. I still think that my dates were wrong, and that my daughter was just not quite ready to come. If you and your baby are fine, I think it's best to let nature take its course.

*Emski*

# Pain management – what worked or didn't work for you?

**I had pretty much everything** going. After a few hours when the contractions started to get really painful I tried gas and air, which helped me breathe through them and took the edge off the pain (I found that standing up was the best position for me). Then as they started to get quite intense I had a diamorphine injection. That relaxed me so much I actually slept in between the contractions. I had a second injection when that one began to wear off after a few hours but, although it certainly dulled the pain, I'm pretty sure it slowed things down as well because after about 15 hours I was still only 4–5 cm dilated.

The midwife then ruptured my hind waters and suddenly everything speeded up – the contractions were coming every three minutes or so and were incredibly painful. I was screaming for an epidural and by the time it was done – maybe 40 minutes later – I was fully dilated. It was a great relief to have the epidural but it meant I couldn't feel a thing for the pushing stage, which was tough. It was only when it started to wear off a couple of hours later that I was able to push the baby out. Next time, if there *is* a next time, I'd be inclined to skip the diamorphine (although the naps were quite nice) and have an epidural a little earlier, with the hope that it had worn off a bit by the time it came to pushing.

*Nancy*

**Mumsnet fact**
Only six per cent of women opt for a completely natural birth.
National Birth and Motherhood survey 2002 (*Mother & Baby* magazine)

**I went into hospital utterly terrified** of pain and determined to have every form of pain relief possible. The pool was wonderful and I only left it because the midwife promised that I could have morphine. Unfortunately, when she examined me, I was already 10 cm dilated. I wasn't allowed back in the pool and had to proceed with no pain relief whatsoever. They even confiscated the gas and air as it seemed to stop me pushing. So, despite having been utterly convinced that I would need pain relief, I now think that next time I would certainly try to manage with nothing at all.

*Harrysmum*

**Gas and air,** which is actually a 50 per cent mix of nitrous oxide (laughing gas) and oxygen has a very short half-life. That means that there are virtually no side-effects except in very prolonged use. When it is breathed in, it must be started at the beginning of the contraction so that it is working before the height of the contraction. It has no lasting effects on the baby after birth, unlike diamorphine/pethidine, which cause the baby to be sleepy and might lead to feeding problems in the first few days.

*Mears*

**I was allowed to keep the gas and air** during pushing, but I still screamed anyway. The problem was, I screamed through the mouthpiece, which seemed to echo down the pipework and sounded quite eerie. I was pretty embarrassed afterwards when reception told me that they could hear me. Screaming does help you though.

*Lil*

**I intended to have as natural a birth** as I possibly could, but to be honest I was so frightened that I opted for an epidural early on. My labour lasted 10 hours but for most of it I chatted quietly with my husband or lay back reading my magazine. The birth was fine. I was tired afterwards but it was nothing like I imagined. In fact, I would easily do it again, and I really felt that the epidural allowed me to enjoy it. It took the fear out of my labour and I had a lovely little girl at the end. I was not woozy or sick, just happy to meet her at last.

*Aoibh*

---

**What the experts say**
Medical progress has given women greater choice in childbirth and they no longer have to accept that extreme pain and suffering are unavoidable.

Kate Figes (*Life After Birth*)

The advantages of drugs are often greatly outweighed by their disadvantages, both to mother and to her baby.

Sheila Kitzinger (*The Experience of Childbirth*)

---

**I had pethidine** with my first baby and was so grateful for it. It didn't actually reduce the pain directly, but it made it much easier to relax between contractions, which made the pain go away more quickly. I found that during both my labours, physically relaxing my body reduced the pain – not the intensity, but the duration.

I would have been quite happy to have had pethidine again with number two, but I held on so long thinking that the pain was bound to get even worse that by the time I asked for it, it was too late and my daughter was born 15 minutes later.

*Azzie*

**I had pethidine** and don't think I'll bother again. I felt a bit out of it but didn't actually get any pain relief. I also managed to knock myself out on gas and air so will restrict that too. However, as we all know, it's easy to have these resolutions now but when it comes to 'that' amount of pain again and a smiling midwife offers a slight improvement in the form of a jab, will I really say no?

*Lizzer*

**I've had pethidine** and found its pain-relieving qualities non-existent. It made me so woozy that I 'came to' in the middle of huge contractions, without the normal build-up. I felt completely out of control and had memory blanks, which I hated. I was determined not to have it the next time and coped with gas and air instead. I'm not convinced that works either, but at least it's something to do.

*Baabaa*

**Mumsnet fact**
70 per cent of women find that pethidine offers ineffectual or inadequate pain relief.
Janet Balaskas (*Birth and Baby Diary*)

**I had diamorphine** with both labours as gas and air makes me feel nauseous. The morphine did make me very woozy, but also extremely relaxed. It certainly calmed me down and helped me get through the next few hours. I felt able to 'wake' myself up to push and the birth was no problem. I did feel a bit spaced out afterwards but I don't think it interfered with bonding.

*Eulalia*

**I had pethidine for my first labour** (only gas and air for the subsequent two) on the advice of the midwife who was delivering me. She felt I was losing control and thought it would help me. It is not supposed to be administered within four hours of giving birth and my midwife thought I would not be giving birth until the following morning (this was about 11.20 pm). As it turned out, I gave birth at 11.35 pm and the paediatrician had to be called to give my daughter the antidote to the pethidine, as it can make babies drowsy and late to respond.

*Bumblelion*

**Mumsnet fact**
Narcotics given during labour have been detected in babies' blood streams eight weeks after birth.
William Sears and Martha Sears (*The Birth Book – Everything You Need to Know to have a Safe and Satisfying Birth*)

**I had a TENS machine** and would definitely use one again. I put it on when I was getting irregular contractions in the morning, stayed at home all day, went into hospital the following morning at 2 am and wore it until it was no longer giving me any relief at about 6 am. I had my son at 7 am. It definitely helped me, but whether it was actual pain relief or a placebo I don't know or care. I could feel a huge increase in the pain during examinations, when I had to stop the TENS and it would take a while to become effective again. I know people who have found them helpful and others who say they have felt no effect. I think that if they are used early enough in labour they are most beneficial as the pain relief builds up. I enjoyed being free to move about with the TENS machine.

*Eefs*

**I thought TENS was wonderful.** I used it all the way through, with gas and air for the last hour. I was still relaxed, walking around, chatting when I was 5 cm dilated and I think TENS had a lot to do with that. It may have been all in the mind but that's fine with me, just so long as it works. I even found it helped when I was having my stitches done.

*Phillipat*

**I used TENS for my first son** but thought it was fairly pointless until it was taken off and I realized that it had been taking the edge off the contractions. It is also a useful thing to have to take your mind off the pain.

*Hughsie*

**I used a TENS machine both times,** but if I am honest, I think it was used more to give me something to do other than to relieve the pain. When you are pushing that little button you feel like you are 'helping' somehow. In my first labour, my battery went dead and it took me about an hour to notice. The second time it worked for about 20 minutes before I went on to the gas and air and my son was born not long afterwards.

*Susanmt*

**I had essential oils massaged** into my back, and the birthing pool, which was lovely. My mum also borrowed a machine that scented the room with lavender. I had soothing music playing, which I had been listening to throughout my pregnancy. My husband was the best help though and gave me all the support I needed at all the right times.

*Peanuts1*

**I tried homeopathy;** I was recommended chamomillum to take non-stop during the labour. I thought it helped, although it was still a painful experience.

*Pupuce*

**I didn't use my birth ball** much before the labour, only to sit on it when my back was playing up. But during my labour, you couldn't get me off it. It was the only place I could get comfortable. I took it to hospital and sat on it there and my waters broke on it too! I was told afterwards that it probably helped my cervix dilate quicker as in that position your pelvis is more open.

*Corky*

**Mumsnet tip**
Don't buy a birth ball. Buy an exercise ball from Argos or Index. They're exactly the same but half the price.

*Bobsmum*

**I could not have imagined** not using my birth ball. It was very good to be on all fours in labour with my head against the ball. It was really relaxing.

*Sweetypie*

**I bought a birth ball** and wouldn't say it was essential, but it was useful. You're supposed to use it to sit on as much as you can prior to the birth as it strengths the pelvic floor muscles and I did try and do this, but not enough. When I went into labour I used it a fair bit during the early stages, but I could have managed without. However, once I was in really strong labour I didn't want it anymore. My other reason for buying it was to use it for stomach exercises afterwards but it didn't come with any instructions on how to do these. I ended up deflating it as it takes up too much room.

*LizC*

**After having my daughter** and relaying my birth story, I found that people were almost surprised that I didn't take any drugs, in any form, like 'How did she do it?' During the first stage I was at home, on a lovely shag-pile rug on the floor, propped up against the bed. My husband gave me honey and hot water to keep me going because I was there for a few hours. Each time a contraction came I got up on my knees and leant forward on the bed and my husband rubbed my lower back. I was like this for hours, and I was really comfortable, and the pain was only bad when the contractions peaked. But when they died down, it was almost pleasurable. When I got to the hospital I was 9 cm, and two hours later she was born. I was only pushing for 25 minutes. The crowning was really painful, like fire, but I didn't tear, thank god! I've heard so many scare stories about women who've had an epidural early on, which has lead to other forms of intervention or a C-section because they were so drugged up that they couldn't push the baby out. Labour is painful no matter what, and I reckon it's better to feel the pain and control it than to have some drugs control it for you.

*Boogs*

**My birth was relatively 'easy'** and I put that down to the yoga and active birth classes, plus keeping as active as possible throughout pregnancy. I sat on a chair the 'wrong' way round for early labour, did lots of hip swaying early on too, tried all fours but didn't like it, and eventually found that being at about a 45-degree angle worked! Unfortunately for my husband, this meant that I leant against his chest standing up for the last two hours of my labour. He had to have a pillow eventually as my head was bruising his chest! The best thing about having an active birth is feeling in control. I understood everything, and once I got into the second stage, I got my 'business-head' on, and I felt totally on top of what I needed to do.

*Lalaa*

**I had a very good second labour** and I think it was due to being more relaxed and practising the breathing I had learned. Try to practise breathing like this: breathe in while letting your tummy out and breathe out while pulling your tummy in. It's called belly breathing. My husband, who plays the trumpet, says that this is how you should breathe to get maximum breath control.

*Bee*

**What the experts say**
Many women find that the harmony they create between the contractions and their breathing gives them real delight. Even when the contractions are very fierce – at the end of the first stage of labour when the cervix of the uterus is almost fully dilated – by synchronizing the breathing with the rhythm of the contractions it is possible for labour to be pleasurable, much like swimming in a stormy sea.

Sheila Kitzinger (*The Experience of Childbirth*)

**I found it helpful to know** that the uterus is the strongest muscle in the body and the only one that doesn't revert to its previous shape when it relaxes. This means that every contraction is a step forward, with no steps back. Every contraction takes you a bit nearer the goal of a muscle thinned and stretched round the base (round the cervix), and bunched up and pushing at the top. It's quite easy to visualize this as it's happening and I found it helpful.

The other useful tip I picked up was that the pelvis is at its widest when you are kneeling up, facing backwards (holding onto the bedhead). This gives you an extra couple of millimetres at the crucial moment. You don't need to do it all through labour, but my 'blocked' baby came shooting out like a champagne cork when I eventually remembered this!

*Copper*

**Use plenty of deep breathing,** but most of all keep focused and calm. During the labour of my second daughter, I lost it at one stage, and felt the panic and fear about the pain take over. Try taking it one contraction at a time and crossing each one off an imaginary list in your head.

*Batey*

**You should definitely remain upright** and mobile as long as possible and use abdominal breathing between contractions, and for as long as possible during contractions. Apparently the body naturally goes to abdominal breathing when you are completely relaxed and so forcing abdominal breathing is supposed to trick the body into being relaxed. Whatever the reason, when I remembered to do this breathing, the pain was much less than when I forgot. I spent most of my labour standing up in a hot shower, which was a great help. Also one of the midwives suggested rocking my hips from side to side during contractions, so I tried it and it did actually help. I had planned to have gas and air if needed, however, with all the concentrating on breathing and hip – rocking, my baby was born before it even occurred to me to ask for pain relief!

*Chelle*

## What the experts say

One of the main causes of unnecessary pain in childbirth is the use of the reclining position. Even if you are propped up by pillows, you are like a stranded beetle – completely helpless – and the contractions of your uterus will hurt more. Other postures, such as kneeling forward, standing, squatting or sitting upright actually relieve the pain and help you tune in to what is happening inside you. You need the freedom to use your whole body to discover how to make yourself comfortable.

Janet Balaskas (*New Active Birth*)

**I found that I could almost** self-hypnotize with the very deep breathing. My other suggestions would be to move about until you find a position that's comfortable, use water, whether a pool or very deep bath, turn off the lights, light a candle and float around. And if none of this works, ask for pain relief from your midwife. There are no medals for suffering.

*Emmagee*

# Epidurals – for or against?

**Actually having my epidural** was horrible but once it kicked in I was able to relax and chat away with the midwife. I stayed on my feet as long as possible when I had it and so things progressed very quickly. I let it wear off a bit when I got to the pushing stage but ended up having a bit more in the last 20 minutes. I'd love to have the nerve to totally refuse it but for a first-timer I think it was a great choice.

*Rooty*

**I had an epidural with my first** and was delighted to be given it. It did not work brilliantly but was sufficient to make the pain bearable. It was not a mobile epidural, but I did lie on my side and not my back, which, my midwife told me, is a good position for pushing. In the end I had an episiotomy and forceps.

*Jasper*

**I had a mobile epidural** because after 36 hours of labour I was fully dilated but my contractions were dying away, so I was given the [labour-inducing] drug Syntocin on a drip. I was too tired and too afraid to turn down an epidural as the 'artificial' contractions caused by Syntocin are considered more painful than 'natural' contractions. Just 45 minutes after the drip was administered, my son was born, without intervention. I sat up in bed, which meant I had the benefit of gravity. I would do the same next time, as pushing even with an epidural isn't totally pain-free so I can't imagine what it's like without one.

*Ap*

> **Mumsnet fact**
> In Britain, 31 per cent of women have an epidural during childbirth.
> *The Sunday Times*

**Epidurals have my vote.** I had twins in a German hospital, where C-sections are not elective, and they have no gas and air available. I was induced and two hours later asked for an epidural, just as I could start to feel the contractions. I then had a nice afternoon nap. A few hours later it began to wear off, which I found helpful because it meant I could just feel the contraction, which helped me to push. I still didn't have any pain. Twin one was born and twin two followed 12 minutes later, with no intervention and no episiotomy. The whole experience was wonderful. I felt that I could take in everything that was going on in a calm manner without having to worry about pain.

*LindaH*

**After 19 hours of contractions** I was exhausted and miserable and they took pity on me. Moments after the epidural kicked in I was chatting happily to the midwife and inviting her round for dinner. I was totally aware of what was happening; I could feel sensation but no pain so the pushing and the actual whoosh of the birth was enjoyable. I would definitely recommend it and would have had one with my second if she'd waited long enough!

*Sobernow*

**The epidural worked very well for me.** It's your choice whether you get it topped up. I let it wear off towards the end so I could feel to push and could also deliver on my knees, which was much more comfortable.

*VJR*

---

**What the experts say**
The epidural is generally when pregnant women get their personalities back. They become nice and loving to their partners, and chatty with their midwives and friends.

Vicki Iovine (*The Best Friends' Guide to Pregnancy*)

..........................................................................................................................................

It is neither safe nor healthy for a woman to be disconnected from her sensations during labor. Pain has a purpose.

William Sears MD and Martha Sears RN (*The Birth Book – Everything You Need to Know to have a Safe and Satisfying Birth*)

---

**I definitely wanted an epidural** and I wanted it early. I really couldn't see the point of waiting until I was in agony, although obviously you have to wait until labour is established. I was experiencing mild, period-type pains when I had mine. I think they are wonderful. I had hours of no discomfort whatsoever and then spent 45 minutes pushing at the end. There was no real pain at all.

There is SO much said about 'natural' being good as if it's somehow preferable to suffer. Prior to having an epidural I kept looking for the 'catch' – it seemed a bit too good to be true. I remember telling anyone who would listen for the next few weeks after the birth that for my next career move I was going to work for the epidural marketing board.

*Bayleaf*

**I had an epidural during my first labour** I could still move my legs, kneel, go on all fours, but was a little too wobbly to stand and walk around. If you head down the epidural path, my tip is to tell your anaesthetist what you want from it. They can then set the infusion running to give you the pain relief you need. Being totally pain-free often results in no mobility and thus perhaps a greater chance for intervention later, whereas a lighter effect allows greater mobility but you may not be pain-free.

*Honeybunny*

**What the experts say**
An anaesthetist must administer an epidural. The good part about this is that no amateurs will be puncturing your spine and crippling you for life. The bad part is that not all hospitals have anaesthetists on duty 24 hours a day, so there may not be one around when you want one... if there is even a remote chance that you will want an epidural, tell your midwife several times during pregnancy, and remind her when you call announcing that you are in labour.

Vicki Iovine (*The Best Friends' Guide to Pregnancy*)

**I had an epidural quite early on** in labour – I'm a total wimp when it comes to pain and the pethidine had worn off. It was totally wonderful. I didn't feel a thing and the midwife helped me push by putting her hand on my tummy and telling me when the contractions were coming (which I could also feel very mildly). I think the epidural also helped recovery because I couldn't feel the stitches for a couple of days, which eased me in nicely. It's not for everyone but it made my birth a happy memory.

*Jolou1*

**I have a hunch** that my emergency C-section was due to having an epidural. The Caesarean was required after three hours of pushing and making no progress at all when my son started to show signs of acute distress. Having an epidural means that you have to labour flat on your back – the position in which your pelvis is most closed, and which does not take advantage of gravity to get the baby out.

It's pretty much accepted that moving around during labour can facilitate movement of the baby through the pelvis, so staying active can make a difference. In my case I needed a drip to increase the strength of my contractions as well. It was an absolutely classic case of 'cascading intervention', as it is termed: get one form of intervention and all of a sudden you need a whole lot of others.

*Amber1*

**What the experts say**
Every woman should know that having an epidural increases the chance of forceps delivery. In a study made of those who decided beforehand to have an epidural it was discovered that forceps deliveries were five times as common, and that the baby's head was in the wrong position three times as often in women who had epidurals as compared with those who did not.

Sheila Kitzinger (*The Experience of Childbirth*)

**My labour with number one** was only two hours 40 minutes. I was on the drip and was fully dilated in under an hour. I had a mobile epidural but it didn't work. This was supposedly due to the fact that mobile epidurals work their way gradually down your back following the pain – however, my pain was too fast and it didn't catch up. I found the 40 minutes of pushing agony because I had no pain relief at all.

*Pamela1*

**Epidurals are wonderful things** when needed but it is not always a good idea to plan to have one before labour has started. You might find you are able to benefit from other means of pain relief such as a birthing pool, which gives you much more freedom of movement. Unless your hospital offers mobile epidurals, having an epidural early on in labour can really slow the process, increasing the likelihood of needing other interventions. With an epidural you need a drip to correct a potential fall in blood pressure, continual blood pressure recordings every 15–30 minutes and continuous monitoring of the baby. It is much better to be established in labour with regular contractions prior to having an epidural sited so that the anaesthetist knows he/she has managed an effective block. If it is done too early it can be difficult to assess if it is working properly. There is nothing worse than an epidural that does not work effectively. It's soul destroying for mother and midwife.

*Mears*

**I had an epidural** when I was almost fully dilated and the pain was pretty unbearable. It was fairly hairy getting it in for the anaesthetist, as the contractions were coming thick and fast and I was supposed to be still and it took a while to take effect – 15 minutes, I'd say – but when it did, the relief was immense. The downside was that I found the pushing stage really hard going as I couldn't feel the contractions at all. It was only when it began to wear off – a few hours of fairly fruitless pushing later – that, just as everyone was giving up hope, I was able to pop the baby out. So, in my case it probably would have been better to have had the epidural a bit earlier, and to insist it wasn't topped up too much.

*Nancy*

**I had an epidural with my daughter** after a long, protracted first labour. It was slightly uncomfortable as it was administered, but nothing compared to the pain of a contraction. The relief was quick and gratefully received. As is often the way with epidurals, I ended up with an assisted delivery (ventouse) as I had no 'urge to push', and consequently found it difficult. However, I weighed up the situation at the time, and an epidural was right for me then. Don't make up your mind beforehand, just go in with an open mind.

*Leese*

# Ventouse and forceps – what does it involve and how long does it take to recover?

**I had a ventouse delivery** at 36 weeks with my first baby, who decided he wanted to put in an early appearance. I had an epidural early on because it was recom- mended. I was therefore flat on my back and had no feeling whatsoever and had to be told when I was having a contraction, so I never had the urge to push prop- erly. My son was also in a posterior (back to back) position so the wrong part of his head was presenting. When I made no progress in the second stage I was taken into the assisted-labour room, put in stirrups and given an episiotomy for the ventouse, which worked very well. It's rather undignified but you don't care at that point. I had two midwives, two paediatricians, a doctor, a teacher and several students all looking on. I didn't feel a thing due to the epidural being so strong.

My son had a slightly pointy head for a day or so and was a bit bruised for a while. He ended up in special care with a chest infection but this probably wasn't linked to his delivery. He didn't seem to suffer any problems and always slept well as a tiny baby. I got a slight infection from my scar and I'm not quite the same down there as I was before but it hasn't caused major problems.

*PamT*

**Mumsnet fact**

In 1989 forceps were used in 83 per cent of instrumental deliveries and ventouse in only 17 per cent. By 2000, 65 per cent of instrumental deliver- ies were by ventouse.

NHS Maternity Statistics, England 1998–1999 and 2000–2001

**The idea of ventouse or forceps** terrified me throughout pregnancy, but when it came to the crunch and the midwife and doctor said, 'We need to get this baby out', I couldn't have cared less how they did it as I'd been in labour for hours. I actu- ally thought they were going to do a C-section and was quite relieved. They used a ventouse as the cord was around his neck and under his arm. This was affecting his heart rate so they pulled while I pushed. It was all over in a couple of pushes and pulls and all he had was a bit of a squashy purple bruise for a few days.

*EmmaTMG*

**I was induced at 39 weeks** as I have diabetes and ended up having both ventouse and forceps to get the baby out. After 26 hours in labour I didn't care what they did as long as he came out safely. He did have a bit of a swelling on the back of his head for 24 hours, and a scab, which dropped off after about a week, but other than that he was absolutely fine. It meant we had to stay in hospital for an extra night though.

*Hoxtonchick*

**My first son was forceps** with the accompanying stirrups and episiotomy. I have to agree that at that point you really couldn't care less about what they are going to do because at least they are getting the baby out and the end is in sight. My son had a bruised, elongated head and I blamed his poor sleeping on the forceps and tried cranial osteopathy but my second son and my daughter turned out to be just as bad and had normal deliveries so it's just the way I make them!

*Miggy*

**I had a ventouse delivery** and it really wasn't that bad. The episiotomy didn't hurt at the time, and I was lucky it healed well. The stirrups weren't too bad, and I was only in them for a short time. It's not like you're confined in that position for hours.

*Jane101*

**Something to bear in mind** if you have a ventouse is that it's not unusual for the vacuum seal between the ventouse cap and the head to be broken. This makes the most terrible noise and sounds like something ghastly has happened, but it's nothing at all to worry about – they just have another go!

*Isbee*

**I believe that the more intervention** you have in labour, the more you are likely to require an assisted delivery. So, if they do suggest a procedure to you, I would really query if it is necessary. This is easier said than done when you are in labour, as you are very vulnerable. So get something down on your birth plan about it and discuss it with your birth partner in advance.

Having an epidural makes it more likely you'll need an assisted delivery, but you might decide the benefits outweigh the risks. I gave birth to my first son with the aid of a ventouse, and there wasn't a mark on him. He also had a very high Apgar score – after nearly three hours of pushing. I think a ventouse is preferable to forceps – I remember the consultant wanted to use the latter, but the midwife talked him out of it.

*Khara*

**Mumsnet fact**
In a study made of those who decided beforehand to have an epidural, it was discovered that forceps deliveries were five times as common.
Sheila Kitzinger (*The Experience of Childbirth*)

**I had a ventouse with my daughter.** I had been in labour for 37 hours, she was posterior (came out face up), and when she was born she was 9 lb 12 oz. The ventouse was an alternative to a section. I had requested no episiotomy as I preferred to tear, and the tear ended up being smaller than an episiotomy would have been. The ventouse did give my daughter a bit of a cone head but it was gone in a couple of days. The horror stories about brain damage come from the days when 'high' forceps were used to 'pull' a baby out. These days they are not used and a section is done if the baby is stuck high up.

*Susanmt*


**As a midwife, I can reassure** you that the decision to use ventouse or forceps is taken only if there is a need for your own efforts to be aided: sometimes because the baby is not tolerating the pushing stage well and sometimes because the baby is not advancing very well when pushing. If the baby's heartbeat is okay, then you will be able to continue trying yourself.

I have had women asking for assistance from the doctor because they don't have the energy to keep going. You should try not to think of the baby as being 'wrenched out'. Ventouse/forceps just guide the baby out, assisted by your own pushing when progress is slow. To try and avoid an assisted delivery you should remain as mobile as possible during labour and avoid an epidural, but doing this does not mean you won't need any assistance.

*Mears*

---

**What the experts say**

Forceps should be used only when valid indications exist. Most commonly these include prolonged labour or prolonged second stage labour, maternal distress (the mother is exhausted; can't push well; or has heart, muscular, neurological or respiratory disease that prevents her from pushing); an abnormal foetal heart rate; vaginal bleeding from a suspected placental abruption.

Murkoff, Eisenberg and Hathaway (*What to Expect When You're Expecting*)

---

**I had forceps and my son was born** looking like he'd just done a round in the boxing ring. He had black eyes and bruising all over the side of his face. Bruising results in a breakdown of the red blood cells and therefore often leads to higher jaundice levels due to excess bilirubin. He ended up with really bad jaundice, which meant that we were in hospital for a week.

In order to bring down the jaundice level, the baby has to dispel it and thus drink lots of milk. But because the jaundice makes them really sleepy, they don't seem bothered about suckling. My son just used to fall asleep as soon as I put him to my breast. In the end I was advised to give him a top-up feed with a little cup or bottle, which I wasn't over-enthusiastic about, but it did mean that he took a bottle from day one. Photo-therapy also helps break down the bilirubin so that it is more easily excreted and my poor feller lay naked for days under this sun-lamp for photo-therapy. Each day he would have the bilirubin test, which is done by a heel prick, to check the level. It was really upsetting and I was so happy when I was told that the level was finally low enough for us to be allowed home.

*Ra*

**I had both ventouse and forceps** as my son was arm and head presentation (his arm was tucked behind his head) and I had been pushing for six hours. I was so relieved the doctor was going to get the baby out and that it would be over quickly. I had an episiotomy and a lot of stitches afterwards in theatre whilst my husband held our son outside. My son had a slightly long head, which went in a day. He had two scratches on the side of his face from the forceps, which disappeared within a few days. He also had a nasty blister on the back of his head from the ventouse, which had gone by 10 days. Apart from this, he was absolutely fine following his birth. We did take him to a cranial osteopath to get him checked out but he hadn't suffered any ill effects. He was a good feeder and a fantastic sleeper.

*Gem13*

**I didn't think it was possible** to have a positive ventouse experience until the birth of my third. After a quick first stage of labour, I was pushing for one and a half hours and the baby, although well down, was showing no signs of coming out. The doctor came in to examine me and gave me the choice of either pushing for another half an hour or a ventouse there and then. I went for the ventouse as she felt convinced it would be straightforward. She used a very small 'cap', which was neatly fitted on the baby's head. From then on it reminded me of my driving instructor teaching me the rudiments of reverse parking: 'push, push, stop, breath, breath, breath, push, push, push...' and the next thing he was out. It left no marks, I didn't need an episiotomy and it certainly beat a further 30 minutes of pushing.

*Bon*

# Episiotomy and tearing – can it be avoided and if not, how long does it take to heal?

**The position you deliver in** can make a huge difference. You are less likely to tear if you are on your side or out of bed because there is more flexibility in the coccyx, which allows the head to glide out rather than be forced upwards on exit (this can cause labial tears). Breathing the head out instead of actively pushing helps. Entonox (gas and air) is very helpful when getting through that stage. Some women are just not very elastic down there and will tear, no matter what they do. I had episiotomies first and second time – done at the last minute because I had started to tear. Mind you, that was a few years ago when nearly everyone delivered propped up on their backs. I didn't know as much then as I do now.

*Mears*

**Mumsnet fact**
In a study of 11,000 mothers, only 18.7 per cent of those who gave birth vaginally emerged with an intact perineum.
Birmingham University Hospital

**I had a third-degree tear** with my first child, along with an episiotomy, which was caused by having to push my daughter out very quickly because they couldn't find her heartbeat. I suffered terribly until the birth of my second child almost five years later, when I only tore slightly. With the last two I didn't need stitches at all, and I think it was due to the fact that I had midwives who were a bit more vocal about when I wasn't supposed to push.

*Lou33*

**Tearing is often due** to women pushing the body of the baby out too quickly after the head is out, so listening to the midwife is really important. I know that some people massage their perineum before birth and I have read a Canadian clinical study which showed that this was helpful in first labours. Also, being in water helps avoid tears as it softens the area.

*Pupuce*

**What the experts say**
Use your own hands to feel the baby's head when it begins to crown and to ease the tissues or even massage them with a little oil. Interestingly, mothers who use their hands to help the baby out rarely tear!
Janet Balaskas (*New Active Birth*)

**It's certainly hard not to push** when the overwhelming urge is just to go for it. The most important thing is to control that crowning stage, which is when the baby's head is born. If you pant rather than push, it allows the head to be born more slowly – usually it just eases itself out – and in turn this gives the perineum a bit more time to stretch, resulting in less trauma to that area. However, whether you tear also has a great deal to do with other factors: the size of the baby, the speed of the labour and delivery, your perineum, etc. Some women still end up with some tearing however controlled they are whilst the head delivers. Other women shoot through labour and deliver really quickly with one massive push, and still end up with an intact perineum. The length of the first stage of labour (as your cervix dilates to 10 cm) doesn't really have that much to do with the stretching of the perineum. That occurs more in the second stage as the baby's head descends and starts to stretch it. Also, some babies are born with hands alongside their ears or face, which can also result in some grazing.

*Leese*

---

**What the experts say**
There are grounds for suspecting that episiotomy has become obstetric fashion. If medical staff indicate that they think an episiotomy is necessary during labour, you should ask why it's being done.

Dr Miriam Stoppard (*Pregnancy and Birth*)

---

**I used almond oil** (and then grape-seed oil when I got worried about allergies) religiously for about three months before I gave birth. I still tore and needed an episiotomy – though neither were any big deal and I healed fine.

*Oldmummy*

**I really recommend lavender oil** to speed up the healing of stitches. Also arnica pills, as it is possible that there might be some deep residual bruising too. I clearly remember my midwife having a look at my stitches a week after I'd given birth, tutting and saying, 'Now, that looks a bit brutal.' If anything was guaranteed to give me a complex, that was!

*Enid*

**Mumsnet tip**
If you're suffering with stitches or a tear after giving birth, invest in some baby wipes – they're far more soothing than ordinary toilet paper.

*Holly*

**I would recommend a warm bath** with lavender oil as often as you possibly can and, gross as it sounds, drying with a cool hairdryer rather than a towel.

*Candy*

> **Mumsnet tip**
> Take a jug into hospital with you when you give birth. You can pour luke-
> warm water over yourself when you first go to the loo afterwards, minimiz-
> ing the sting!
>
> *Milkbar*

**I was terrified of the stitches,** having never been stitched anywhere in my life before. I can't even watch people being stitched up on telly. But my stitches were beautifully done, healed up so very quickly and didn't pull. I cannot recommend continuous running stitch enough. Put it in your birth plan. When going to the toilet after the stitches, I poured a plastic bottle of water over the area whilst peeing in the bath. Otherwise the acid in the urine can cause incredible stinging. I used to have a shallow bath every morning to bathe my stitches.

*EmmaM*

**I had the continuous running stitch** and they pulled so badly I nearly had to have the whole lot removed and restitched.

*Molly1*

---

**What the experts say**
Research shows that those women who have been stitched by an experienced midwife or doctor suffer less perineal pain afterwards, as do those who have been stitched with a continuous running stitch rather than with interrupted tran-scutaneous stitches.

Kate Figes (*Life after Birth*)

---

**I had an episiotomy** and quite frankly I found the stitching up far more stressful and traumatic than the actual giving birth. They took nearly two hours to stitch me because they kept undoing the stitches as they felt they wouldn't heal right. The first time I felt brave enough to get a mirror and look I was horrified and I'm sure it has psychologically scarred me. A friend of mine eventually got the doctor to recommend she was re-done and said it was worth it. It took me nearly a year to 'get over it' and even now, if I think about it, I have difficulties in feeling 'normal'. Everyone I've spoken to has also taken time to get over having an episiotomy. The one bit of advice I would give is not to look down there!

*Selja*

## Baby positioning – can you turn the baby before birth and does breech mean Caesarean?

**I found out at 37 weeks** that my baby was breech. My midwife suggested I try and turn the baby by going on all fours, with my bottom pushed up into the air and head near the floor, which I did a lot. It's a strange position to watch telly in, but it worked for me.

*Maisy1*

**I had a horrible transverse birth** with my first daughter and swam twice weekly whilst pregnant with number two and am convinced it helped. She was head down, normal delivery.

*Enid*

**Jean Sutton, who co-wrote** the *Optimal Foetal Positioning* book, recommends cycling shorts to correct transverse lie. You need to buy the proper sort that are really tight across the abdomen and leave the baby with no choice but to go head down.

*SueW*

**Mumsnet fact**
If you're over 35 you have twice the chance of having a first baby in breech position, compared to younger women.
*Pregnancy and Birth* magazine

**My second daughter was transverse** and then breech. I found a website which told you various methods to turn a baby. Amongst the more amusing suggestions was shining a light up your bottom (the baby is supposed to turn to the light!) but the one which seemed to work for me was lying on my back with my bottom raised up in the air on several cushions. It was pretty uncomfortable but it really worked – I was lying there one day when I felt all this squirming around. Sure enough she had turned round.

*Caroline5*

**There are some easy yoga postures** that are good for getting the baby into the right position. It involves spending as much time as possible in forward leaning positions. You're supposed to try and be forward-leaning even when doing things like using the computer or watching TV. Try sitting backward in your chair or kneeling on the floor leaning forward onto your birth ball, for example. I also found these positions were a lot more comfortable as I got bigger.

*Rkayne*

**It is now recommended** by the Royal College of Obstetricians and Gynaecologists that women with uncomplicated breech babies at term should be offered ECV – External Cephalic Version – to avoid Caesarean if at all possible. It may be performed under ultrasound guidance, often after medication has been given to relax the uterus.

*Mears*

**My baby was breech** and I was planning a home birth, so was really not up for a C-section. I was offered an ECV at 37 weeks and it was fantastic! A wonderfully skilled consultant turned my little boy in less than a minute. It felt quite peculiar, and the side of my tummy was slightly sore afterwards where he'd had to press his fingers in, but the turn itself wasn't painful or uncomfortable. I was so relieved that something that had been worrying me so much could be solved in such a short, simple action that I burst into tears immediately afterwards!

*Gooby*

**I had ECV to turn my baby,** it didn't hurt and my baby stayed head down. The procedure is carried out after an ultrasound scan to check on where the baby, cord and placenta are. You and baby are monitored before and after for any signs of distress. I didn't have any drugs and the consultant gently put his hands on the baby and helped her move around. It really was gentle – I think she liked him!

There are risks involved with ECV but these are mainly associated with attempting the procedure before 37 weeks and when the placenta is anterior (on the back of the womb). There are other small risks, the main one being that you could go into labour and may then need a section. My advice would be to ask to speak to the person who would carry out the ECV and ask them about their success rate – it does vary depending on the skill and experience of the obstetrician.

*Cadi*

**At our maternity units** ECVs are done by consultants and have a 50 per cent success rate. If it fails they do allow women who they feel could have an uncomplicated birth to go the vaginal route. I think second-time mums, for example, who have already had a vaginal birth, find it far easier. I believe they put you in stirrups at the end as it ensures that your pelvis is wide open for pushing. Personally I'd try turning with accupuncture. Even consultants in our units recommend it as it can be very successful.

*Pupuce*

**I went into labour on my due date,** the same day I was booked in for a scan to check the position of the baby as the midwives just could not tell! We discovered that he was extended breech and were advised to go for a C-section. However, my consultant was all for my attempting a vaginal delivery on the agreement that they'd perform a C-section if there were problems.

I was fortunate in having a very rapid labour for a first-timer – about five hours, and got through it with only a TENS machine. I had an episiotomy, but avoided the forceps and it was a small price to pay. It's hard to say if breech is more painful than normal – for me, it didn't feel like 'pain' as such (presumably helped by the fact that, for a breech, the baby was very well positioned and came out bum first). The worst part was getting his head out. I admit that I did scream at that point, but anyone having a natural birth has to go through the same thing – for some it just happens at the end instead of the beginning.

A few weeks after he was born, I discovered a lump on one side of my baby's neck. A check with a specialist showed that it was a torn muscle caused by the force of pulling him out at birth. Not a serious injury nor is it permanent – exercise will solve it – but it's worth being aware that this is not uncommon in breech deliveries.

*Racheljw*

**I had an undiagnosed breech** after 12 hours of labour. I really wanted a natural birth. I had a TENS machine but was adamant I wouldn't have any other medical 'interference'. I had my birthing pool all run and was literally just about to climb in when they discovered the baby was breech. I didn't feel freaked out but just got on with what needed doing. I did think it was a bit ironic that I had been so against medical intervention and ended up having a Caesarean.

*Bo*

**What the experts say**
There is evidence to show that most mothers deliver breech babies vaginally with hardly any difficulty at all, and caesarean section is only justifiable in about one in six patients.

Dr Miriam Stoppard (*Pregnancy and Birth*)

**My baby was transverse** *occopito posterior* (about as wrong a way round as you can get), which wasn't spotted until I had been trying to push her out for over two hours. They explained that they could give me a Caesarean, but would like to try to deliver the baby 'naturally'. Well, they succeeded, but only by turning the baby with forceps and then dragging her out with a ventouse. I found the experience completely horrific, especially as I wasn't offered an epidural. My daughter was born with huge bruising and a very swollen head and I felt very traumatized for months after. We are both completely fine now, but believe me, I would much rather have had a C-section.

*Caznay*

**I had an undiagnosed breech birth** and then a Caesarean. To be honest, I can't remember if they asked me or not whether I wanted to try and give birth naturally.

I was in agony, trying to push out a baby who was the wrong way round with no pain relief. Thank God for the Caesarean and the spinal that came with it and thank God for a healthy baby.

*Bebee*

**Mumsnet fact**
Around 24,000 births each year – 4 per cent – are breech and the Royal College of Obstetricians and Gynaecologists advises that babies are 75 per cent less likely to die if they are delivered surgically.

*Daily Mail*

**I had a C-section with my eldest** child who was breach. The hospital were fantastic letting me go into labour normally but I did end up with a Caesarean, which was a good experience; calm, relaxed, the staff were very supportive and I have very fond memories of the whole thing. The important thing was that we had discussed what would happen if I had a section just as you would for a normal birth and all our wishes were followed right down to the music. Incidentally, I subsequently had two normal deliveries.

*Philly*

# Labour tips for dads – what should they do or not do?

**I think dads should** try not to be too vocal. My husband started off by 'talking me through' each contraction. Saying things like, 'well done – it's nearly over now, you're over the worst' until I 'asked', through gritted teeth, how the hell he knew... After that he kept quiet but was very useful to lean on during contractions and did a nice little massage routine on my lower spine. So always ask if what you're doing is all right, don't take offence if it's not and don't, whatever you do, try the gas and air whilst chewing gum (as mine did) – it's not supposed to be your drama!

*Roberta*

**My only tip would be to avoid** doing what a lot of dads do (which is meant with the best of intentions) but actually isn't hugely helpful... which is to ask their wife during the transition every few minutes, 'Are you all right?' Physiologically for labour to happen as smoothly as can be, a woman needs to be left undisturbed at the end of her labour to let her hormones be at their peak.

Unfortunately, the more you speak/interrupt, the more they produce adrenaline, which slows down their oxytocin level (that's the one that makes you contract). What you will probably notice is that she will not want to engage in conversation... she will want peace and quiet – unless she is frightened, and then of course you can reassure her with a few words. My husband said that it is quite frightening to see how very painful it can become for the mother. He held my hand until I heard the midwives laughing. I looked up and he was in agony... I was squeezing his hand so hard he was about to faint.

*Pupuce*

**Use a cold flannel** as a compress on the head, neck or lower spine. This seemed to help but be warned, things can change. What's pleasant one minute can become aggravating the next. Be prepared for the midwives to ignore you: they are not rude, however their priority is the mother and baby. Speak up for your partner, she will be relying on you, so be assertive. In the final stage of labour, your partner will not look human. Eyes rolling, teeth bared and animalistic grunts are to be expected. If blood doesn't worry you, take this chance to see the head emerging. It's amazing. Otherwise, look away! Prepare to be absolutely stunned at your wife/partner's bravery, resilience and stamina, and to come out of the experience feeling rather humbled.

*Newdad*

**My husband massaged** me so firmly that the next day I was bruised all along my lower back. Needless to say, I barely felt the massage!

*Edgarcat*

**Mumsnet fact**
In parts of Brazil, fathers cut themselves during their partner's labour, in order to share in their pain.

*Expecting Our Baby* magazine

**Back massage suits some people,** but I know that I was happy for my husband to be curled up in the chair in the corner whilst the midwife and I got on with it.

*Rosy*

**My husband seemed to have some** running banter going on with the midwives. I was really pleased that they were chatting as I just wanted to retreat to my own little world and not have to acknowledge anyone around me. For me, his presence was important (there's no way I would have let him leave the room) rather than his practical help. That said, he was useful in passing me water and energy tablets when I needed them.

*Bon*

**In the third stage of labour,** it's very common for women not to want to be touched – don't take it personally! There is some research which shows that women with partners who are prepared for labour (i.e. know some basic info about it, such as pain relief options), and are supportive, report less pain in labour... so we are of some (limited!) use.

*Tom*

**What the experts say**
A well-timed joke raises the spirits of the whole birth team and breaks the monotony of a long, tedious labour.

William Sears MD and Martha Sears RN (*The Birth Book – Everything You Need to Know to have a Safe and Satisfying Birth*)

Although a man cannot ensure that everyone is quiet during contractions, he can indicate politely by his own silence and attention to her that he is not available for conversation during contractions and by doing this can help her to enter a 'circle of solitude' with him and the baby who is coming to birth.

Sheila Kitzinger (*The Experience of Childbirth*)

**My best friend asked me** to be her birthing partner for her little boy as her partner was squeamish. I had to be there in case he passed out. It was the most amazing experience I'd ever had. Whenever she wanted something, there was always someone to give it to her and she was never left alone. I helped her in and out the shower after the birth whilst the father got to know his new son. I took their first family photo and was the first person outside their family to hold the baby. Her partner was fine and didn't waiver one bit at the sight of the placenta being delivered, which I found quite horrible.

*EmmaTMG*

**My husband was just amazing.** We had talked both labours through in advance, so he knew exactly what I wanted. They were very keen to give me an epidural first time but I really didn't want it and he was able to explain my wishes. The second time they were going to do an episiotomy. He was able to explain to the midwife how I would rather have a tear than a cut. It was helpful to have a real advocate, someone who could talk for me when I couldn't!

*Susanmt*

**I don't know how** I would have got through my two labours without my partner. Not only was he brilliant at getting me to relax, but his presence meant that I could concentrate on the business in hand and be sure that he wouldn't let anyone do anything that I didn't want. He made me feel really safe – he'd done his homework and knew what was going on. He was absolutely vital to me and helped to make both experiences about as good as anything so painful could be! So all you dads just remember – whatever your partner says to you in the heat of the moment, the fact that you're there and trying to help really means something.

*Azzie*

# Vitamin K – should you let your baby have it after birth and if so, should you opt for injection or oral vaccine?

**Vitamin K is given post-delivery,** to combat the effects of Haemorrhagic Disease of the Newborn – which is extremely rare – more 'common' in premature babies, or those who have a more traumatic delivery (i.e. forceps) – but even then extremely rare. It is a clotting factor which babies lack. Most units offer Vitamin K by injection as the routine, but it can also be given orally, if requested. A study in the early 1990s by Professor Jean Golding suggested a link between Vitamin K given by injection and childhood leukaemia. The study was leaked before it could be completed, and thus it never could be completed, as it caused a storm of controversy. Lots of units went over to giving Vitamin K orally as a safeguard until further tests were carried out. Subsequent research has not proven a link.

*Leese*

**I opted for oral vitamin K** as I felt it was less traumatic for my sons than having a needle stuck in them when they'd just been born. I also didn't want to take even a theoretical risk of a link with childhood leukaemia.

*SoupDragon*

**My son had the jab.** Quite frankly, a little pin prick after a three-day labour, being stuck and squeezed and finally an emergency C-section, hardly seemed a big deal to me or to him. I was just pleased that they were giving him something that would prevent something nasty.

*Ghosty*

---

**What the experts say**
We don't yet know which is the safest way of giving vitamin K, whether by injection or by mouth.

NHS (*The Pregnancy Book*)

---

**In theory, the jab should only be necessary** if the baby has a traumatic birth (e.g. trauma to the brain from forceps or ventouse) or it doesn't breastfeed straight away as colostrum contains lots of Vitamin K, but if the mother has a diet which is low in vitamin K, then her colostrum would also be low in it. So you could always plan on oral vitamin K, and then opt for the jab if the birth is problematic. The jab is supposed to be absorbed more quickly.

*Zebra*

**I opted for oral vitamin K** although I was told it was fairly unnecessary. I am a non-meat eater although I eat fish and had a healthy diet whilst pregnant and an un-traumatic home birth. I also felt it was less traumatic for a newborn than an injection.

*Calcium*

> **Mumsnet fact**
> In a study the oral administration of Vitamin K rose from none in 1970 to 58 per cent in 1993. The proportion of babies routinely given intramuscular Vitamin K increased from 23 per cent in 1970 to 58 per cent in 1982 and dropped to 38 per cent in 1993.
> Neonatal Nurses' Association Survey

**My son had vitamin K orally** as well. The only problem we had was that neither the doctor nor the midwife had ever had anyone request the oral solution before, so they had to look up on the Internet how to do it.

*Megg*

**I was concerned that oral** administration whilst breastfeeding could be tricky and also that my baby, who was very sicky, may have brought the vitamin K back up and thus negated the good effect.

*Clary*

---

**What the experts say**
[Vitamin K] can be given orally but it is not so well absorbed into the body this way and will need repeat doses at one and two months.
Kaz Cooke (*The Rough Guide to Pregnancy and Birth*)

---

**Vitamin K was introduced** because babies who developed haemorrhagic disease of the newborn (HDN) invariably died. I have read that in Australia, when oral vitamin K was introduced, the number of babies who developed bleeding problems increased so the policy was changed back to the injection. The injection is a one-off and is more effective than the oral vitamin K, which needs to be given as three doses for breastfed babies. I give the vitamin K now when the babies are skin-to-skin after delivery with their mums and very few even cry. Being skin-to-skin has been shown to be less traumatic to the babies and breastfeeding is a painkiller. When I trained, only babies that were pre-term or were forceps/ventouse got the injection but that changed to all babies because some babies developed the disease after an uncomplicated delivery. Certainly, in the past, babies received it without parents' consent. That does not happen now – consent is always asked for.

*Mears*

**We decided not to give it to our children.** The first time we were told: 'This is what we do in this country.' The second time, the midwife was more sympathetic – she said, 'If you plan to stay at home and not transport your baby everywhere for the first weeks, then it should not be needed.' In several countries they do not give vitamin K.

*Pupuce*


**My oldest two didn't have vitamin K** as it wasn't in use then. When the leukaemia research was published I asked my GP if my daughter had received it in hospital and it turned out she had been given it without my knowledge or permission. I was so angry.

When my second daughter came along I looked into it and also asked every midwife I came across whether they had ever seen haemorrhagic disease in a healthy, full-term baby. None of them had, so I decided to decline the offer. The 'heavy brigade' was sent in after the birth to change our minds, but after I'd outlined our thoughts the paediatrician said, 'Fair enough. If you do decide you want it, just let your midwife know and she'll administer it', and left it at that.

*Baabaa*


**My son had a non-traumatic birth** and he was breast-fed immediately afterwards. I talked to my midwife and listened to the reasons for this vaccination, and didn't think my son was particularly at risk, which is why I 'opted out'. I was happy with my decision until a doctor came to see me and demanded to know why I had not given my son vitamin K – she really made me question my decision. My daughter, born four years ago by emergency C-section, was given the vitamin K as I thought she was more at risk.

*Hebe*


**I didn't feel particularly strongly** about vitamin K after my two were born, but my husband, who's a chemist, did not want them to have it. We were not 'allowed' home until he had had a careful discussion with the paediatrician about it, but he managed to argue his case and we were 'let off'. I was comforted to know that there is vitamin K in breast milk, so from the moment they are born, babies do start getting a natural source of vitamin K.

It does seem like a 'nanny state' reaction to deal with a tiny risk with a one-size-fits-all approach.

*Catt*

## Labour – was it as bad as you expected and what do you wish you'd known beforehand?

**Giving birth was nowhere near** as bad as I thought it would be. There were things I wished I'd done differently, like deciding beforehand whether to agree to have my waters broken, and discussing birth positions before the contractions got too close together for talking. But I can honestly say that, although of course it hurt, it wasn't the unbearable agony that I thought it might be. I'm a complete coward and planned to have an epidural if I felt I needed it, but it never got to the point where I couldn't cope.

*Jane101*

**You should be excited** rather than fearful. I think the worst thing is not knowing what will happen, so give in to that, go with the flow and you'll be fine. The best pain relief I had was when my partner started kissing me very gently. This obviously may not work for you, but think of the things that do work and go with those.

*Seapea*

---

**What the experts say**
Birth is surrounded with mystery, and people fear what they don't understand. Women who know more about birth fear it less.
William Sears MD and Martha Sears RN (*The Birth Book – Everything You Need to Know to have a Safe and Satisfying Birth*)

---

**The pain was, it has to be said,** quite frightening in that I felt I couldn't cope with it. But I felt so exhilarated by the whole experience that, after reliving it in my mind for the next 48 hours, I knew I would certainly not be put off having another go. And that cup of tea whilst being washed by the midwife was sheer heaven!

*Tinker*

**The first time round** I went into it thinking that it can't possibly be as bad as people suggest. I was then completely overwhelmed at how much it hurt. Second time around, though, I was far better prepared for it mentally and really didn't find it bad at all.

*Ringer2*

**Both of my experiences** were good (painful, but good). My second labour especially, because I had much more of a feeling of control – I knew what I was doing. At the end of both I felt very positive – sort of 'If I can do that, I can do anything.'

*Azzie*

**The midwife said to me,** 'If you run away from the pain it will follow you, but if you turn towards it, it can only reach halfway.' It was just what I needed to hear, and it really helped. I felt amazingly all-powerful after I had given birth.

*Sobernow*

**I loved giving birth!** Yeah, it hurt, but what an amazing experience! I had great care (even though I was in a big hospital) before, during and after. I was totally in control and everything went just the way I wanted it to, from the getting a good parking spot in the hospital (this was a big worry) to the pain relief.

*Philippat*

**Most people are surprised** when I say that giving birth wasn't too bad. I think they are used to all the horror stories. I also think my expectations were very low (possibly due to all the horror stories) so when everything went normally, it all seemed great to me! It was faster than I thought it would be, and although I had been saying I would have every sort of pain relief going, I had nothing at all, not even a gasp of gas and air.

*Whellid*

---

**What the experts say**
The intense and thrilling sensations of the descent of the baby's head, which can be not only painless, but enormously satisfying and enjoyable... again and again I have heard women describe the keen sensuous pleasure they obviously experienced – and which often surprised them with its delight; it is not a question of just feeling the contractions and knowing when to push, but of the gradual opening up of the vagina like the uncurling petals of a rose.

Sheila Kitzinger (*The Experience of Childbirth*)

The danger of linking sex with childbirth is that women who have yet to give birth only have their largely pleasurable experiences of sex to compare it with. Childbirth may be exhilarating, intense and extraordinary but for most women it isn't nearly as much fun as having sex.

Kate Figes (*Life After Birth*)

---

**I have never felt so alone** in my life, although my very supportive husband and two midwives were there. But it wasn't a lonely kind of alone. It was the kind of aloneness you feel when running a marathon or studying for an exam – determined and concentrated.

*Inga*

**Throughout each contraction** of my second labour I focussed on what my baby was going through as he was being squeezed and pushed out of me – the new sensations and the fear. I tried to send reassuring thought signals to him. Concentrating on him definitely distanced me from my pain.

*Frank1*

**One of the things** I found helpful after my first daughter's birth (which was pretty traumatic) was just writing down what had happened. Obviously, this depends on having the time and opportunity to do this (I was lucky as my daughter was a very obliging baby who slept a lot). I found that once I had put onto paper what had happened to me, I could mentally 'draw a line' under it, so to speak.

*Gillymac*

**I had two not so good labours** and I'd still go through it all again. You forget it so easily once you have your baby in your arms. The thought of the end result kept me going all the way through. Pain, for however long the labour is going to be, is worth it for a lifetime of happiness with your children.

*Floops*

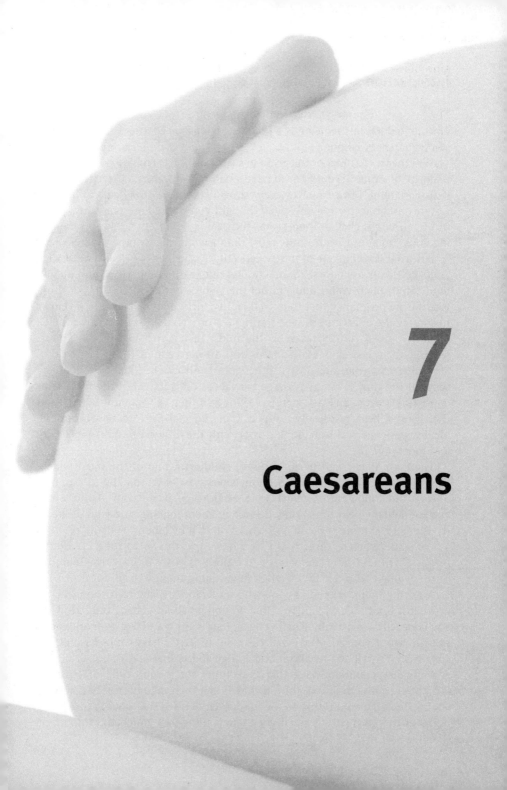

**7**

# Caesareans

# Introduction

The words 'Caesarean section' can inspire fear, disappointment or unbounded joy in the heart of a pregnant woman, depending on what stage of pregnancy or labour she is at.

Whether it's instinct or the result of brainwashing there's no doubt that the majority of women would opt to have a natural birth over a C-section – even if that 'natural' birth involves every drug at the midwife's disposal, an episiotomy and forceps. Whatever you thought you wanted pre-pregnancy, once those hormones click in there seems something definitely noble about pushing your child out with nothing more than a whiff of gas and air to help you.

But what if you're one of the 21 per cent (Department of Health figures for 2000–2001) of women in Britain who, for one reason or another, end up giving birth through your middle rather than where nature intended? For those told during pregnancy that their well-crafted birth plan will have to give way to surgery the effect can be devastating. For others, the decision to go the C-section route is hastily taken in the midst of chaotic or difficult labours (emergency Caesareans make up around 50 per cent of those carried out, according to Department of Health figures). Although, invariably, it made sense at the time and was perhaps crucial for the survival of the mother or child, Caesareans can leave women feeling as if they've somehow failed – and that they've been physically ravaged. Can you make a C-section a positive birth experience and how do you cope with the aftermath, both physically and mentally?

There are many myths surrounding childbirth, one of the most widely believed being that once a C-section, always a C-section. This is patently untrue, but following one birth by C-section, what are your chances of a vaginal delivery next time? How do you go about making sure your desire to try the natural route is heard and what is a 'trial by labour' really like?

For some women, though, a C-section is the answer to their childbirth prayers. Written off by some as the 'too posh to push' brigade, the majority of the women who opt for electives have sound mental or physical reasons for wanting them. Indeed anyone who undergoes a Caesarean soon discovers that it's not an easy option. How do you go about getting one? How do you cope with a new baby when you can hardly lift it and feel as if you might split in two if you do? And what can you do if you have an older child to cope with, as well as a newborn and a large abdominal scar?

Mumsnet members have had C sections for a multitude of reasons. Delighted or disappointed, they all have their own take on the best way of coping, but all would testify to the fundamental truth that once you're holding your newborn baby, how it got there is ultimately much less important than the fact that it's finally arrived.

# Having a caesarean – what's it really like?

**I had an elective C-section.** The operating theatre doesn't look that different to the labour rooms. There are quite a few people around – the surgeon, anaesthetists, nurses, etc. so it's fairly busy, but I found everyone friendly and unless you have to have a general anaesthetic you will be able to have your partner with you all the time to hold your hand and distract you. If you have an elective rather than an emergency you may have to wait a while as any emergencies take your place in the queue – which is understandable, I suppose, though I got very hungry! I was scheduled for the morning but didn't get seen until after 6 pm.

You sit up to have the anaesthetic (epidural or spinal), then you're asked to lie down and are tilted to one side, with a sort of wedge. An epidural is a constant drip of local anaesthetic so you remain attached during the op. A spinal block is a single injection of anaesthetic and works faster and wears off faster (usually about an hour). I really wanted a spinal block as I wanted to get the sensation back as soon as possible.

I don't remember feeling any pain whatsoever the first night (lovely morphine, I expect!). You have a catheter, but I have to say it didn't bother me, and you will be attached to a drip for a while too. Most units encourage you to be up and about within 24 hours. I had my section at 6.30 pm and was up the next day, feeling rather sore and walking like Quasimodo, but otherwise fine. The stitches are nothing really, and so low down in your bikini line that your scar will be hidden in your pubic hair (at least mine is) so it's nothing to worry about either. My top tip is to take a Walkman or a book or some mags into hospital with you. You can wait for hours and if you don't have much to do you can end up feeling nervous. Distraction is the key, I think.

*Aloha*

> **Mumsnet fact**
> At 21 per cent the UK has the third highest rate of caesarean sections in the world.
> *Practical Parenting* magazine

**I went to the hospital for a scan** and an hour later was having an emergency Caesarean. It feels like someone doing the washing up in your stomach and it is bizarre talking to people whilst someone is rummaging around inside you.

Surprisingly – having never been in hospital, let alone had major surgery – I recovered fine. I was up and about the next day. I was unable to have the surgical stockings so I needed to move to prevent blood clots. The only time I had some pain relief was in the evening as it helped me sleep. In fact, I got annoyed at continually being offered pain relief. I was tender but I think being aware of my stomach being tender helped me not to overdo it. My baby was in Special Care so they kept me in for five days before I finally convinced them to let me go home but I was able to lift her in and out of her incubator.

*Eidsvold*

**I had a semi-emergency C-section** after 24 hours in labour and those three dreaded words 'failure to progress'. I had never considered a C-section during my pregnancy and was not prepared for it. I will never forget the feeling of my innards being pulled left, right and centre, but the stitching was quick and my only regret is I don't remember my son being shown to me immediately afterwards, I was so spaced out. I hope to have a vaginal delivery next time but would have another C-section without hesitation if it were best for the baby.

*Donna1*

**I had an emergency C-section** for my first and only child. I was awake and I was scared! The actual operation did not hurt, but it was uncomfortable and, as everyone says, it felt like someone was doing the washing up in my stomach. Also, I nearly lost it when I heard the surgeon telling her colleague to move my bowel, but a bit of gas and air soon got me under control again.

*Batters*

**I had a fairly straightforward section** with my daughter. I had already been induced, drips, epidural, etc. so I was quite relieved as I was more frightened of the alternatives. The operation was a bit uncomfortable (a rummaging sensation) though I was fairly drugged up by then. It's all a bit of a haze and thankfully my husband videoed us in recovery as otherwise I would not have remembered much. My only regret was the surgeon's conversation meant we knew the sex before we could find out ourselves, so if that's important to you, mention it beforehand. I recovered well and the plus side was that because I was in hospital with nothing else to do, I cracked breastfeeding.

*CathB*

**My C-section was also** very straightforward and pretty lovely – on schedule, music in the background and a very calm atmosphere. I would say the sensation is a bit more uncomfortable than someone doing the washing up in your tummy, but certainly nothing like natural labour. The babies needed to go to special care but I still got a hug in before they were whisked away and everyone was very kind. My husband tells me he got to see the placenta and even my womb, which was lifted onto my stomach to be cleaned out apparently, so he clearly had an experience to remember in more ways than one!

*Nancy*

**I had an emergency C-section.** I was terrified – but there was no reason to be. It was fine and the moment I heard our beautiful daughter scream I forgot everything.

As for the birth, our doctor asked my hubby if he'd like to cut the cord (he said a very strong 'No'!) but I guess some people would love that and they handed the baby straight to me (lying down) so I got the first cuddle. The only disappointment for me was that I couldn't go to the nursery to see her being weighed, etc. but my husband took the video camera and videoed the whole thing, which was great and a top tip.

*Sjs*

> **Mumsnet fact**
> 75 per cent of births in Brazil are by caesarean section. In the Netherlands the overall rate is less than 10 per cent.
>
> *Junior* magazine

**I found it very peculiar** going into hospital knowing I was having my baby that day, and walking into theatre. But it all went so well, and once the baby is out (and it takes no time at all), what does it matter? You're busy looking in awe at baby whilst they stitch you up, so it feels as though it takes no time at all.

*Maisy1*

**With two emergency C-sections** I was wide awake and able to hear my babies' first cries and see them but just not hold them – the first hold for dad. The hardest thing is having to stay in hospital for five days (the norm), especially if you have children at home. If it's your first then I'd recommend making the most of the help in hospital. Even though it's a major operation it's amazing how quickly you recover and are able to start caring for your baby yourself. I was on my own from the third/fourth week (respectively) and really looked forward to it.

*Rivi*

**I had an emergency section** and was terrified of it happening again. I wanted to try for a vaginal birth but my consultant told me of the risk of rupture, and that I would have to have an epidural in case of emergency again and I ended up having an elective section. This was an entirely different experience from the first time. The nurses were brilliant – lots of jokes, choice of music, lots of happy memories and being able to cuddle my son immediately. I recovered much more quickly and was home in three days.

*Sammac*

**When I had my third caesarean,** there was a training anaesthetist present who was observing my heart rate. He told me that as the baby was lifted out and cried, my heart rate practically doubled – I was completely unaware of it myself. So for those who might be disappointed not to be taking a more physical role in the proceedings, don't worry, the rest of you is right in there!

*Janh*

**My second C-section** was a fantastic experience, although most of my pregnancy was ruined by worry that my consultant wouldn't let me have one. The first elective C-section was for a breech baby, the second purely my choice. I was frightened of the spinal block first time, and was shaking so much that they had to give me morphine as soon as my son was out, but second time around I was not at all scared and chatted to everyone throughout the procedure.

The spinal block is the oddest feeling. You can feel what they're doing, but not feel pain at all. I was given my baby to hold almost straight away, whilst they were still rummaging around inside me. If you want an elective C-section, demand it, and have it put in your notes that that is what you're demanding. After all, how likely are you to succeed at a vaginal birth if you don't actually want to?

*Paula1*

---

**Mumsnet fact**
Caesarean births have increased by 400 per cent in the UK since 1970.
*Daily Mail*

---

**I had an emergency C-section** after a very late discovery of a breech birth ('Oh here's the head, oh no it's not, it's a bum.'). The relief when the spinal took effect was worth the angst of having it put in whilst writhing in pain, and the joy of having a healthy baby is worth anything anyway. I had an elective second time around and the experience was so incredibly different. There's so much panic in an emergency, no time for polite conversation, intense pain (before the spinal takes effect) – it all happens so fast.

With the elective there is something weird about having your baby's birth date in your diary in advance and then going into an operating theatre physically well and stone cold sober – i.e. no adrenaline rush, contractions. You certainly have time to notice all the scary-looking implements being prepared. This anxiety was not helped for me by the fact that it took the anaesthetist seven goes to get the spinal in and at one point my husband had more medics around him than I did (he's not good with needles). The actual 'birth' was quick though (especially compared to full labour followed by C-section) and it's just lovely to walk into a calm environment and moments later be handed your baby.

*Biza*

**My caesarean was due to transverse lie.** I felt confident with the surgical team who handled my op (and sewed me up again when the first lot of stitching came undone three days later... bad 48 hours) but they were a charmless lot who did nothing to make me feel special or even that I was having a baby. One of them cheered up when they saw I'd had a boy as they'd had two boys already that morning and there was a sweepstake on whether number three would also be male.

The anaesthetists were kindness personified, as was the midwife who had had two C-sections herself. But no holding the baby for me; no favourite CD or attempt at making me feel in any way part of the goings-on; no effort made apart from showing him to me to acknowledge the fact I'd given birth. I didn't even get to touch him until an hour later.

Neither of us would have made it through a natural delivery so I am grateful we are both here to tell the tale but it is quite possible to go into an operating theatre a healthy, carefree soul, and come out wondering if you will ever feel well again.

*Clare2*

**I've had two emergency Caesareans** and got infections both times. After the first I was unable to function normally for several months, although the second was much better. However, the second one followed a truly awful labour – it was absolute agony and I can say nothing positive about the pain having been 'worth it' (since I ended up with a C-section anyway). I still wish I had had a vaginal delivery, though, simply because I saw friends a day or so after a 'natural' delivery and they were pretty much back to normal, whereas 10 days after my C-section I was still on high levels of painkillers. I think a lot of people choose elective C-sections out of fear, and that if they were properly informed and supported they might choose differently.

*Amber1*

**I have had two C-sections.** The first was emergency after a failed 32-hour labour. I had a choice with the second, and decided to have an elective. Nature had other ideas, and I went into labour two days before the surgery date. I decided to see how it went, but it became apparent the same problems were occurring, so I was booked for a C-section later that day. When the surgeon made his incision he found I had extensive scar tissue from my previous C-section and it took a long time to get the baby out. (It's horrid I know, but my bladder was adhered to my uterus). I had many post-op infection problems and a recent laparoscopy shows the adhesions are now so bad I could be at risk of an ectopic pregnancy if we had a third child (not likely!).

*Tania*

## Elective C-sections – should you opt for one and if so how do you go about it?

**I have had two elective C-sections** because of problems with raised blood pressure and pre-eclampsia. I took all the medication on offer, including lots of morphine when it was 'on tap'. I reckon any good hospital will get you up and about quickly and it's really not too bad. But it's a major op and a big decision to choose to go through one unless there is some definite medical reason. I sometimes feel sad that I didn't have a vaginal birth – but I try to concentrate on the here and now. I have two lovely healthy kids.

*Kathmary*

**I often wonder if we place too much** emphasis on having a 'correct' birth experience (no pain relief, vaginal delivery, instant bonding, etc.), which makes some women feel like failures if they don't achieve all those things. A friend recently had her first baby in three hours flat with no pain relief (due to speed not inclination!) and is the heroine of her NCT class. Lots of congratulations on doing it 'the best way', but as she says, 'It wasn't anything to do with me!' Others who ended up having a C-section, having planned for ecstatic hypno-birth (seriously!), feel ashamed and as if they have had the 'wrong' kind of birth.

As for recovery, my friend with the fast natural delivery (who feels great and would opt to do it again the same way) is only now, two weeks on, able to walk more than 100 yards without a lot of discomfort from stitches. I recovered just as fast – if not faster – from my very expertly done C-section. It's not a clear-cut issue but I think it does women no favours to imply that natural birth is always a lovely experience and that if it isn't, or you have another kind of delivery, that you have failed or had a second-class experience.

People have asked me if I would recommend an elective C-section. I've never been in labour so I honesty can't pretend to know which is best and there are pros and cons. The longer stay in hospital can be a big factor and not everyone recovers as fast or as well as I did and it certainly isn't a pain-free option, but I do think that how our babies arrive is of very little importance compared to what happens when they get here!

*Aloha*

---

**Mumsnet tip**

If you're feeling disappointed about your birth experience try and remember that birth is nothing really and babies are everything. We spend at most a day or so giving birth, we spend the rest of our lives being mothers. That's the important bit.

*Nick*

**Before both my labours** at about 38 weeks or so I wanted a C-section, I was petrified of the pain. Luckily the support I got from midwives and friends gave me the courage to face my fears and I am so happy I have been able to have vaginal births. My first labour was hell but still I did it again. Second time around was far easier, just as painful but much shorter. We should spend more time listening to women who are scared of labour rather than showing them the theatre door.

*Thewiseone*

**I was determined to avoid a C-section** because it's a major operation. If I'd pushed for it I expect I'd have got one (older mother, large babies common in my family, baby lying badly). Instead I had a very difficult vaginal delivery – the local anaesthetic didn't work for the episiotomy and I couldn't be stitched straight away as there was an emergency Caesarean. I got terrible bruising, infected stitches and took longer to recover than the mothers who'd had Caesareans.

By the time I'd recovered – and I was lucky in the sense that the damage wasn't permanent/didn't need another operation – it was a bit late to think about another child. So I think vaginal deliveries can be over-rated and there is something to be said for elective caesareans.

*Robinw*

**It is perhaps worth noting** that repeat C-sections carry with them increased risks. As a midwife I have seen women request Caesareans following a traumatic first delivery assuming it is routine and risk-free. Unfortunately the resultant C-section has been more traumatic than expected and a decision regretted. First labours can often be a harder experience than expected but often the second experience is much better. The Caesarean is a wonderful mode of delivery when needed due to whatever complication for mother or baby but I do get annoyed when I see 'routine caesarean' written about. Major abdominal surgery is never routine.

*Mears*

**Mumsnet fact**
Although very rare, death of the mother is four times more likely in Caesarean sections than in vaginal deliveries.
**NHS website**

**Those of us who might be** classed as anti-elective Caesarean believe that our bodies were designed to do this job and in an ideal situation can get on with it relatively unhindered. There is no getting away from the fact that you are opting for a major, invasive procedure, when you may not need any medical intervention at all.

*Emmagee*

**It absolutely infuriates me** when people try to persuade women that the 'natural' birth option is the one we should all opt for. My first birth was a truly traumatic experience ending in a forceps delivery with episiotomy and a 3rd–4th degree tear (they couldn't decide which). For those not acquainted with 3rd-degree tears, they are a tear from the vagina right up to and into the anal sphincter. The Royal College of Gynaecologists recommends counselling and offering a C-section to any expectant mother who has suffered a third-degree tear. They go on to say that any subsequent vaginal deliveries may worsen anal incontinence.

I therefore subsequently decided to go for an elective Caesarean. However, I have come under enormous pressure from friends and relatives to opt for another vaginal delivery and being asked to explain my choice of a C-section means I have to talk about my problems with anal incontinence, often to people I don't even know very well. Many friends have spent hours trying to persuade me to have another vaginal delivery. These are, of course, the people who have a five-hour labour and are in Sainsbury's three days later.

*Anto*

**If the medical profession** is all for elective Caesareans (and I know two doctors who have gone for this option) then surely there must be something going for it? As I see it, if the quality of life in western civilization has improved sufficiently that women no longer have to suffer incredible pain to give birth, then whoopee!

*Berta*

**Speaking as someone who's had both** an elective caesarean – my waters broke at 30 weeks and as my twins were very small it was the safest option – followed by a vaginal birth (albeit with tons of pain relief) with my third child, personally I'd recommend the 'natural' route. The Caesarean was calm, relaxed and relatively pain-free, whilst the vaginal delivery was lengthy, pretty painful and involved quite a lot of stitching up.

I recovered much quicker from the vaginal birth, however – I was out of hospital in less than a day and up and about almost immediately – whereas with the Caesarean I was in hospital for five days and felt like an invalid for weeks – not surprisingly as it's major surgery. There is also something very wonderful about pushing the baby out yourself – it does feel right. Having said that, it comes down to the individual. I can quite understand that if you've had a traumatic time trying to deliver naturally you might opt for an elective next time and it can still be an enjoyable and fulfilling experience.

*Nancy*

**I had an emergency C-section** with my first and was absolutely terrified with number two. I was taken in with high blood pressure and asked the doctor if he would perform another C-section, partly because I was scared and partly because we had recently moved away from any family and it would have been nice to schedule the delivery when number one was safely at nursery. The doctor said 'No', which upset me a bit, but in the end a new friend offered to have my son when the time came and two days later, I gave birth with gas and air and an epidural. The feeling of having pushed him out has never left me and I am so pleased I have 'done it both ways', although I wouldn't want the emergency C-section option again.

*Coxy*

**I had an emergency C-section first time** having reached 10 cm dilated without pain relief (undiagnosed breech). I was petrified I'd be forced to try for a vaginal birth second time round. My GP was surprisingly supportive but then she'd seen the effect a bad labour had had on me. At the hospital I 'put my case' early on and they said to wait until 34 weeks and see how I felt about it. When the time came I took my husband (a lawyer) in, who was all ready to say he'd sue the pants off them if they refused a C-section (as they'd cocked up so badly first time round). In the event it wasn't necessary. I told the two (male) doctors in the bluntest possible terms the effect the last labour had on my sex life and mental health, and that there was no way I was leaving that room without an okay to a C-section.

If you feel strongly, stick to your guns. I don't think legally they can refuse you and if one consultant does, just keep on asking for a second opinion. The birth experience with the elective was fantastic in comparison to the emergency – no pain, quick, calm and lovely. The pain comes afterwards and is significant. Although I seemed to have made a speedy recovery – out and at a party two days later – in retrospect I was up and about too soon (I was eager to be home with my toddler). My surface wound started gaping after a week and I had to lie down for a few days. Incidentally the woman opposite me had just had her fifth C-section – and had children aged 18, 17, 10, 8 and a new baby. She was tired but fine!

*Biza*

**I had a C-section at 38 weeks** (due to my son being breech) and would definitely have another one. I was up and about within about 5–6 hours of giving birth, sitting down was a lot easier for me than for the girls who had given birth 'naturally' and I was out of hospital within two days. I had a spinal block and I won't pretend that bit was pleasant – it was very scary – but I think that it was definitely worth it. People talk about it being major abdominal surgery (which I can't deny), but it didn't really feel like major surgery. I hadn't had a general anaesthetic, pain was controlled with pills, and generally it was a very positive experience.

The thought of an emergency Caesarean fills me with dread and I think that is where some of the negative feedback about Caesareans arises from as maybe many of the women have already been through hours of labour before having the operation. After talking to friends I have no intention of giving birth naturally next time and will go private if my consultant won't support me.

*Paula1*

**What the experts say**
You will be asked to consider the difficulties of coping with a newborn baby while recovering from major abdominal surgery. When you have discussed your idea with your consultant and have heard in detail the other side of the argument, you may find that you want to reconsider your decision.
Adriana Hunter (*The Queen Charlotte's Guide to Pregnancy & Birth*)

**You shouldn't have to go private** to get an elective Caesarean. If you feel very strongly about having a Caesarean then it would be difficult for a consultant to refuse you. Even if they did, you could always ask to see another.

I had a bad birth experience first time round. I was so badly bruised internally it took seven months for the pain to finally go and my stitches were so tight it took five months for those to stop tugging. I had my birth plan all written out, I had read the books about holding my baby's hand in my mind and to imagine my cervix unfurling like a tulip, I had drunk raspberry leaf tea, done my pelvic floor exercises religiously and attended two sets of antenatal classes. I was not frightened, I felt calm and well prepared. I will most definitely be opting for an elective Caesarean, should we be lucky enough to have another child and I won't be sad to be missing a vaginal birth. I will be relieved.

*Molly1*

**I had a horrible first delivery** (induced at 42 weeks, failed ventouse and emergency Caesarean with 10 lb 3 oz baby). The hospital has already suggested another C-section and I'm tempted to accept. I suppose technically this would be for 'medical reasons', but for me the considerations are also about 'better the devil you know' and I have a sneaking feeling (that I hate to admit to...) of 'Well, I've already got a scar... why ruin another part of my body?'

*MotherofOne*

**What the experts say**
[Some] choose a Caesarean because they are told they can keep a tight vagina and well-toned pelvic floor that way. Unfortunately, it does not work like this. Just being pregnant may put stress on those muscles, especially if the baby is big.
Sheila Kitzinger (*The New Pregnancy and Childbirth*)

Caesarean: operation to remove baby from the womb resulting in normal and perfect, uncomplicated sex life resuming in no time at all. Celebrate!
Penny Wilson (*Wipe: Survival Tactics for Parents with Attitude*)

**I chose to have an elective Caesarean** after having an emergency one the first time round. The elective one turned out to be far more traumatic than the emergency one had been and I'm not sure that I would choose that route again. I believe that too little is known about the dangers involved in having a Caesarean. I experienced very heavy bleeding post op and no one knew what the problem was. I was told that I needed to go back to the theatre and if the cause of the bleeding could not be found, I would need to have a hysterectomy.

In the end it wasn't so bad – the problem was caused by part of the placenta being left behind. Due to the complications/trauma it took a lot longer to recover from the second Caesarean – five days later and I could still only shuffle around. If you choose the elective route, make sure that your consultant discusses all the possibilities with you and make sure that you are prepared for them.

*Wendy*

**Mumsnet fact**
At London's Portland Hospital, 44 per cent of babies are delivered by caesarean section, most of which are elective.
*The Sunday Times Good Birth Guide*

**I had a planned C-section** due to placenta praevia – so it saved my life and my son's. But apart from that, I thought it was a great way to give birth. He was a big baby but I didn't have a moment's pain. I went into the theatre (which didn't look like one), I was a bit nervous but not afraid, the epidural took beautifully and I felt absolutely nothing – not even a rummage. It was very calm and yet very emotional, my husband was right next to me and we were both crying – my son was beautiful, noisy and had no problems whatsoever, despite being three weeks early. My consultant was able to deliver him onto my tummy and I was able to hold him and feed him right away. I was up the next day and out of pain in three days. I was totally fine and back to normal in two weeks – yes, driving and lifting and everything. My scar is in my pubic hair, and frankly, so few people see down there I never give it a thought. I think so many problems connected with C-sections are due to them being emergencies after horrible labours and many interventions. I lost quite a lot of blood in mine, but that was due to the placenta, not the op and I'd have lost a hell of a lot more with a 'normal' delivery. In fact, I may well have bled to death.

Most people who have a vaginal delivery seem to have tears and stitches – yet nobody goes on about scars and stitches and infections when discussing this type of birth. I'd rather have a controlled cut than a nasty great tear in the most sensitive bit of my anatomy.

*Wells1*

**My first baby was emergency Caesarean**, all very quick and scary after 13 hours of labour. I think because I was so tired I didn't really feel that I was there and it all just happened around me. Because of all the traumas of birth one I was advised to have a Caesarean for birth two, apparently I could have had a trial of labour but the same problems may well have occurred. So I was booked in, which was the strangest feeling. It really did feel as if giving birth was pencilled into the diary. Husband was booked off work, other son was all sorted out at nursery, life felt strangely organized! Going into 'the room' to have my spinal block felt very surreal, especially compared to the panic of the previous time.

I had made a compilation tape, which 'the team' thought was great because they'd had the same Christmas carols tape going for days! When baby was born, the chief man came out of his office asking who I would like to phone. I said, 'My mum' and he produced this phone, dialled my number, and my mum heard the first cries and me sobbing, 'It's a boy, mum, and I've just had him.' Wonderful moment! My husband and I cuddled him whilst I was stitched up.

*Maisy1*

## Recovering from a C-section – how do you cope with the physical and emotional aftermath?

**I think I was very lucky** with my C-section as I had no problems at all, apart from the first couple of days in hospital when I was a little drowsy (I'd had a general anaesthetic). I have a very modest scar and experienced no real discomfort. I stayed in hospital five days, mostly due to my son losing weight so we weren't 'allowed' out. I was home on day six and cooking lunch for guests on day seven.

*Lindy*

**I had an elective C-section,** and was out of hospital in three days. Looking back, I thought that I was a lot better than I actually was. However, I got around really well, and didn't really do anything different to people I know that have given birth naturally. One thing that I would have asked for (if I had realized that it was available) was for the midwives to look after the baby on the first night. I was in a communal ward with just curtains between me and the next person, so every time a baby snuffled/cried, I thought it was my baby, struggled out of bed (which took a while), discovered it wasn't my baby and got back into bed – only for the same thing to happen all night long. Then I had the weepies all the second day.

*Paula1*

**I had two C-sections,** both emergencies for different reasons. What really helps is having friends/family around who can run errands for you. Also accept that to heal quickly you should not be jumping up and down too soon (especially stairs). They told me that stairs would be tricky for about 10 days but I felt able to go up and down earlier than that.

The best advice for recovery is to walk a little and rest a lot. Don't stretch and allow others to pass the baby to you and put the baby down again in the first 24 hours. You can't get out of bed for 24 hours but the painkillers are effective and both times the medics stressed the need not to suffer.

*Rivi*

> **Mumsnet tip**
> If you've had a C-section, keep a changing set upstairs and one downstairs, so that you keep the going up and downstairs to a minimum.
>
> *Biza*

**Get as much help as you can** lifting the baby. Take it slowly, if you think you're fine and then overdo it slightly, the wound won't thank you. I went shopping soon after I was out of hospital. I walked slowly from the car to the shops, arrived in pain and sat on a bench whilst my husband shopped. Then I hobbled back to the car in agony. That made me stop and think, 'Hang on, I've had surgery here!'

The first 24 hours you can't do much, but the nurses soon help you up and out of bed, though you think you will never be able to walk again! You hate them at the time, but walking little and often really helps the healing.

I had the baby in bed with me for half of the first night, which saved getting him in and out of the cot. There were other Caesarean mothers in the ward, so those of us who had been in a while would help those who had just had their babies.

As for driving, they say if you feel you can manage a hard emergency stop, then you should be okay. I could drive after five or six weeks, but before that I would have feared injury or pain if something difficult had arisen.

*Maisy1*

**Accept all help and pain relief** going (just think what you would normally do if you had had major surgery). Don't do anything but look after the baby and yourself and sleep as much as possible. The first night, the hospital offered to take the baby so I could sleep and to bring her back if she cried. I said 'No', feeling I wanted her by my side. It would probably have been better if I had accepted their offer because it was hard to sleep and I couldn't get up for her even if she needed me so I had to call a nurse anyway.

*Sjs*

> **Mumsnet tip**
> The best advice I got was to wear 'granny pants' – the big ones that come over your tummy and hips – they don't hurt or restrict your scar and look great on the washing line!
> *Maisy1*

**You're told to take it easy,** no lifting anything heavier than your baby for six weeks. This is incredibly hard and means all sorts of things like hoovering and shopping are off-limits, so if you can get someone to help out it's really useful. Online shopping's a godsend but it's worth signing up in advance when your brain's less sleep-deprived.

*Janus*

**Arnica tablets are my top tip.** Take them from around three days before the operation to seven days afterwards. Within a day I was walking, holding and feeding my baby and had had a shower. I was in hospital three days altogether and was really scared about going home. But in the end I was fine, it was just me and my daughter as my partner had just started a new job and couldn't take more than a couple of days off.

*Batters*

**I have had two** and wished I could have managed a vaginal birth second time around but in the end I was up after four hours, out of hospital in four days (I wanted to go home earlier but wasn't allowed) and driving in less than two weeks. There are some benefits to Caesareans, but I wouldn't choose to have a blooming great scar!

*Crunchie*

**I found the C-section itself no problem** but the aftermath quite a trial. Initially, I felt pretty disabled and being attached to all that stuff – drain for the wound, catheter, etc. was a pain. It also took me a long time to recover and my scar, five years later, is still quite red and angry in places. I got a terrible backache (possibly from the epidural) that lasted about a month after the birth and my scar was tender and sensitive for about a year – I remember cowering when my babies (twins) wanted to climb on me. I found I was up and about the next day no problem, but I was still hobbling around a bit for the next two weeks and that made me feel a bit low.

*Nancy*

**I wouldn't want anyone to think** C-sections are the 'easy way out' – it is major surgery. I had a home birth booked for my first, but at full dilation they found she was breech, so I was whisked into hospital and had an emergency Caesarean. I know that many of my negative feelings are to do with the fact that I was unprepared for it and that it was the exact opposite of what I wanted, but I also didn't enjoy being so crippled with the pain and being whacked out on morphine for the first 24 hours.

*Emmagee*

**I had an emergency Caesarean.** Having had a big, heavy baby I found holding him to breastfeed put pressure on my scar and hurt – one of those v-shaped pillows in front of me for support was a great help. I wore short Lycra aerobic shorts under some jogging pants if I had to move around much/go out, but it's also important to get air to the scar too, so I tried to wear looser clothes around the house.

I was worried about how the scar would look but they really do fade – two years on and mine is very pale and not massively noticeable. It's not nearly as horrific as you might imagine beforehand, and as a nurse friend (and mother) said to me, 'It's probably the only productive type of surgery where you get something nice to keep after they have removed it!'

*MotherofOne*

## Vaginal birth after a C-section (VBAC) – is it possible and what's it like?

**I was keen to have a natural birth** second time around after my twins had been born very early by Caesarean because of complications. The midwives/doctors were very supportive, though I wasn't allowed to be in the midwife-led birthing centre and try for a water birth, as I would have liked. When it came to the birth, the first midwife I had was pretty negative. Her first words were: 'You do know you'll have to be hooked up to the monitor constantly and won't be able to move from the bed', because of the risk of scar rupture.

Luckily the midwives changed shifts and the next one was more experienced. We agreed that we'd just monitor every hour or so – she told me that if a doctor came in to say I'd just been to the loo. Once I was able to move around during the contractions I was much happier and more able to deal with the pain. I had a long labour – 24 hours – but not complicated. Thankfully the staff gave me every chance to deliver naturally, which I did, eventually, and it was wonderful.

*Roberta*

**I had an emergency Caesarean** under epidural with my first baby and was given the option of choosing an elective for the second. I didn't choose it as the first experience was not pleasant and I didn't want to go through the difficult recovery with a toddler. I had another epidural the second time but it was much better. I ended up with stitches after forceps, which was sore but I recovered much more quickly.

*Ginette*

**I had an elective first time** round because my baby was breech. It went well and was a positive experience, but I was determined to try for a natural birth second time round, mainly because I couldn't bear the thought of not being able to pick up my toddler.

I had an excellent antenatal teacher who explained how your body is designed to give birth naturally and how your hormones kick in to help you. She gave me the courage and determination to do it. Although I was in labour for a long time and I had to agree to be put on a drip to speed things up, I got by without an epidural and I had a lovely normal birth. I was thrilled to be home the next day. As far as giving birth is concerned, an elective under epidural/spinal block is obviously easier, but recovery is slow – after all, it is major abdominal surgery. However, the feeling of satisfaction after a natural delivery is unbeatable and I'm glad I did it.

*Giskin*

> **Mumsnet fact**
> The main risk associated with trying for a vaginal birth after a caesarean is that of the scar rupturing. But the chances of a rupture are rare – about one woman in 300.
>
> VBAC.com

**I had an emergency C-section** with my first child, which was absolutely awful (everything got infected and the cut had to be reopened). I then had three 'natural' deliveries after that, although for the second child I had to beg the gynaecologist to allow me to have a natural delivery as there is only a 21-month gap between the two. It took me months to recover from the C-section but the recoveries after the 'normal' deliveries were much faster and much easier.

*Sprocket*

**Having one C-section** does not commit you to having another second time around if the factors present for the first one are not there, but having a second C-section does. In many cases there is no reason why there should not be a trial of labour. You won't know if you don't try.

*Mears*

**I had a pretty awful time** first time round ending in an emergency C-section. I found it very shocking and had lots of flashbacks, etc. I was quite nervous with number two but had very laidback midwives, who let me go at my pace. Baby two was born without assistance (I had an epidural) after nine hours. It was so much better than the first time and the recovery rate was much quicker.

*Baggie*

**I had a VBAC** and am thrilled that I pushed for it. The midwife explained that the danger with a VBAC is the possibility of rupture of the C-section scar tissue in the uterus during labour. The best way to avoid this is to do constant monitoring during labour and the best way to keep you still in order to do this is to hook you up to an epidural. However, all the research indicates that women on epidurals are much more likely to end up having C-sections because they aren't walking around. I decided that the risks involved in a C-section are higher than the risks involved in a scar rupture (even if there is a rupture, it doesn't necessarily mean problems for the mother/baby). I had only gas and air and was only in labour for 51/2 hours (versus 40 hours the first time). I actually had a haemorrhage after the birth but it turned out to be unrelated to the previous C-section.

*SofiaAmes*

**What the experts say**
Only about one woman in four who had a Caesarean with one birth even tries for a VBAC (vaginal birth after Caesarean) with her next.

Sheila Kitzinger (*The New Pregnancy and Childbirth*)

**Having had one emergency C-section,** I really wanted a vaginal delivery second time around and got myself into a birthing centre (no doctors, no epidurals just birthing pools, aromatherapy, etc.) to try to get it. But my labour was exactly the same – fully dilated fairly quickly (eight hours or so) and then several hours pushing with the baby not even properly engaged at the end of it. Sometimes even the best will in the world just won't help.

The upside of the second time was that it was comparatively guilt-free – I knew that I had done everything I could. The downside was that in an attempt to stay active and maximize chances of a vaginal delivery I didn't get an epidural until I had been in second stage for one and a half hours. The pain was indescribable – I was honestly trying to figure out if I could throw myself out of the window without anyone catching me. So, far from the warm and fuzzy experience I had hoped a natural delivery would be, I had an extremely traumatic labour, which passed every extreme of pain and horror I could possibly have imagined beforehand. It was undoubtedly the worst experience of my life.

The interesting thing was that the second C-section was much easier to recover from – largely due to the fact that I had better support in hospital – for example, the nurses raised and lowered the bed for breastfeeds and changed nappies for the first day. First time around I was on my feet, lifting babies, cranking beds, etc. within hours of the operation.

*Amber1*

**I really wanted to go the natural route** – yoga, antenatal classes, no pain relief, water birth, etc. and I ended up with an emergency C-section and a very long recovery time – months and months. All very disappointing and shocking and painful.

But then I had a second baby with no pain relief – the 'natural' birth I'd wanted (without the water). I have to say it was bloody awful, zillions of stitches and a really long recovery time too! I was glad that I could give it a go, but if I had a third I may consider elective Caesarean.

My top tip after a stressful first birth is to try and get an appointment with someone to get a debrief. I didn't and really wish I had. It would definitely have helped to have had some answers to all my questions.

*Monkey*

> **Mumsnet fact**
> Vaginal birth after a caesarean can be achieved in around two thirds of cases.
>
> *Practical Parenting* magazine

**I wanted so much to deliver** my second child 'naturally' that I even hired an independent midwife and planned a home birth to give myself what I considered the best possible chance. When I went overdue I decided to opt for induction in hospital (waters broken – no induction drugs) and went into labour rapidly. Unfortunately the second labour was identical to the first and I simply couldn't get him out, so after pushing for more than two hours we went for another C-section.

When someone recently asked if I was disappointed to have had another C-section, I said 'No', because at least only one part of my body had been ruined by childbirth – my pelvic floor muscles were in good shape.

*Mo2*

**I had an emergency C-section** for my first, and delivered 'naturally' for my second. It was very quick – and extremely painful. I still have pain 'down there' and sex is really painful. If I do have a third it'll definitely be an elective Caesarean. I was really scared about giving birth for the first time with my second baby and I wish I hadn't been so determined. I don't mean to be negative, but I think folks deserve honest answers from lots of different perspectives.

*Bo*

**I've had four C-sections!** My first delivery was a non-emergency emergency section. The doctor decided the baby was stressed and should be delivered (she was fine, just small). As I had a transverse scar (rather than vertical, which carries a greater risk of rupture), I was allowed to have a trial of labour with my second – my doctor never mentioned any danger of rupturing. However after two prostaglandin pessaries had no effect at all I actually asked for another section, which I had never intended to do. I was disappointed at the time but I don't care now! Having had only sections and no labour at all I have never had any pain or problems 'down there'.

*Janh*

> **Mumsnet fact**
> Successful vaginal births have been achieved in women who have had three or more caesareans.
>
> *AIMS*

**Having had an emergency C-section** I was undecided whether to have an elective or try for a 'natural' second birth. In the event I went into labour naturally and coped with gas and air before having a low-dose epidural, which meant I was still able to move and stand up even with a foetal head monitor. All was going well and in seven hours I had reached 10 cm and was ready to push. The baby's head, however, was stuck in the pelvis and the baby was showing signs of distress, so out came the knife.

It was disappointing but at least only seven hours as opposed to 37 with my last child – I felt very positive and in control of the labour (unlike last time) and understood a Caesarean to be the safest option and one I was familiar with. A month on and it doesn't seem to matter anymore – everyone is just one happy family!

*Lezlee*

**8**

# Coming Home

# Introduction

So the big event is over – all that preparation and anticipation and you've finally met your lovely little bundle(s) and perhaps even got round to giving him/her/them a name. You have a few moments to bask in the miracle of it all and then the realization dawns. This isn't the end of the questions and anxiety; it's only the beginning.

Being a first- (or even a second-, third- or more) time parent is like being plunged into the toughest of tough new jobs whilst recovering from climbing Everest (with or without gas and air). Whilst the most precious bits of your anatomy are tender, leaking or downright hurting, you're being subjected to sleep-deprivation techniques that medieval torturers would have been proud of. You're most likely chuffed to bits but that doesn't stop the first days being more than a little bit scary.

When should you go home if you had your baby in hospital? And what if your baby has to stay because of health difficulties – how do you cope with having a baby in Special Care? Or perhaps all didn't go quite according to your carefully crafted birth plan – are there any coping mechanisms that can help you come to terms with a traumatic birth?

The nine months you spent reading every magazine article and book you could lay your hands on and trotting off to antenatal classes were all geared to preparing you for labour and birth, but how on earth do you survive the first night, let alone a whole week of actual parenthood? And what of your partner (if you have one)? You've done the hard labour – but what can they do – or specifically not do – to help you recover?

Perhaps birth wasn't a new experience and you had been there, done that before – but dealing with a newborn and an older child is completely different to being able to indulge a single baby's every whim. Where do you start?

Then there's the thorny and emotive issue of how you're going to feed your little mite. Breast or bottle? If breast – how do you get started and, once started, continue even if it's hard going? If, for whatever reason, you choose bottle-feeding, how do you cope with censure (real or imagined) from the medical profession or your peers? And what's the best approach to the military operation that is sterilizing and preparing enough feeds for the day (and night!).

The great news is you've made it this far. You've had your baby(ies) and that makes all the anxiety of pregnancy worthwhile. The other great news is that when the going gets tough – which, with sore nipples, sleepless nights, stitches and everything that goes with being a new parent, it inevitably will – there are plenty of folks on mumsnet, who have been or are going through exactly the same traumas and who are only too happy to offer advice, support and a (posset-stained) shoulder to cry on.

# Hospital – when should you go home?

**When I had my first child** a five-day hospital stay was usually the norm but I had a couple of days each with my first two. Times had changed by the time I had my third child – I was only in hospital for four hours. It was nice to go home and settle straight into a routine and have my home comforts around me. I think it depends on the individual but in my opinion, the less time in hospital the better. Let's face it, hospital food is disgusting and the places are full of infections.

*Doormat*

**I think more people would stay longer** in hospital if the aftercare was better, bathrooms were nicer, call bells were within reach and visiting times were a bit more sensible. My aftercare was awful and I effectively insisted on going home and once there my community team rescued me. No one in hospital showed me how to care for my baby or how to breastfeed.

*Podmog*

**Post-natal stays are an ordeal to me.** I need lots of peace and quiet to properly recover and the bustle and noise of a ward isn't the place to get it. No one explains the 'rules', like where to get anything or where the phone is, plus in my case the day room was full of smokers. Even with my first, when I had no clue what to do with this tiny human being, I was desperate to go home. I was absolutely terrified too, but making mistakes in the privacy of my own home seemed the lesser of two evils.

*Baabaa*

**For my first pregnancy I was in hospital** for four days. I didn't really want to be there at all, but I felt safer being there because it was my first baby. My second time I was home six hours after delivery, which was nice because I was able to relax more at home. The decision should be up to the individual and how they feel in themselves.

*Washer*

**My son was born early on a Tuesday** morning and we were sent home at midday on the Wednesday. The birth itself was horrendous but the aftercare was pretty good. We ended up going back in on the Thursday for a very long four days as our son was jaundiced. I swore then that when I had baby number two I'd be going straight home. She arrived late on a Friday night and there was no aftercare at all. By 6 am on Saturday morning a midwife came in and said, 'So you'll be wanting to go home then.'

I'm glad I went home early but I hated feeling as if I was on some kind of production line. The care from the community midwives was a lot more helpful. I had no help with breastfeeding in hospital but once I was home a lovely midwife visited who spent an hour helping me with breastfeeding and I'm still feeding almost 13 months later.

*Angel78*

**I was in for five days** with my first daughter and less than eight hours with my second. I loved being able to go home so quickly. I had a very uncomplicated birth and just couldn't wait to get back to some home cooking and a good sleep in my own bed. I had a fairly helpful partner and a very unhelpful three-year-old but I really made an effort to stay in bed once I got home, although physically I felt fine – a bit battered and bruised but nothing too horrendous.

*Enid*

**A word of advice** – you can leave whenever you want. Hospitals cannot keep you in if you want to go, even if you are on the verge of death – it would be false imprisonment! They may not be happy about it, but it is entirely up to you when you leave. You just discharge yourself. They could only prevent you taking the baby if there was a serious and urgent risk to their health and they got a Court Order. I am always amazed when people talk about being 'allowed' to go home. They can only advise you as to whether it is safe or not. It is up to you whether you take the advice. If I have another child I certainly aim to be home in a couple of days. I was well enough the first time and I doubt anything would be different the second time.

*Aloha*

**It's all well and good** for second-time mums to be let out quickly but most women have no idea what to do first time around and (like me) some are probably still in shock! A few days in hospital offers a good period of adjustment before being thrown out into the big wide world to cope. I had hardly even held a baby when I had my daughter and had no idea how to change nappies, bath, dress and feed – my stay in hospital taught me these basics. I would recommend at least two days for first-time mums.

*Grommit*

**I stayed five days** when I had my daughter six years ago. I had been very nervous as I wasn't looking forward to sharing a ward with other women. As it happens, I had a great time. The other woman in with me had also just had her first – we used to have lovely evening chats over supper in the day room and I look back on that time as special. We were both in the same boat muddling through. I had no idea what I was doing and felt that at least in hospital I'd have professionals on hand to help me out.

*Linnet*

**I think that mothers** should be able to stay as long as they wish, within reason. I gave birth on a Friday morning, and left on a Monday morning, by which time I was ready. I did not feel like I knew enough, but wanted to be at home. Having said that, my milk came in that night, and it was terrifying, because my boobs were too full for my son to latch on. I spent a horrible night and think that I would have dealt with it better if I had been in hospital.

*Chinchilla*

**My first birth** was an emergency C-section and I had such a bad time in hospital I couldn't wait to go. It was hot and dirty and there was practically no post-natal support. I was miserable and booked myself out after a day and a half.

My second child was a 'natural' birth but with a huge episiotomy and third degree tear. I stayed in hospital five days and it was fine, although sharing with just two others is still too many. I'm now expecting number three and considering splashing out on a private room. I suppose I would go home if I had help and support there, but I know that I'll just be back in the thick of it, with three to look after. I'd rather have a week in to recover and find my feet.

*Monkey*

---

**What the experts say**
If you feel you need more time in hospital – either because you're still not feeling one hundred percent or because you don't feel ready to cope with the baby on your own – talk to your midwife and explain that you need to stay a couple of extra days.

Kaz Cooke (*Rough Guide to Pregnancy and Birth*)

...get home as quickly as you can. It's cleaner, more comfortable and far more conducive to sanity.

Penny Wilson (*Wipe: Survival Tactics for Parents with Attitude*)

---

**In today's hospitals** with large post-natal wards and people being wheeled in and out at all times, and other peoples' babies screaming, I don't see how anybody gets more rest there than at home, no matter how many screaming toddlers they have.

Having said that, as a first-time mother, in some ways, I welcomed the fact I had to stay in hospital. I got wonderful breastfeeding support from one midwife, who sat with me for about two hours during the night, providing reassurance that I was doing it right. It was lovely to have the reassurance of somebody who knew what they were talking about, telling me that the red rash on my one-day-old baby's back was heat rash rather than meningitis – I'm not sure I would have believed anybody telling me to calm down over the phone.

*Prufrock*

**I would have hated** to be booted out of hospital after 24 hours and I had normal pregnancies and easy births both times.

I loved being in the ward. Luckily, I can sleep through anything, which helped. The happiest five days of my life were spent in a public ward in Greenwich hospital just after the birth of my first son, resting and getting to know the ropes. I had no idea how to care for a newborn, I needed to be shown (not referred to a book) and I wanted the reassurance of 24-hour back-up in the ward. Even the best home support network can't provide that.

I truly felt that left alone at home, even with a supportive husband, I could have easily succumbed to post-natal depression. The slightest thing could have toppled my confidence. I also did not want to face all the hoo-ha, the cards and flowers and visitors. I just wanted time alone with him, lots of routine, set visiting hours, set meals, and no danger of unpredictable things happening. After three days my husband was begging me to come home. He had cleaned the house from top to bottom, but I resisted for another two days. When I came home I felt ready and had enough core knowledge to see me through.

*Frank1*

# The first night home from hospital/post birth – a survival guide.

**The first night was terrifying.** I looked at this tiny little bundle and said, 'Oh, he's here for ever, isn't he?' I know it sounds stupid but I hadn't thought beyond the birth and realized the enormity of it. The thing that helped me through those first few days (not coming back from anywhere since my son was born at home) was having my mum there. She shopped, cooked, cleaned, reassured me and let me sleep as much as I wanted. It made all the difference. So get help if you can.

*Wickedwaterwitch*

**We carefully put the little car seat** in the middle of the floor, stepped back and just looked at her. Suddenly the house seemed a lot smaller! We woke up at 3 am with her and thought, 'Where is everyone?' It was then I realized that, basically, we were on our own.

*Enid*

**I felt that the hospital** should not have left me alone with my baby. I kept saying to my partner, 'But it was harder to get the cat from the RSPCA!' My main memory of the first night (after all the phone calls and euphoria) was being afraid to fall asleep in case she cried and I didn't wake up. (Ha! that's how inexperienced I was!). I lay in bed with my partner on one side and daughter in her Moses basket next to me and swore I would not sleep until she was 17. So, my tip is to look at your sleeping babe for just as long as it takes for you to drift off.

*Sobernow*

**Make sure the heating is turned on** so when you get back late, having waited for hours to be signed out of hospital, the house isn't an icebox. If the only way the baby will fall asleep is on your partner's chest, let them and don't fret about routines/bad habits. They are only this tiny for a small amount of time and hard as it is, you'll miss it when it's gone.

*Haley*

**For a healthy newborn** one layer of clothing more than you have on is sufficient and – apologies for being so graphic – buy some care mats/padded towels to sit on in the car/on the sofa, etc. to stop bloodstains.

*Codswallop*

**Make sure that your partner** has remembered to actually take out of the freezer some of the wonderful meals you cooked beforehand – otherwise you can wait a long time for them to defrost. Beware of thinking you'll save yourself the trouble by ordering a takeaway. The pizza delivery boy will ring the doorbell very loudly just as your baby has gone to sleep. If you do order out, stand guard!

*Prufrock*

> **Mumsnet tip**
> If your baby slept in the hospital but will now not sleep unless you hold and rock them, don't worry – it's normal.
>
> *Hmb*

**I came home the day after my son was born.** We arrived home at lunchtime and I fed him. He then slept and slept and slept. After eight hours we rang the midwives on the labour ward and asked if this was normal. The midwife we spoke to said that we had to wake him up, give him a bath, etc. – but wake him. Her tone made us panic so we duly undressed him and gave him his first bath. When he still refused to wake, we rang the hospital back and spoke to a much calmer midwife who said that after his traumatic birth it wasn't surprising he was so tired. And why were we awake? Of course, by the time we were ready for bed he started to stir...

*Gem13*

**We had a similar story,** but at night-time. Our baby slept for 10 hours but I couldn't sleep for worrying/breasts aching. Served me right as it was the last time she slept through the night for about two years.

*Biza*

**If you expect the house to be cleaned** and filled with flowers – ask for this specifically (yes, bitter experience). However, I was in hospital for four nights after my C-section (and a month beforehand) so for me being home and eating home food and sleeping in my own bed was such bliss I don't even remember the baby waking up – though I'm perfectly sure he did.

Make sure you've got clean sheets on the bed – so lovely after horrible hospital bed linen. If I ever go to hospital again, I'm taking my own duvet and pillow!

*Aloha*

**Make sure you have somewhere** to change the baby other than the floor or your bed. I was told that changing tables are a waste of money and the best/safest place to change a baby is the floor. Sadly, no one mentioned that in the days immediately after birth it would be near impossible/very painful to try to get down to the floor with baby and then try to clean up all that meconium from that position.

As soon as your baby appears to be at all settled (which might well be straight away if still sleepy from the car journey), have a lovely, relaxing bath with some lavender oil or something similar and allow your partner to get to know the baby whilst you wallow in your own bath – so much more appreciated after the hospital one. Continue with this routine in the next few days.

Finally, do not let your partner sort out your leaving hospital clothes. I left hospital in chunky walking trainers, no socks and a skirt in February with snow on the ground. As if I didn't look bad enough with that sort of moving-gingerly-new-mum-waddle.

*Bozza*

**My sister gave me exactly this advice.** When she saw the clothes her husband had brought to the hospital for her to wear, she burst into tears. I took the advice to heart and packed my own bag beforehand with suitable things. Then he forgot to bring it and I went home in my nightshirt. So when you've packed the bag, put it in the car boot along with the baby seat.

*Eemie*

**Make sure you have formula** in the house, even if you're breastfeeding! I came home 10 hours after my first baby was born and was breastfeeding. My daughter was feeding constantly and was simply not satisfied by colostrum (my milk came in three days later). She was so hungry that she was still crying even when my partner took her out for a two-hour long drive at 2 am! We went out the next day and bought some of the ready-mixed stuff to tide us over. I would definitely get some in beforehand, given my time again.

*Wickedstepmother*

**Alternatively,** if you're really committed to breastfeeding only, don't have formula in the house. That way, even if you're tempted, you can't give in.

*Nick*

**I wish someone had told me** about Muslin cloths beforehand! I had to send my husband out to buy more sheets for the Moses basket as my son kept posseting on them and they needed washing so I was running out. My mother-in-law came to visit and spotted 100 sheets on the washing line (slight exaggeration) and suggested laying the baby on a Muslin cloth. Why didn't I think of that?

*Northerner*

**Stick a note on the door** telling everyone your baby's details with a note saying, 'Please do not disturb unless urgent'. I also had one later which said, 'Mother and baby feeding or asleep – please do not disturb unless urgent'.

*SoupDragon*

**If your baby was born in hospital** (very noisy places), it may not be able to sleep in dead quiet. Have a radio on very low in its room for the first couple of nights (turn down gradually) until it gets used to the quieter home surroundings – it works like magic. The longer you stayed in hospital after the, birth the more your baby is likely to panic at silence in the middle of the night!

*Princesspeahead*

**Mumsnet tip**
Have a pack of dummies in the house. Even if you are adamant you are never going to let a child of yours have a dummy... you might change your mind at 2 am!

*Kmg1*

**I don't remember much about** the first night but I do remember putting this tiny little bundle into the cot – he looked so small and so lost in there – and just feeling for the first time that he was mine and I didn't have to ask the midwives' permission to do the things I needed to do for him.

My advice would be to enjoy those precious first few days/weeks – they don't last long and before you know it, you've got a big, fiercely independent, almost-five-year-old.

*Anais*

# The first week – survival tips.

**You will cry and cry and cry** over something during that first week. Warn your partner about this beforehand and tell him you won't need advice, just a hug and reassurance that you are/will be the best mother who ever lived. My husband looked very startled when I sobbed so much – I think he thought I was going to have a fit.

If the baby won't stop crying, go out. Dummies are not the work of the Devil. Get help. Mums, mothers-in-law, neighbours, anyone who will help on your terms, not theirs. Someone who will take the baby out for an hour whilst you sleep is a godsend. Someone who comes round and expects you to make them tea, isn't. When people come round, tell them the kettle and teabags are in the kitchen, then they'll make you a cup of tea, which is much more preferable.

Ask your partner to take the baby with him when he goes to the supermarket. You get a little rest and the baby will sleep all the way round. Oh, and whilst the baby's still in it's sleepy phase (if he/she has one), go out for lunch or dinner together as a couple with baby snoozing in pushchair/car seat to remind you that there's some of your old life left.

*Aloha*

**The best thing anyone told** me was to minimize housework – prepare meals in advance that can be stuck in the microwave (or stock up on microwave meals and takeaway menus) and leave the washing up or buy paper plates. If you need people to talk to (as I did), don't wait for them to call you – many will assume you don't want to be disturbed. Oh, and it turns out that dummies are in fact the greatest invention of all time.

*Lucy123*

**Invest in an answer-phone** if you haven't already got one then you can screen calls. Have a notice saying 'Mother and new baby asleep' for the front door and tip your postie off in advance so he/she knows not to hammer on the door at 7 am.

*Clare2*

> **Mumsnet tip**
> When feeding, have every single mail order catalogue you own positioned strategically around you – bubba in one arm, pen in the other and shop. Retail therapy stimulates milk production – honest!
>
> *Bobsmum*

**We had a fab postman** who put the letters through if they looked dull, rang the bell once if it looked nice (cards, etc.) and twice if there was a parcel. He then left the parcels behind a flowerpot so I could get them in my own time. We hung a huge blue bow on the front door when my son was born. That way, neighbours knew that the baby had arrived and that he was a boy. I'm sure it saved a few unnecessary 'pop rounds'.

My parents live quite far away and came down for the birth but booked into a nearby hotel for a few days so they could be around all day but give us some time alone in the evenings. They gave us all the support we needed plus that added bonus of 'us-time'.

*Bruntwig*

**Beware of exploding breasts!** On day three I couldn't work out why, even though I dried myself over and over after a bath, my feet were still wet. Turns out I was dripping milk all over them. On that note, get in a BIG supply of disposable breast pads – washables are great, when the supply has settled down. Every time you sit down to breastfeed, position a big glass of water, the remote control, a cordless phone and tissues right next to you.

*Batey*

**Don't try to be Wonder Woman** and do everything around the house (as I did). Don't feel guilty if you don't get dressed all day. In fact I wished I'd stayed in my pyjamas for the first couple of days and concentrated on getting to know my baby.

*Northerner*

**If a really good friend,** or your Mum can baby-sit, don't feel guilty about going out for a meal or to the pub. You only need to be gone an hour or so and it'll help you feel human again. I spent the last part of my pregnancy making casseroles and Bolognese sauces, etc. and freezing them and it was really worth it.

*ThomCat*

**Sleep when the baby sleeps.** You will regret not doing so when you have baby number two and can't do this because of your toddler.

*Codswallop*

> **Mumsnet tip**
> If it's your second or more child, when you sit down to feed, get the older sibling to fetch a story to read. My son had never had as many stories in his life as when I was breastfeeding my daughter.
>
> *Dannie*

**Start keeping a diary** – your feelings if you're into that or just sleeping/feeding times, etc. if you're not. Then, when you're going berserk later, you can see that the little darling always has the abdabs at 4 pm and you won't feel so bad.

*Eeek*

**If you can do it without sounding mercenary,** tell people to bring a prezzie for you, not the baby – a voucher for a facial is much more welcome in my house than another pink babygrow. If you've got folks travelling from a distance to see the new arrival, either get them to visit you in the hospital, or wait until the little one is a few weeks old to visit you at home. I learnt by bitter experience that hosting a minor family reunion with a five-day-old baby is very bad for the baby blues.

*Lilymum*

**We had two parties,** one for family and another the next week for friends. We issued invitations, 'The Sluglet will be available for viewing on Saturday between 1 and 3 pm', or something like that. It worked very well as there was a definite time when people knew they were expected to leave and during one of the sessions I snuck off for a half-hour kip, secure in the knowledge that there were plenty of broody women around just dying to change a nappy!

*Slug*

**Train your husband to say** to his parents, 'She's very tired, goodnight.' Preferably before they've sat there cooing at the baby for three hours the first night home. Or better still, 'No she's not up to visitors this evening, call back tomorrow.'

*Tallulah*

> **Mumsnet tip**
> Keep the ironing board up so that if people bore you, you can say, well, I must get on with the ironing – true friends do it – others leave!
>
> *Codswallop*

**We had the first night on our own** (I think I spent the whole time stressing about whether he was latching on okay) and then the next day my mum came for a week. She was a godsend: she made tea for visitors, she cooked for us, she took the baby for walks in the pram and she answered the door and the phone when I didn't want to or when I was asleep. And better still, she, being a midwife, showed me exactly (by hands, on demonstration!) how to express milk to avoid engorgement. I know not all people have midwives for mothers but if you can bear people staying in your house, get help for a few days so that you can enjoy your baby and get some rest.

*Ghosty*

**The best advice I got** was from a neighbour with five children, who said she made a point of staying in her pyjamas for the first week after giving birth. It reminds everyone what you've been through and that the baby was not delivered one morning with the milk.

*Rolypoly*

## Being helpful in the first week(s) – essential reading for partners.

**For my first son** my husband decorated the house with boy banners, balloons and flowers. The second baby was a home birth but he still managed to put up the banners. It was lovely that everyone who walked past the house knew, and even strangers would stop, smile and wave at us.

*Hughsie*

**The partner's main job is as gatekeeper** – to allow in the visitors you want, keep away those you don't, throw out those who have overstayed and make tea for all of them. Ditto screening phone calls – he can take most of them and only pass across those you want to talk to.

He should also provide the new mother with a constant supply of water, tea and coffee (don't wait to be asked), ensure she eats, take baby whilst she does eat (as babies somehow know to scream every time food hits the table) and keep fridge stocked up with necessary foods.

Tell her that everything she is doing is fantastic, you are very proud of her, you think she and baby are wonderful and you love them – self-confidence is very low in new mothers and they need as much boosting as possible. Do as much with the baby as you can, (nappy changing, winding, taking it for walks, baths, etc.) but don't take it personally if she appears to criticize the way you do it all – ride with it and tell yourself it will get better soon. If you find her in tears for no reason at all, it's probably just hormones – just keep telling her how wonderful she is.

Make sure that when the baby is settled the new mother gets as much sleep as possible – during the day as well as night – and is not rushing around doing pointless 'essential' tasks like cleaning the worktops in the kitchen. Put her to bed if necessary. Write as many thank you letters for presents and flowers as possible so she doesn't have to do it.

If your mother arrives to help, keep a close eye on how it's going. If she appears to be winding your wife/partner up, whether or not you think it's justified, try to step in and defuse the situation.

*Princesspeahead*

**Take charge of who is allowed to visit** and for how long. I was too tired and emotional and people just called or turned up and stayed/talked for ages. I wish my ex had answered the phone/door and said, 'Thanks for stopping by/calling but now's not such a good time.' As it was, he just sat in the corner watching TV and left me to deal with entertaining the guests. Probably why he's my ex!

*Pie*

**Buy flowers or a present** – I told my partner after giving birth to my first son that I was not impressed he didn't get me any but did he remember second time around? No! What do I have to do to get a present?

*Kaz33*

**My husband was a star.** Whenever my son needed a night-time feed he would make me a cup of tea and a biscuit. Then he would re-swaddle him for me (I was hopeless at swaddling!) and put him back in his Moses basket, often changing him too. It felt like we were really in it together and it was lovely that he was such a part of the night-time routine despite having to get up for work, etc.

*Jessi*

**If your partner is off work,** and you are bottle-feeding or expressing, persuade them to do all the night feeds – you need your sleep more than he does – especially if recovering from a traumatic birth or C-section.

Do not make new mothers laugh – it hurts their stitches. It's normal to cry, and be paranoid about being a good enough parent. Don't try to solve every problem they come up with – sometimes they just need your sympathy, not a resolution.

*Prufrock*

> **Mumsnet fact**
> Roughly 60–80 per cent of new mothers find themselves feeling at least a little blue at least occasionally during one of the happiest times of their lives.
> Murkoff, Eisenberg and Hathaway (*What to Expect When You're Expecting*)

**The most important thing is to tell** the mother how brilliant she is, how wonderful their baby is and how delighted you are to be a dad. It's also a good idea to do all the washing, drying and putting away that a new baby seems to generate. Get everything organized so that nappies, cream etc can be found when they're needed. Realize that to a new mum the world is a suddenly scary place full of dangers to her baby – especially if you've been in the hospital for a while.

Oh, and the classic – work out how the car seat fits in advance – yes it was us panicking on Christmas Day in the snow. Luckily our son seemed unfazed by it all. Be in charge of taking flattering photos of the new mum and baby so there's something to treasure (mine are truly awful). Give a cuddle and reassurance before (as opposed to after) the tears start. And above all, be there – two weeks minimum.

*Eeek*

> **Mumsnet tip**
> Drive over speed bumps very slowly on the way home from the hospital.
> *SoupDragon*

**Don't ask your boss and his wife** to lunch the day after you come home from hospital (after an emergency Caesarean). Or at the very least, if you do invite the boss and his wife to lunch, please get the meat out of the freezer as requested. I have to disagree about partners staying off at least two weeks – thank God mine went back to work after two days!

*Lindy*

**At one of our NCT meetings** there was a discussion about whether eating enough carbohydrate could help stave off PND. I don't know if there is any truth in it but my husband was concerned enough to make sure he put two rounds of sandwiches in the fridge everyday before he left for work. Thinking back, a flask of tea would have been useful too. He also made a sign for the front door asking cold callers not to ring the doorbell. When a new mother is bawling her eyes out at 1 am screaming, 'You can't still be hungry, you've been feeding all evening', give her a big hug and sit with her until the small demon is asleep.

*Twink*

**Mumsnet tip**
Don't ever, ever, ever say to a new mum who has been trying to breastfeed a screaming newborn for about an hour, 'I think the baby's hungry.'

*Biza*

**If you can afford it** and you think she's the sort that would appreciate it, hire a post-natal Doula for a few hours a week to give your partner the 'womanly/motherly' support that she might need. They can do things like debriefing her birth, giving support when breastfeeding and doing whatever would suit the mum like cooking, bathing older kids, school runs, etc.

*Pupuce*

**Put a message on the phone** telling everyone the bare essentials and asking them not to leave non-urgent messages so you don't have to ring back/listen to them. Organize a friend who can give your circle of friends updates and therefore avoid calls. Don't contradict the new mother or do competitive tiredness. If breastfeeding hurts, it does and if she is tired, she is! A 'maternity ring' is always welcome, no matter what it costs. It's a lovely memory and token of respect. Sleep in separate bedrooms if you can' t cope with lack of sleep but do everything else and let her do the baby.

*Codswallop*

**Don't complain** about lack of sleep...or sex!

*Babster*

**Be proactive about** doing your share, don't just hover while she does things. Take time to sit, hold the baby close and fall in love. Your partner's had nine months of contact with this baby – now it's your turn to get to know him/her.

*Philippat*

**Don't leave the new mum in hospital** around mid-morning to go home, phone everyone you know and then fall asleep all day and evening – no matter how tired and traumatized you are (new mum meanwhile getting frantic with both phone and mobile switched off), then turn up at 9 pm to get told off by concerned mid-wives. The first day is for sharing! The best thing my husband did was to take our son downstairs in the middle of the night (for weeks) and swing him to sleep in the hammock so I could get some sleep.

*Gem13*

> **Mumsnet fact**
> The number one cited cause of marital distress in new mothers is feeling unsupported and misunderstood by their spouse.
> Kate Figes (*Life after Birth*)

**From a dad's perspective:**
Get stuck in to as much childcare as possible – if you only have two weeks off, it'll be the only chance you get to develop your infant care skills (apart from holidays). Don't let your partner dictate the way you do things with the baby – holding, changing nappies, comforting, etc. – you need to develop your own ways, and men and women hold and care for babies differently. Her way is not the best way for you – your way is – all it takes is practice. Realize that baby care is a learnt skill, not an inherent one, and it's the same for men and women, so the more you do the better you get. Be there for all meetings with midwives and health visitors, so you get all the info as well. If you're off work, get up at night to help with feeds (this will happen anyway if it was a Caesarean).

Be aware of the benefits of breastfeeding and talk to her about it, but be totally supportive of your partner's feeding – just support her choices. Talk through the options with her and don't push her.

If your baby is bottle-fed, send your partner off on a day trip and take over for a whole day. If your baby is breastfed, encourage your partner to express, then when you've enough for a feed, send her off for a shopping/cinema trip as soon as she finishes a feed, so she can get back for the one after that.

If she's breastfeeding, make sure she's got a drink and she's comfy – ask every time if there's anything she needs... TV remote, chocolate, tea, etc.

When you're back at work, finish on time and get home, and don't expect a break. If you can afford it, hire a cleaner at least for a couple of weeks and some-one to do the ironing. Take personal responsibility for parts of the baby's day – e.g. bath-time, bedtime.

Expect the quality of your relationship to suffer in the short term – anything up to a year. Don't moan about the lack of sex.

*Tom*

> **Mumsnet tip**
> When a new mum is crying, don't say, 'Oh, I've read about this bit, you're becoming clinically depressed, you'd better get some help' and then go straight out to work.
>
> *Sobernow*

**Take turns to sleep.** For us, that meant my husband sleeping all night and during the first feed in the morning. Then I would go back to sleep and he would entertain and settle baby during the day, so I could nap whenever I wanted.

*AliFar*

**During the night-feed nightmare,** my husband made me a thermos flask of hot tea/coffee, a jug of iced water and a plate of biscuits each night to make the breastfeeding a little bit easier to cope with. This little gesture of support made me smile every time. The best advice for new dads, though, is to talk to your partner so she can tell you specifically what she wants/needs.

*StripyMouse*

**Turn up at the hospital after the birth** with flowers at least, if not, expensive jewellery (and edible food too). Find your special skill. My husband was brilliant at burping and settling our daughter in those first few weeks. Thinking back, he probably wasn't any better than me, but he was patient and willing to try and I was really tired and very grateful.

*Sjs*

**Remark, quite spontaneously,** on how much thinner and babe-like she's looking (this is important). If tempted to remark on how tired/stressed out you are, check your own bottom for stitches and/or general battering, and shut up. Take over all the cooking, even if that means just ordering in a pizza.

*Motherinferior*

**Listen.** In those first days let your partner talk: about her, about the baby, about her and the baby, about you, about you and her, about you and her and the baby. Let her talk it all out until she stops needing to. Then it's your turn.

*Frank1*

# Special care – how do you cope emotionally and practically?

My daughter was born nine weeks early, weighing 3 lb 5 oz. She spent about five days in an intensive care incubator, then progressed to breathing by herself, NGT (tube into stomach) and finally into a cold room cot and attempted breastfeeding. She stayed in special care for six weeks as she didn't put on weight and was eventually given a blood transfusion, which seemed traumatic at the time. She was finally discharged weighing 4 lb 2 oz. It was all quite distressing but she's now a happy, very intelligent seven-year-old with no signs at all of her less-than-perfect start in life.

*Judetheobscure*

**My daughter was born** at 351/2 weeks and was only 4 lb so she spent the first few days in an incubator being tube fed, and she was jaundiced. At one stage they even wrapped her in bubble wrap to keep her warm. I couldn't breastfeed her for a week. It was all so scary (hospitalized at 32 weeks with pre-eclampsia) that it took ages before I could think about it without crying. But she is a chunky, happy, smiley baby who sleeps through and is generally pretty calm. I often come across babies who spent time in special care, and who are very placid and contented and soon fall into routine, probably because of the routines in hospital – it's just their parents who have the unhappy memories.

*Sobernow*

**I remember running about everywhere** when my son was in intensive care (only five weeks early but ventilated). You have to remember that you need to get lots of rest even though you are not physically caring for a baby at home – try and get some people to look after you!

*Mears*

**Other people don't seem to know** how to react. It's hard going out and about and seeing neighbours, etc. who don't know what's happened – it's obvious you're not pregnant any more but there's no baby – I guess they don't know what to say. Hospital visiting is also hard and I cried every time I had to leave. The Special Care Baby Unit (SCBU) was next to the labour ward so most times I saw mums coming out with full-size new babies ready to take home and couldn't help feeling like a failure. Why couldn't I keep her in a bit longer?

It's particularly hard if your child isn't progressing. My daughter had severe feeding problems and was surrounded by much younger and smaller babies who were feeding away like anything. In my case it helped to be told some good news. For example, I heard of one baby who took until two months after his due date to feed properly but was then fine. Just hearing a story with a happy ending helps you cope.

My daughter finally came home, seven weeks after being born. The relief was unbelievable – I felt like I'd woken up from a terrible nightmare to find everything was okay after all and vowed never to complain about the sleepless nights!

*Jodiesmum*

> **Mumsnet fact**
> Mothers who've previously given birth to a premature baby have a 15 per cent chance of giving birth to another premature baby in a subsequent pregnancy. While women who have experienced two premature deliveries have a 32 per cent chance of giving birth to another premature baby in any future pregnancies.
> Ann Douglas (*The Mother of All Pregnancy Books*)

**I had a daughter at 34 weeks** (now a happy, bouncy, chunky eight-month-old) following severe pre-eclampsia and got 48 hours notice of a C-section birth. We just 'coped' whilst we were in hospital and SCBU, and for me expressing milk every three hours quickly became the norm. Not that I'm saying I looked forward to being milked like a cow, but at the time I just did it to try and give my daughter something of mine that no one else could provide.

It's only afterwards that you realize you could have done with more support. My immediate advice to anyone whose baby has just been whisked off is to risk being annoying to staff and ask, ask, ask about everything, even if you think you won't understand their responses. Write a diary and then go over it when you can. It will help keep things in order in your mind (which will be all over the place). Later on when you feel you need answers, this will help to form the 'story' of your child's birth.

*Moomicat*

> **Mumsnet tip**
> When you finally get to bring your baby home from SCBU, decorate the outside of the house with loads of pink/blue balloons or ribbons, just so everyone gets the hint and feels safe to come and talk to you again.
> *Judetheobscure*

**Although I knew my daughter** would have to go to special care when she was born, we were not really prepared. She was born two weeks early after a routine ultrasound showed my placenta had not been functioning effectively. Within two hours of the ultrasound I was a mother.

Make sure you look after yourself. After I was finally discharged (and our daughter was still there) I would go in the morning and spend time with her – come home around lunchtime and sleep, and do what needed to be done. Then when my husband got home from work we would go to the hospital together. I think taking that time out in the afternoon helped me recover from the Caesarean as well as I did. I feel it also put me in a better position to care for her when she came home three weeks later.

Also, be aware of all your child's care – if you don't understand at first, ask until you do. See if there is anything you can do in terms of your child's care. We started with nappy changes whilst she was in the incubator, moved to topping and tailing, tube-feeding, medication, etc. until we did it all if we were there.

I also found it helpful to talk with other mums who had babies in special care. One little boy was born at 20-odd weeks and had struggled for weeks to live. He had been there for almost a month and a half when my daughter was born, was still there when we went home and was still there when I visited the hospital to let them see how my daughter was getting on. His mum was one of the most positive, uplifting women I know and we always made a point of asking after each other's little ones. Support from someone who is sort of in your shoes is helpful.

*Eidsvold*

**Mumsnet fact**
About 100 babies are born prematurely every day in the UK.

Tommys.org

**When my daughter was about five months** I suddenly got concerned that I hadn't bonded with her when she was in special care. I had actually been quite relieved that I didn't have to look after her myself for the first few days after a Caesarean. Five months on, that seemed such a hard-hearted approach. I blamed myself terribly for not being by her bedside every minute I could and got the idea into my head that I'd spent very little time with her. I was told a lot of parents feel like this.

One thing that helped was that I had kept some notes about my daughter's first 10 days or so and re-reading them made me realize that we had lots of time together, that breastfeeding had gone really well, that she used to do these really cute little fat smiles after a feed and that I did love her right from the start.

Talking to my health visitor helped, as did accepting that what happened happened and focusing on my relationship with my daughter now. I was told I was grieving for the not-quite-perfect start my daughter and I had, which to some extent is true. Although grieving is rather a dramatic word, the stages I've been through are similar to the grieving process.

But I'd recommend keeping a diary, especially writing down the way you feel about your child, because usually you're so shell-shocked that you can't remember very much about it otherwise.

*Emwi*

**What the experts say**
It's important to spend as much time as possible in the special care baby unit with your baby. It will help demystify the technology and helps you bond with your baby.
Dr Miriam Stoppard (*First-time Parents: the essential guide for all new mothers and fathers*)

**My son was born at 35 weeks,** weighing only 4 lb and was tube fed in the Special Care Baby Unit for the first four days. Breastfeeding was rather difficult but we got there in the end. For the first day I imagined him lying in his incubator crying and no one giving him a cuddle, but in reality he spent those first few days (weeks, actually) pretty much asleep. He is now a very cheeky two-and-a-half-year old and you soon realize that those first few days – worrying though they can be – are nothing in comparison to the days, weeks, months and years that follow.
*Titchy*

**I was forewarned that my baby** would be in special care, because I was sent to hospital at 27 weeks with pre-eclampsia. We hung on for four days, until both of us were being 'compromised' and then I had a section. I had been able to visit the day before, so at least I knew what the room would look like – in intensive care your little one is wired to all sorts.

I couldn't sit for hours watching the cot. I used to go in, read all the charts and ask copious questions. I was detached from it all and I just felt so guilty. My body had let me and my baby down, and I blamed myself. Reading information about the grieving process helped me more than anything else could and made me realize that I was normal, and that there are many ways that we cope.

Having a premature baby is like a sudden death. To start with, there is shock, then denial, thirdly anger, fourthly grieving (for the perfect pregnancy, or what should have been) and fifth acceptance. Each one of these phases can last just hours, days or even months – I guess four years later I am at the fifth stage.

The shock lasted a lot longer than I realized and was combined with denial. I kept saying, 'but I never get ill' and 'these things just don't happen to me'! Anger definitely reared its head when she didn't seem to be progressing as quickly as I thought she should, or when my husband wasn't allowed to hold her one night. I was so angry with the staff – nothing anyone did was right for my baby!

Grief took a long time coming and a long time to go and boy, did I grieve for the 'perfect baby/pregnancy'. I don't think I really let go of it until my second baby was born two years later. I think acceptance came three years after my first baby was born and I realized she was fine, I hadn't hurt her – or rather her 'pre-maturity' hadn't.

I am not proud to admit it but I think I am closer to my second baby (though I love them both dearly). She was my baby from the start – my first daughter didn't become my baby until she was 14 weeks old and even then the routine she was in wasn't mine, I never had to muddle my way through those early days.

One of the most upsetting things was coming in when she was about 10 or 11 days old, and she was dressed. Up until then she had been naked, save a nappy, but I didn't choose her first clothes, or dress her first. Even now that brings tears to my eyes, as it was a special moment that was denied me. I would advise anyone with a child in special care to make it clear that when the time comes to dress them, you want to be the one to choose the clothes and if possible, put them on.

A year ago I saw my sister-in-law go through a similar thing. She went the opposite way and couldn't leave the bedside and was sobbing over the cot whereas I was off at the cinema, watching awful movies and eating out because I just couldn't cope with being nearby. But she still went through the same process, it's just her coping mechanism was different to mine.

*Crunchie*

**My daughter was born at 32 weeks** and was in SCBU for five weeks and my son was born at 28 weeks and was in for six weeks. I wasn't able to hold either of them until they were a week old. It was horrendous, my memories of it are terrible, but without ventilation I would have lost them both. Do I think it affected my 'bonding' with them and their 'contentedness' in the long run? Absolutely not!

*Mabs*

## Coming to terms with a traumatic birth – what helps?

**I had a horrible birth** that left me feeling cheated, scared and humiliated in equal measure. I pushed for three hours before the midwife examined me and realized that my daughter was completely the wrong way round. Instead of a C-section, they decided to turn the baby in utero using 'high' forceps – something which I have since found is not routinely practised these days. Unfortunately, I had had no pain relief and wasn't offered an epidural. It was horribly brutal, painful and completely terrifying.

My daughter recovered quite quickly. I, however, suffered bad panic attacks and had something that I self-diagnosed as post-traumatic stress disorder (replaying the event over and over again in my mind, feeling desperately sorry for pregnant women, etc.).

I didn't really come to terms with it until I was pregnant again. I talked endlessly about it to my midwife and was amazed to realize that it hadn't been a normal birth. The doctors played it down at the time and I was left with the impression that what I had gone through was just a bit bad and I should stop complaining. She was genuinely amazed that I had decided to go through with another pregnancy. She assured me that they would do everything they could to make sure the new baby's position was closely monitored. It was only when my second daughter was born, quickly, normally and with no pain relief, that I realized how horrific the first birth had been.

What finally helped me over it was talking to my lovely long-suffering health visitor – a trained cognitive behaviour therapist. She taught me positive ways of thinking about the birth – the amount I bonded with my first daughter, the fact I didn't have a C-section (this was quite important to me) and the fact that I coped with it at all must mean I had great inner strength (not sure about that bit, but it made me feel better!).

I wrote a very long letter to the hospital and felt better the minute I had posted it. I got a not-very-interested letter back although they were clearly ashamed about their forceps technique. I suppose stories like mine might scare mums-to-be, but honestly I would have welcomed reading anything that showed me the 'dark side' of birth (after the birth, that is!).

*Enid*

> **Mumsnet tip**
> If you're feeling battered by the whole birth experience, don't feel guilty about treating yourself. Remind yourself (and those around you) that it is very hard work bringing a child into the world and you deserve lots of praise and treats!
>
> *Haley*

**For various reasons** I ended up having an emergency C-section. All was well and my daughter was healthy, however as they were stitching me up, I began to haemorrhage. After two and half horrific hours they said that they were going to have to give me a general anaesthetic and that I had to sign a consent form to say that they could perform a hysterectomy – this was my first child so I was understandably reluctant, but of course I signed it.

Nine hours later I woke up in intensive care surrounded by my family. My husband was deeply traumatized, he had been convinced that I was going to die. We both still feel that what should have been the happiest day of our lives was in fact the worst. However, we are so delighted with our beautiful daughter that we are considering going through it all again soon! We got through it by talking about it and crying a lot together. In a way it has made us much closer, we have realized how much we love each other and how precious life is.

Most pregnancy books concentrate on the 'nice' aspects of childbirth and gloss over the nastier possibilities. If I had been made more aware of things like inductions taking a week (as mine did) I would not have felt so disappointed. Also, having the haemorrhage was very scary and I had had no information about this. No one wants to scare pregnant women, and what happened to me is thankfully rare, but being aware of what might happen in rare instances is, I think, useful.

*SamboM*


**Always, within reason, question what is being said** or suggested to you so you can really understand what the implications are, and make a decision. With both my births (which were hospital, induced, epidural, but basically fine) various interventions were suggested, which I questioned and eventually refused, and know that if I hadn't refused things would have gone on a downward spiral.

It's difficult because you have to take advice in these situations, but look closely at who is telling you to do what. If it is a senior house officer, ask to see a registrar. If it is a registrar, ask to see a senior registrar or consultant. If the senior registrar or consultant agrees, ask them what the risks/implications are of not following the advice. Listen carefully and then make your decision. I'd generally go with what a senior registrar or consultant says – they are the experts after all. Always remember that a senior house officer may be two days into his six-month rotation and have less obstetric experience than you do.

Make sure your birth partner knows the plan before you go in as when it comes, it is likely to be him/her doing the questioning and demanding to see a senior registrar, not you!

*Wiltshirelass*

---

**Mumsnet tip**

I had hypnotherapy before my second son's birth to wipe out the memories of the first birth. I found it really helped.

*SoupDragon*

**Basically, my daughter helped.** I adore her so much that looking back, it doesn't look so bad. I'm currently 28 weeks' pregnant again and am concentrating on not thinking about the last birth! I've also decided that hospital intervention didn't help and therefore am considering a home birth. I found looking at what went wrong and thinking of ways to prevent it doing so again has helped. Also, not having such high expectations post-birth. Last time I was desperate to find my feet, be a supermum, breastfeed, etc. and thus ended up with full-blown post-natal depression that was not diagnosed for nearly two years. This time I've arranged for my husband and mother to look after my daughter and for me and baby to retire to bed for a month (not sure I can manage this as I don't do staying still, but heck, I can plan) and any signs of the blackness and I'll be off to my doctors for pills.

Ultimately, my daughter was worth it and I wouldn't change a second if it would mean being without her. Understanding that has really helped me – the rest is about trying to ensure it doesn't happen again.

*Wills*


**I only started to recover** when my GP, not known for being overly sympathetic, said she thought I was suffering from post-traumatic stress disorder and referred me for counselling. It only took one session with a counsellor and I was so much better – just someone telling me that what I went through wasn't normal, that my anxieties about another birth were understandable and that they'd do everything they could to help me achieve the birth experience I wanted next time, made a big difference. Shame you have to go through trauma to get that treatment, but at least once I'd had it I could contemplate getting pregnant again.

*Nick*


**I had a bad birth,** with an awful midwife. A doctor friend later told me that what had happened to me was a catalogue of mismanagement and neglect; another said that barbaric was the only way to describe my experience. Perversely, this is what made me feel better about the whole thing. It's the acknowledgement that I had been treated badly and was not someone who was just too lazy to put in the effort (midwife's comment). However, I can't bear the thought of ever going through it again. I know labour would almost definitely be easier next time, but I just can't run that risk.

*Slug*

---

**What the experts say**

Childbirth reminds a woman of her own mortality. Many women feel close to death in labour, and some even beg the midwife to kill them rather than give birth.

Kate Figes (*Life After Birth*)

You can be shell-shocked after birth, too, and if you feel like this, you are not being weak, self-centred or ungrateful, though some people will imply that you are. Women suffer this unhappiness because they are disempowered in childbirth. Post-traumatic stress after birth is iatrogenic – a medically produced disorder.

Sheila Kitzinger (*The New Pregnancy and Childbirth, Choices and Challenges*)

---

**When I think about my son's birth** and read bad birth stories it makes me want to take a baseball bat to those responsible for turning a child's birth – what should be the best day of our lives – into a nightmare of such hellish proportions that we relive it not with joy, but through flashbacks. But I've had counselling, so I won't.

No one wants to scare mums-to-be but equally, knowledge can be empowering. If there is ever a next time round for me, God help anyone who doesn't do their job properly. I will be straight on the phone – from the operating table if needs be – to the chief executive's office if things start to go pear-shaped. My advice is to scream the place down if people don't do what you want. There are some fantastic people working in the NHS and there are some who shouldn't be allowed in a pet shop, let alone a hospital. If you encounter the latter, let them have it with both barrels and let them know you will take matters further and they will be held accountable for their actions. So what if they think you are a difficult old hag? All that matters is that you can look back on the birth of your child with joy.

*Willow2*

**My son was born after nearly 43 hours** of labour and several failed epidurals, plus an undiagnosed osterior positioning. I couldn't talk about the birth without crying for weeks. I attempted to get answers on the undiagnosed OP and failed epidurals from the community midwife on home visits. I was 'threatened' (that's what it felt like) with being registered with PND for wanting to discuss it. The only response was, 'You've got a lovely healthy baby' – sub-text, 'So what does it matter?'

My notes said, 'extensive discussion of labour' – in reality it was about 10 minutes. Needless to say, I just lied about my state of mind on her next visit. Luckily, I have no nightmares or other symptoms of post-traumatic stress disorder. For months afterwards though, I cried whenever friends had babies and was haunted by feelings of failure. I am miserable when anyone brags about not having had an epidural.

But – we are trying to conceive again at the moment. I can contemplate this because there is no lasting physical damage, either to me or to my son, plus I am much more aware of optimal foetal positioning and know that second labours proceed much faster – usually. Writing my labour story down also helped. Above all, as the midwife said, I have a beautiful son, and a couple of dreadful days were worth it.

*Proudmother*

**It wasn't as if I wasn't warned** about birth. My antenatal teacher was so into talking about all the hard facts that as a group we used to get quite depressed about it all and switch off during the bits about PND, episiotomies, sore boobs, etc. We were an optimistic bunch, all determined to have natural drug-free labours, packing our labour bags with homeopathic stuff and socks with tennis balls in for massaging lower backs.

Of the seven couples, only one managed a natural labour, most of us had episiotomies or tears and we were all deeply shocked at how much it hurt! I used to feel that I could never go through labour again. However, time is a great healer and now, two years on, I have laid those ghosts to rest and am hoping to get pregnant again soon. I feel I know so much more now and don't have those rose-tinted spectacles on anymore, so I reckon I could cope better second time around.

*Jessi*

# New baby and a toddler – how do you manage the first weeks?

**I have had three children** with a two-year gap and I now wonder how I did it! If you don't have family near, look into getting some help – a post-natal Doula or maternity nurse. Failing that, make sure you eat well and don't push yourself too much. I also took the extra days I was allowed to stay in hospital and got to know my new little boy before rushing back home to my toddler.

*SAB*

**Keep the toddler in routine** at all costs. The new baby won't mind being left to cry a bit, but a toddler is easily unsettled. I was panicked about bath/bedtime on my own with two. I found the best way was to feed the newborn whilst the toddler watched a video, then leave the baby in the Moses basket downstairs whilst I did our routine – bath, story and bed – with the eldest. I could often hear the baby crying, knew he wasn't hungry and chose to ignore it (I could never have done this first time round, but needs must). More often than not when I came down the baby was asleep, so an added bonus was I got to have dinner and an hour or two with my husband when he came in. I did the same at nap-time. Fed and changed the baby and left him whilst I settled the toddler.

Don't worry if you find yourself looking for routines for your newborn early on – it's just the way it is – you don't have time to feed all day (as I did with the first one).

*Nick*

> **Mumsnet tip**
> Have lots of little prezzies wrapped up for when the toddler comes in to visit you in hospital – just stickers or a lolly – and give one on arrival and one if necessary to ease the going home without you time – something we both found hard.
>
> *Haley*

**I found having someone** to get our toddler up and breakfasted has made all the difference. I am usually up and about by 8–8.30 am or so but not having to get up with him at 7 am was crucial. As far as food is concerned, I filled our freezer before the birth and it has been an absolute godsend. Not only are our evening meals in there but I keep a good supply of bread for breakfast and lunch, which has reduced the need to go to the supermarket.

When I am on my own with both children, I definitely try and focus on the toddler and I'm afraid the baby does get left to cry more than the toddler ever did. However, it seems to me that on balance this is the best way of coping. Even at just over three months, the baby loves watching her brother and is happily entertained by him, especially in the bath.

Breastfeeding is an ideal opportunity for story time. You'll be amazed at how easy small babies are and, if you are anything like me, wonder what all the fuss was about first time around.

*Ringer*

**If you have a napping toddler,** guard that nap-time jealously. Stick a note on your front door saying that a new baby's asleep and not to visit. I used to take the phone off the hook too for two hours every afternoon to relax myself and watch tacky TV. I didn't pre-cook or freeze food. I used to make supper with my toddler when the baby was asleep (around 4 pm, when the toddler was up from her nap). This worked for me, but it depends on the child!

*Crunchie*

**I only had five days** of help before I was left to my own devices. I wept when mum left, feeling I'd never be able to cope, but I did, and you will too. Looking back, my expectations of myself and baby were way too high and that was probably the most difficult, so my top tips are:
- Lavish as much attention on elder child as possible.
- Chill out (ha – easier said than done) I never managed it, but it would have been great if I had done!

*Monkey*

**Buy a present in advance** and let the baby 'bring it home' for the toddler. If people bring loads of presents but only for the baby, either open them later or let the toddler help and share.

Let the toddler have some special days with daddy – we found a trip on the tourist open-top bus around Cambridge followed by ice-cream, was a huge hit. If your hormones catch you out and you burst into tears all the time, or scream at your toddler for no reason, don't be afraid to apologize, just say that you're feeling a bit miserable at the moment and why don't you all have a bit of chocolate or whatever to cheer you up? I found the transition from no children to one much harder than from one to two.

*Bee*

**Mumsnet tip**
Don't tell him the baby will be a new playmate because newborns really aren't a lot of fun for a toddler. All they do is eat, cry, and take what seems like too much of mum and dad's time!

*Mullipups*

**My husband managed to take** a couple of weeks off work, which meant he could do lots of extra fun things with our eldest so he didn't feel too left out. He also did most of the cooking for the first four weeks. I really missed it once the honeymoon was over but the important thing is to get help where you can.

I know they don't work for everyone but Gina Ford's routines really worked for me. Within a week the baby was in bed for 6.30 pm, which meant I could do all the usual bath/bedtime routine with my eldest and have some quality time alone.

The other thing I would say is to really treasure the last few weeks with your first little baby. I couldn't believe how mine seemed to age overnight when I got back from the hospital. He seemed so big and old compared to the tiny baby I now had.

*Maia*

**You will be pleasantly amazed** at how your new baby will thrive on half the attention you gave your first.

I gave my daughter a doll so she could 'feed' as I was finding that stressful at first. She wanted to climb on my lap whenever I had the baby with me. One day, my partner came home to find me breastfeeding the baby and bouncing the toddler in the air on my outstretched legs (great for your thighs).

I kept the baby in a chair on high surfaces for the first few weeks (yes, I know...) because I was terrified my daughter would hurt her by accident. Now I put her in the playpen so they can see each other but all physical contact is heavily supervised.

Get the baby into the toddler's routine as soon as you can. You've already established what works for you both, so any more just have to go with it!

*Sobernow*

**In the weeks pre-birth** cook double lots of meals (casseroles, etc.), half to eat now and half to freeze in microwavable containers. Accept any offers of help gracefully – it does not mean you cannot cope – any help is a godsend in the first few months. Talk to your toddler about the baby, let him help you set up and choose a few little items. Go through his baby photos and show him how tiny he was, and how he couldn't do any of the great stuff he can do now, like run and jump and feed himself. Explain that little babies need looking after when they are new. Buy him a few little gifts and have them wrapped and tucked away for when visitors or relatives bring/send presents for the new baby but nothing for big brother.

Try to set him up with an activity or video nearby before you start feeding, or if you can manage one-handed, you can even read him a book. That makes it a special time for you all, rather than a time he will be trying to get your attention away from the baby.

Avoid the Supermum syndrome – you really can't expect to have a spotless house and effortless routines when you have a toddler and a newborn – so give yourself a break. Only do the essential stuff and try not to get stressed about the rest. Recruit your toddler as your helper – he will love having a go at dusting, polishing or sweeping, and it doesn't really matter if he doesn't do it properly. Lastly, relax! You are great mum and you will be just fine.

*Mollipops*

# Starting breastfeeding – tips (and encouragement) for the first week.

Let the baby feed as long as it likes and don't expect to get anything else 'done'. (Which means when you do get something done, it's quite an achievement!) Understand that it's a learning process and confused as you are at the beginning, you'll be an expert at it by the time your baby's 6–10 weeks old.

There's a big myth that 'it never hurts' if you're doing it right. I ran around trying to get help, trying to get the perfect latch, worrying all the time about why it felt like someone had stuck a TENS machine turned up high to my chest every time the baby fed. I'm sure it's worth checking if things are painful because lots of women can feed with no discomfort. But in my case there wasn't anything wrong with the latch. I just didn't very much like the feeling of 'let-down' (when the milk starts flowing). It was extremely tingly! But it wasn't agony either, and I got used to it once I learnt to relax. It went away after five weeks and never happened at all with my second baby.

*Zebra*

**Try out different positions.** Feeding lying down was a relief at night, but I needed a midwife to show me how, as the pictures and descriptions in books just didn't make sense. Feeding with the baby tucked under my arm was also great when I had a blocked duct in the first week as it put the pressure on the right place.

*Sprout*

> **Mumsnet tip**
> Breastfeeding is a great way to get rid of unwanted visitors and get out of housework – use it wisely.
>
> *Eefs*

**You may find your boobs are sore** watermelons first thing in the morning – I always expressed some to make them 'softer' and more comfortable – this helps the baby get a good latch and not bounce off!

The mysterious 'let down' feels like a tingling sensation in your boobs, and if you breastfeed from one, the other may leak milk. Use a sterilized breast shield or bottle top to collect the drips – after a morning feed I could collect enough to fill a 4 oz bottle for the next feed without expressing.

You could leak milk any time, any place, anywhere... be prepared with breast pads and/or a spare top. I had no discomfort starting breastfeeding and consider myself very lucky. The one thing that got me down was feeling like a prize dairy cow for the first few weeks. As your baby gets older s/he gets better at feeding and you will find what used to take an hour reduces to 10–15 minutes.

*DebL*

**My baby had bottle-feeds** for the first 24 hours because nothing I or the midwives could do would make him latch on for a breastfeed (his head was badly hurt). I worried myself sick that this would mean I would never be able to breastfeed, but after 27 hours he managed to latch on and I kept breastfeeding him for 17 months.

So, whilst it would be better not to give a bottle at first, don't give up all thought of breastfeeding just because they've had one! Even if you are intending to breastfeed exclusively, make sure you get a couple of bottles and have some idea about sterilizing. It never crossed my mind until I was in hospital, but if your baby needs cooled boiled water, or even antibiotics, you may need some kind of equipment. I ended up having to stagger out on my first day out of hospital and buy a ridiculously expensive sterilizer just because I hadn't had time to find out about cheap stuff like sterilizing tablets.

*Tamum*

**Jelonet and Lansinoh!** Jelonet is a paraffin gauze square that you can put onto sore blistery nipples to help heal them. It's a bit like putting lip salve on lips to stop cracking. It's very soothing and very effective. Lansinoh was unheard of when I fed my first son and I had to get it sent from the USA. Now it's on sale in most good baby shops. It's a really sticky goo to apply to nipples to keep them supple. It's 100 per cent pure lanolin and can work miracles.

I had horrendous problems feeding my first son and got no help until he was five-and-a-half-months old, by which stage the damage to my right nipple was irreparable. I had presumed he and I should have known how to do it because it's the natural thing to do. I didn't have a clue and unfortunately nor did he. My positioning was so bad that I'm sure he was existing on foremilk. Getting help was the best thing I could have done for both of us. I went on to feed him for 17 months and only gave up because he wanted to stop.

Do not panic if you take your baby off and find traces of blood! With my first child I didn't think to look at my nipples and presumed he was haemorrhaging from somewhere... then saw it was from me, then I thought was poisoning him, etc. Likewise, when the baby possets and there are blood specks in it, remember if you had bleeding nipples that they are the cause. I have very fair skin and very soft pink nipples so some nipple trauma was inevitable considering the force of his suck. Treating it straight away with a Jelonet/Lansinoh combo helped me most.

*Bruntwig*

**If you're in pain,** use nipple creams – I'd recommend Lansinoh or Mustela. I also used Mustela plastic disks, which kept anything from touching sore nipples. They weren't shields for feeding, but rather they simply let your nipples 'air out' whilst I was not feeding. Don't listen to negative comments! My mother kept saying, 'I don't think you're producing anything', despite the fact that my daughter was feeding for half an hour on each side every other hour, it seemed. I almost gave up because I was concerned my daughter wasn't getting any nutrition, and also I was in so much pain (cracked, sore nipples). In addition, I had a blocked duct on one side, which gave me flu-like symptoms. I did persevere, and it turned out my mother was wrong. Stick with it and stay confident. Also, for blocked ducts, the best thing is a warm, wet compress and get your little one to feed on that side as much as possible – cleared it up for me within a few hours.

*Tinyfeet*

**In the first week of breastfeeding** you may feel slight contractions – this is totally normal and a good sign that your body is starting to recover (no one warned me these might be quite strong and I was convinced something was wrong when I first got them). Get help from a breastfeeding counsellor – you may be doing it right for the first few days but it helps to have your positioning checked when feeding after your milk comes in as your breasts will change shape (again).

If your counsellor seems full of negative comments, smile politely and ring another one – you can do without the doomsayers at this time. Your breasts will appear to have been swapped for rock hard footballs when your milk comes in – don't panic, it won't take long for them to settle back into a more normal shape. It hurt like hell for me as my baby wasn't latched on right. I was so tempted to give up, but found that by bottle-feeding expressed breast milk for a few days my nipples had the chance to heal and when I started to breastfeed again it was a new, pain-free experience. Be warned, expressing breast milk is a very time-consuming process in the first few weeks – it will get easier when your supply is established.

*Eefs*

**The most important thing** is to get the latch right. Demand that a midwife sits down with you and watches you putting baby on and off, showing you different positions, etc. It's a lot easier to stomach the endless feeds if you know at least that you are doing it right. Get your partner on-side – whilst getting established you will need lots of support as well, of course, as lots of nourishing food, glasses of water/wine, the TV remote control, comfy cushions, cuddles and chocolate.

*Kaz33*

**Don't worry if it takes a couple of days** for your baby to get the hang of things – mine didn't really seem to latch on at all for the first three days. For me the turning point was going home from hospital where I could just relax without people sticking their noses in to check my 'latch'. I snuggled up in bed with a hot drink and loads of cushions before starting the feed and it worked!

*Morocco*

**It's not easy, but it's worth it.** Get as many different midwives to show you how to do it – it was the fourth one I saw at 3 am when my daughter was four days old who finally showed us a position that really worked for us. Plus, if like me, you must sleep naked, lie on a towel. Otherwise your mattress will never dry out.

*Prufrock*

**Whilst you are still in hospital,** don't feel guilty about calling for a midwife each and every time that you try to latch your baby on. It can take up to eight weeks to get the feeding going smoothly – so don't give up in despair before then just because it is taking too long. It will get easier.

*JanZ*

---

**What the experts say**

Starting off with breast-feeding keeps your options open for the long term while giving the baby a boost of benefits in the short term.

Penelope Leach (*Your Baby and Child*)

The world is filled with women who rank failure to breast-feed right up there with child abuse, and they love telling you about how they fed their own children until they were ready to start school...Is breast-feeding better than bottle-feeding? Sure I guess so. But then, so is baking your own bread, making spaghetti sauce from fresh tomatoes and never drinking coffee.

Vicki Iovine (*The Best Friend's Guide to Pregnancy*)

---

**Remember that midwives** have a basic training in breastfeeding but they are not lactation consultants. If you are consistently having pain and trouble, then come hell or high water, get a lactation consultant (by this I mean a fully-trained and experienced breastfeeding counsellor) to come and watch you for a whole feed. With my first I made sure a midwife was there every time I started the feed, but every midwife had a different piece of advice, and none of them picked up on the true trouble.

It was important to me to be absolutely sure that after the first few weeks I could safely go away for two or three hours (if only for coffee and a haircut) and not worry about a starving baby and it was important to have the bottle-feeding in place for when I went back to work. A bottle of expressed breast milk a day was perfect – it gave me a break at night (I went to bed early whilst my husband got some baby time) and kept my son willing to take a bottle. When I did go back to work there was nothing to worry about on the feeding front, and he was fully-fed on breast milk. Having a baby that could take a bottle was the reason I kept breastfeeding for over a year.

*Amber1*

**A friend's baby had a cleft palate** and couldn't suck well; she had one breastfeed a day and all the rest were expressed breast milk in a bottle. After her mouth was fixed at eight months or so, my friend stopped the bottles and 14 months on she's still breastfeeding. I didn't give my daughter bottles for fear it would mess up the breastfeeding, and then when I did my daughter refused. She never took a bottle – so I never got a break. Next baby, I'm going to give a bottle a day from about week two. Work at making sure your baby has a full feed and doesn't just have a snack and fall asleep. My baby fed every 90 minutes for five months and it's hard work.

*Zerub*

**Have confidence in your breasts** to supply everything needed – if in doubt I used to hand express a little and the shot of milk in the eye normally convinced me! If you can, get to a breastfeeding group before having the baby. I wish I'd done this just to see the positions, etc. Also – it's not always like it says in the books. Be prepared for feeding frenzies in the evening, possibly morning or other time of day – this really is normal. In the first few weeks I found the constant need for the breast harder than the pain, but it does settle down and you can soon have a life and breastfeed as well.

*Ninja*

**We're told it takes 6–8 weeks** to establish breastfeeding, but you may well find that it seems to take longer. At least, you may have the milk supply sorted out by then, but your body is not convinced. It took me nearer three to four months before my appetite and thirst returned to normal, and before that I felt my milk supply was not immediately affected by not getting enough food/drink/rest, and also before my breasts stopped feeling like engorged melons.

A tip for second-timers – it's a different baby so he or she may feed very differently to number one. With my first I couldn't understand why everyone said breastfeeding was painful. Apart from some soreness on one side (which was quickly resolved with some positioning advice from a counsellor), I never had any pain whatsoever, no sore nipples, no engorgement, no blocked ducts; just hypersensitive breasts. The second time round – ow, ow, ow! And although the various pains were at their worst for the first couple of months, the little darling is still very rough on my poor breasts at six months old.

*Boyandgirl*

**I breastfed for a year** – but it was a nightmare establishing it. I really wanted to do it, but came very close to giving in. I was desperate for 'permission' to stop, there seems to be such a big guilt trip linked to breastfeeding. In the end a midwife, realizing my son was losing weight, said to put him on the bottle. That same night, as I was waiting for a bottle to cool down, I put him on the breast just to try and stop him screaming – and he finally got the hang of it. Things got easier from that point on, but this was nearly two weeks in. So yes, it worked for me eventually, but those first two weeks were horrendous. I think everyone should be supported in her choice, whether it is breast or bottle.

*Willow2*

**Mumsnet tip**
When you're still learning and not ready to feed in front of visitors, don't leave them on the comfy sofa while you hide upstairs to feed. Tell your visitors to go stand in the kitchen/garden/bathroom because you require the living room!

*Zerub*

**Some women don't ever leak breast milk.** Some women don't ever feel a 'let down'. Some women don't ever feel engorged but will still be producing milk sufficient for their baby. As my wise and wonderful midwife said, 'You have a baby, your breasts produce milk, like night follows day, because that's what breasts are for!'

The more the baby sucks, the more milk you produce, but you don't need to sit for hour upon hour with baby at the breast if you don't want to. In the early days if you get fed up, get someone to take your baby away and don't even worry about providing expressed milk. Your baby will be fine for an hour or so and it will do you the world of good.

*Jasper*

**Many new mothers** find breastfeeding much, much harder than they expected. Such a rosy picture is painted before birth and when the reality kicks in and it's painful early on (even if you've got it right sometimes your nipples need to 'toughen up') you can feel a failure. You then feel that you are somehow different to all the happy breastfeeding mothers shown in the literature and you give up. Perhaps what is really needed is a bit more realism in the way breastfeeding is presented to new mums – admit that it might hurt and give people strategies to deal with it. Make them feel normal. The odd one or two (though not many, I bet) might decide not to try it but I'm sure a lot more would persevere if they weren't set up to feel failures.

*GillW*

## Bottle-feeding – advice for those who can't or don't want to breastfeed.

**I can't breastfeed for medical reasons** (I take immunosuppressant for Crohn's disease) and there are many other drugs that you can't breastfeed on. The main problem for me was the attitude of the medical profession. Midwives would come up to me in hospital, see me with a bottle and tut at me without bothering to look at my notes or ask me if there was a reason I was not breastfeeding. It makes me feel very sorry for those who choose not to breastfeed as I can see the problems they face.

Also, the never-ending posters, leaflets and lectures about how breast is best make you feel a total failure. I almost came off the drugs against my doctor's advice because I felt so awful about it. Even in antenatal classes I was told that the hospital was 'baby-friendly' and that they would not discuss bottle-feeding as a result. My doctor finally persuaded me by pointing out that millions of children are successfully bottle-fed and my daughter would miss out more if she had a bed-ridden, sick mother.

In practical terms I always sterilize everything in the morning and make up the bottles for the day. Cool them in a sink of cold water and refrigerate. All the literature says use within an hour of getting out of the fridge – this is not always possible if your baby is a slow feeder. I think two hours is fine personally – my daughter never had a problem.

The best way to feed in the night is to sterilize a bottle and put it together with no milk in it. Take it up to bed with you, along with a mini carton of pre-prepared milk. Then just pour the milk in and feed away! It will be room temperature so there's no need to heat.

Obviously breast is best but it isn't always possible and it's hard enough being a new mum without that added pressure. On the plus side you can eat and drink what you like and go out and leave the baby with someone else without worrying about the feed.

*SamboM*

> **Mumsnet tip**
> Put your partner in charge of bottles. It's good for them (and good for you!).
>
> *Codswallop*

**Establish a routine for making the bottles.** I found doing it last thing at night meant I could start each day fresh without a panicked rush in the morning. I also found that if I made the last bottle at night with boiling water and brought that up to bed, by the time the first feed of the night was required I had a bottle to hand that was the perfect temperature.

Try to start feeding with cold/room-temperature bottles – it will save so much hassle in later months as a bottle-warmer/hot water is not always available.

Get to know the different types of formula available – they all have different qualities. Some babies take a dislike to certain formulas so don't be afraid to try another brand. Make sure you take turns at night (if possible) so that you can have the occasional night of uninterrupted sleep – it will help you recover so much faster. Ignore people who say you will not bond as well if you bottle-feed. Babies nearly always stare at the feeder whilst being fed and it's a wonderful feeling. It is also possible to mix feed (some breast/some bottle). For some people it can interfere with establishing milk supply if you do it in the first six weeks but in my case it was fine.

*Eefs*

---

**What the experts say**
You don't have to breast-feed to bond with your baby. If this was necessary, fathers and grandparents could never fall in love with the baby and all adoptions would fail.

Dr Christopher Green (*Babies!*)

---

**Don't use too many pre-mixed** cartons as it can lead to constipation – they seem richer than the ones you mix yourself. Only put in exactly what it says i.e. one scoop per fluid ounce and no more.

It's hard not to feel guilty although I had no choice as my daughter was tube fed for the first two months of her life and I just could not express for her after a few weeks. I just reminded myself that I was doing the best I could in the circumstances.

*Eidsvold*

**I desperately wanted to breastfeed** especially as my son has eczema, but finally had to admit defeat at three months when he had failed to gain weight (1 oz in the previous three weeks and not much before that). The advice from everyone to continue with breastfeeding because 'breast is best', was well-meant, but wrong for us. Within hours of having his first bottle of formula he was a different child – happy, sleeping well, smiling – it was like flicking a switch.

I felt double guilt then because I had failed at breastfeeding and caused my poor child to suffer all his life through hunger. However, once my hormones had calmed down and I'd had some sleep, I could see that bottle-feeding my baby was the best thing for both of us. Breastfeeding can be wonderful, but it doesn't always work however hard you try (and I tried very hard) and sometimes it's not the best for the baby.

*Vivie*

**What the experts say**

...contrary to some breastfeeding gurus' advice, your baby will not suffer physically or emotionally if you decide to change to formula milk.

Gina Ford (*The Contented Little Baby Book*)

I know that stating these facts can be painful or even enraging to some women who have not breastfed their children, but the continual denial of the superiority of breastfeeding and breast milk, supposedly to spare women's feelings, is a patronising deception.

Gabrielle Palmer (*The Politics of Breastfeeding*)

**I think mixed feeding** should be more widely discussed – the either/ or attitude to breast/bottle-feeding helps no one.

*Eeek*

**I really wanted to breastfeed** and tried so hard to make it work but finally resorted to bottle-feeding after about three weeks. It is one thing having all the reasons for breastfeeding made clear to you and offering practical support, but my team of midwives were so pro-breastfeeding that I ended up feeling hounded by them when they saw I was struggling. I felt violated as if I was a faulty milk machine that they had come round to give a prod and a kick to get working! Not one seemed to care about my emotional well-being, they failed to notice that I was giving myself a hard enough time about it and didn't need daily reminders of all the benefits etc.

To sum up, I was left feeling a failure and even bullied into continuing much longer than was good for me. By the time my husband begged me to stop, I was getting to the point where I resented having my baby at all and was very depressed. I wished it could have been different but it has turned out fine – an allergy-free (fingers crossed), healthy, happy and bright little girl. For my next child (fingers crossed), I will again give breastfeeding a try but will be far less hard on myself if it fails again and definitely not allow the midwives to push me around. I know one girl who used to hide her bottles away when her midwives and health visitor came round to see her.

*JayTree*

**Mumsnet tip**

Don't assume babies will drink the same amount of milk, equally spaced throughout the day. Some times of day they are hungrier than others!

*Daisylawn*

**As a midwife** I much prefer women to say they don't want to breastfeed than skiddle around pretending that they do want to, only to change to the bottle the minute they get home. However, many women choose to bottle-feed without knowing any information about the choice they are making. That is why there is an emphasis on giving women information.

I have known women who have bottle-fed previous children then thought they would give breastfeeding a try and have found they have loved it. I have also known women who have given it a try and absolutely hated it. If you don't try, you don't truly know. If you have read the information, don't want to give breastfeeding a go, then state that clearly. I had this discussion with a friend of mine having her third baby. She said she knew that breastfeeding was best but she had absolutely no desire to do it. She did not suffer from guilt one iota.

*Mears*

**Nutritionally speaking, breast is best** but in my opinion it's not best for the baby if the mother hates it or is depressed by breastfeeding, or resents having to feed her baby herself. I think there's more than nutrition involved in giving your baby the best.

*SoupDragon*

**I am one of the few people** who didn't even try to breastfeed. Most people say they tried and gave up for one reason or another or had a medical reason. This makes me feel very, very guilty and I know that people think that I was selfish. I started out my pregnancy with the intention of breastfeeding as I have asthma, hay fever and had childhood eczema but as time went on I just knew I couldn't do it. I had nightmares about it, which only stopped when I decided not to try. However, I do think that had more support been available during pregnancy, and I mean support – not midwives telling you you must breastfeed because we say so – then I may have given it a go. I knew no one who had breastfed and only heard stories of how awful it was and how I would not be able to cope with it from friends and family.

Towards the end of my pregnancy I began to change my mind and thought I would try mixed feeding but was told that this was not possible (something I now know is rubbish). I felt that the midwives had their policy and were not prepared to find out what was best for my particular situation and feelings. I wish that I could say that I bottle-fed and my daughter is perfectly healthy, etc. but she has asthma. So this is a decision that I will have to live with for the rest of my life.

*JulieF*

---

**Mumsnet tip**

Keep a carton of formula milk in the freezer just in case you run out and can't make the shops.

*Eeek*

**I fully intended to breastfeed** my first child but he never managed to get a single drop of milk from my breasts – even though the milk was there. Health professionals all thought this could be overcome but one after the other they gave up – as did the breastfeeding counsellor and my Active Birth teacher. After a week (it seemed so much longer) a kindly midwife said, 'Stop beating yourself up and give the poor hungry mite a bottle.' He blossomed. I expressed for two weeks before my milk dried up and then he had formula. So I had a happy baby but I felt a complete freak. Everywhere I turned – books, the media and other mothers – all told me that my baby was going to get all sort of diseases, that I was failing him and was an uncaring mother. There was no information on bottle-feeding and no help to be had. I was miserable and to begin with it ruined what should have been a wonderful time.

My son has not been affected adversely in any way and neither has my relationship with him. Bottle-feeding mothers are not evil. There is far more to producing a contented, healthy child than simply breastfeeding.

On top of that there are benefits to bottle-feeding. Fathers can take over a night-time feed – I used to get to sleep between 10 pm and 5 am (bliss). Plus grandparents and friends absolutely love giving feeds. You can mix up all the day's bottles in one go and once you're practised it takes about as long as it does to clean your teeth. They can either be kept in the fridge and pulled out when necessary or filled with boiled water and powder added just before they're needed. You can buy special containers to store the powder and dispense from. Keep spare supplies of cartons and disposable bottles in the pushchair/car just in case you're out longer than you think – it's great for peace of mind.

When feeding, try to get as much body and facial contact as possible to encourage bonding, especially in the early days. Bottle-fed babies are much more prone to dehydration (check if the fontanelle is depressed) so you will probably need to give some cooled boiled water even to young babies in the summer. Most brands do a version for older, hungrier babies. Mine switched at three months and was better for it. Remember that formula has been used for thousands of years – tribes in the Amazon made up a version using almonds – so don't feel bad. There's something wonderful about watching your baby guzzling down milk with obvious enjoyment, it's very special.

*Nobby*

# 9

# When Things
# Go Wrong

# Introduction

Sadly, it doesn't always turn out as the books say it should and not everyone who falls pregnant goes home with a baby. It's a well known but tragic statistic that around one in five pregnancies ends in miscarriage (*Junior* magazine) and yet whilst there are shelves full of books on everything from massaging your perineum to the best sex position for a full-term mum-to-be, miscarriage remains a taboo subject.

Given that it has been estimated that only 1 per cent of pregnancies miscarry after 13 weeks of gestation (Professor Lesley Regan *Miscarriage*), the tradition of not publicizing pregnancy in the first trimester 'just in case' is perfectly understandable, but it does mean that when the unthinkable happens you can find yourself isolated, with no one to turn to and unable to explain to colleagues, friends or family why you're feeling so miserable. It can feel as if you're the only person in the world who has ever had to watch your longed-for baby make an all too premature appearance.

The first sign of bleeding during pregnancy – however slight – is enough to send any expectant mother into a blind panic but it doesn't always indicate that a miscarriage is imminent. So, what does a miscarriage really feel like? How long does it last and, if you find yourself in the throes of one, is it best to go for surgery and risk an anaesthetic, or allow the baby to 'pass naturally' and risk losing your baby into the toilet bowl?

It's an unfortunate fact that just as your hopes and plans are abruptly halted you find yourself in the midst of hormone hell, so it's easy for guilt to creep up on you. Everyone searches for reasons why their baby didn't make it, but the consensus seems to be that there is little anyone can do to avoid a miscarriage or prevent a recurrence. So once you're no longer pregnant, when can you or should you think about trying again?

What if you make it past the magical 12-week mark, only to be told that your child has a high risk of being born with special needs, shows signs of severe abnormalities, will not survive birth or, worse still, is already dead? It's not a scenario anyone, and particularly a pregnant woman, wants to dwell on for any length of time, but how on earth do you cope with it?

Inevitably, amongst mumsnet's thousands of parents, losing a baby before term is a sad but relatively common occurrence. The only positive outcome from these personal tragedies is the wealth of empathy, experience and understanding they have generated. Nothing and no one can fully prepare you for the mental and physical pain of losing a child but if you're anxious about it, have already lost a baby or are in the midst of a miscarriage or post-test trauma, take comfort in one thing – you are not alone. Others have been there before you, grieved and survived, and in most cases gone on to have happy and healthy future pregnancies.

# Bleeding in pregnancy – does it always mean miscarriage?

**If you bleed don't despair!** I had lot of sudden bleeding and clots at 13 weeks and an ambulance came for me at once because they assumed miscarriage. I was crying and showing the ambulance man the photo of the last scan. They decided not to admit me but booked me in for a scan the next day, and told me to come back as soon as possible if I bled any more. However, all was well and I had a healthy son in due course.

*Amma*

**I've had bleeding in all my pregnancies.** Three went to term and the first two ended in miscarriage. Unfortunately, there is no real way of knowing what bleeding means without going to an early pregnancy clinic or an A&E unit. It's a very worrying and upsetting thing to happen, but bleeding certainly doesn't always mean that all is lost.

*Oxocube*

**I am 24 weeks' pregnant** and had some bleeding at seven and 11 weeks from what they thought was a low-lying placenta. Fortunately for me it's moved out of the way as my baby has grown and I'm fine now.

*Honeybunny*

**I bled on and off between** six and 18 weeks with both my first two pregnancies (both boys, both low placentas). At times I wished that I would miscarry so that I could stop worrying and get on with my life. Everything turned out okay in the end but my second son had to be delivered early when I started bleeding badly at 31 weeks due to placenta praevia. It's always worth getting it checked out when you bleed.

*PamT*

**I had a significant bleed** lasting for about one and a half days at around five weeks and I assumed it was my period. I was very surprised to discover I was pregnant a couple of weeks later – I didn't get any strong pregnancy symptoms until I was about seven weeks. The rest of the pregnancy was fine.

*Eulalia*

**I had bleeding at about six weeks,** coupled with a very sharp pain. I was convinced I'd lose the baby, but luckily it settled down after two days. I was away on a Hen weekend at the time and spent most of the time in bed in tears.

*Sweetie*

## What the experts say

It used to be thought that the best thing was to go to bed and stay there until the bleeding stopped. There is, however, no evidence that this helps at all. So do whatever makes you feel more comfortable.

Sheila Kitzinger (*The New Pregnancy and Childbirth*)

**I started bleeding at six weeks** but was unsure if I was having a miscarriage as friends said miscarriage involved bleeding for about 10 days and terrible cramps and I had no pain at all. I since found out that some people miscarry painlessly (physically). In the end I went for a scan. The baby was still there – like a knobbly baked bean – and I stopped bleeding.

*Anoushka*

**I bled at six and eight weeks** and called out the emergency doctor, who said I was miscarrying. I then went to have a scan just to be sure and they found a heartbeat. My mum had three periods/bleeds whilst carrying me and my brother and me were both fine. Some women just do seem to bleed in pregnancy.

*Tillysmummy*

**Mumsnet fact**
Ninety-five per cent of women who bleed in the first trimester and then have a scan that shows all is well, go on to have a normal pregnancy.

*Practical Parenting* magazine

**I'd already had a miscarriage** and D&C before having my daughter and when I went to the loo and lost a small clot of blood in my subsequent pregnancy I didn't hold out much hope. My doctor was very reluctant to organize an early scan so in the end I went through accident and emergency. We had a long wait and finally got a scan. Almost instantly they told me they could see the baby and the heartbeat. What a massive relief! The bleeding was coming from a tiny area and they weren't worried but said it may happen again. It isn't always bad news.

I think the waiting is the worst bit. My first miscarriage was awful because, although there was no heartbeat and the baby was far too small for the dates (which I was certain of), the hospital re-scanned me weekly for three weeks before even suggesting a D&C and even then said that they could scan again. I suffered from terrible depression mainly due to not knowing what was going on.

*Ames*

**If you do experience bleeding** and want to know what is happening, press your GP to get an early scan or just go direct to the hospital. I was fobbed off, left bleeding over Christmas and the New Year, and was almost out of my mind at the end of it.

*Hmb*

**I feel so sad and frustrated** for people who get badly treated when they have an early bleed. I bled at six weeks with my first pregnancy and was devastated. I phoned my doctor in tears and they just said, well, it's very early, isn't it? To me it wasn't – a sixth of the way through seemed a reasonable amount. I got my husband to phone and they gave him the number of the local early pregnancy unit and I had a scan that afternoon and a problem-free rest of pregnancy, although I didn't stop worrying for a minute.

Why are so many 'health professionals' so callous when it comes to miscarriage and worries about bleeding in pregnancy? I remember them discussing 'viable pregnancy' with me and I was thinking, 'this is my baby we're talking about.'

*Monkey*

**One thing to bear in mind** if you have a bleed and are rhesus negative is that you should see the GP straight away, as you will need a dose of anti-D (to prevent you making antibodies against the baby's blood type). You should have this within 72 hours of a bleed.

*Leese*

**I'm 24 weeks' pregnant** and have had a number of bleeds in this pregnancy, as I did in a past pregnancy. I was told it was a cervical erosion but, after a bleed at 17 weeks and a scan, I was then told the loss was from my placenta. I had to spend the New Year in hospital after yet another bleed, which was again from my placenta. I find it very amusing reading pregnancy magazines that say I should feel wonderful at this stage.

*Ariel*

**At six and a half weeks' pregnant,** I started bleeding. It started off just brown, like the beginnings of a period, but after a couple of days became a lot heavier, brighter red with some clotting. I went to the doctors and they arranged an early scan. My first pregnancy had gone without a hitch so I was surprised to have bleeding this time.

It's strange, but despite three positive pregnancy tests I had had niggling doubts that I was actually pregnant because I hadn't felt sick at all and I was nauseous and sick all the way through last time. The scan confirmed my fears and showed the uterus to be 'clean' – most of the material had already been expelled. I think it's better if it happens earlier rather than later and although I'm sad, I do believe it's for the best and 'nature's way'.

*Donna1*

**When I started to bleed** I hadn't even signed up with the midwife, so I just rang the hospital directly and they were happy to fit me into the Early Pregnancy Unit. I had a scan at six weeks and six days approximate gestation. They picked up a heartbeat, which was reassuring, but I carried on bleeding and miscarried anyway. I had awful cramps, but my cervix dilated to expel everything in the uterus. I also didn't 'feel pregnant', no nausea or food aversions, etc.

When you start bleeding everyone tells you to put your feet up. This might make you feel better, but won't make a blind bit of difference to the outcome. If a miscarriage is imminent there is nothing you can do to stop it. So if you do miscarry, please don't feel that anything you did contributed to the bleeding. As a positive postscript, I am now nine weeks' pregnant with a completely different, normal, nauseous pregnancy – after being convinced I would never conceive again.

*Enid*

**I started bleeding at seven weeks** and miscarried in a very 'low key' way – I bled less than a normal period and had no pain. But after four days of stopping and starting – hopes raised then dashed – I suddenly just felt different and not pregnant. I'd had misgivings about the pregnancy. The test at the doctors had showed a pale thin line not a vivid fat one like my other two pregnancies and I had had no particular symptoms – apart from tiredness – but that's me most of the time. So in a way I don't feel that I actually lost a baby, I just think that the chemicals weren't doing what they should have done in the first place.

It was still a really upsetting time and I cried the other day telling a friend about what happened. I'd sailed through two pregnancies and although I know all the statistics – I had just assumed I wasn't one of them. It was sad enough to miscarry at that stage but I tried to console myself with how much worse it could have been if it had happened at a later stage. I was still surprised though at how deep the sadness goes.

*Maras*

**I've had three miscarriages** – two involved heavy bleeding, pain, the whole lot. The other one had no symptoms at all, tiny amounts of spotting and no pain. I knew in all cases I'd miscarried as my breasts deflated immediately and I could touch them without pain.

*MABS*

**My first pregnancy miscarried at seven weeks** and it seems to me that we know about them more because of efficient pregnancy test kits. Women of our mothers' generation may just have thought they were having a late period. It's a form of progress in that the earlier we find out we're pregnant the better we can start to look after ourselves, but it does bring heartache with it

*Sobernow*

## What's a miscarriage really like and when can you try again?

**I had an early miscarriage** two years ago. I only realized several months later (when I learnt that even a very faint line on the pregnancy test means you're pregnant) that I had miscarried. It was the most painful 'period' I had ever had – I normally get cramps, but this was doubled-over-almost-in-tears stuff. Fortunately, the worst was over in half a day, and I think I escaped the emotional trauma of it because by the time I realized it had been a miscarriage I was pregnant again. I had another miscarriage earlier this year and that was a different kettle of fish as I found out at the scan that the baby had died. Don't assume, though, that just because you have an early miscarriage it won't affect you. It's still a big deal and a hard thing to cope with.

*Amber1*

**My first miscarriage** – around seven weeks – was like a very heavy period and by the time I had a scan, all signs of the baby had gone. When I miscarried at eight and a half weeks I bled unimaginably heavily for several days, and had a lot of pain. After about 10 days the blood turned smelly and it turned out I had an infection, which is something to watch out for.

I was surprised both times that the pregnancy symptoms continued post-miscarriage for quite a while. To still have morning sickness and sore breasts when there's no baby seems so cruel and unfair. If you're sent home to miscarry 'naturally', you need industrial strength sanitary pads and someone sympathetic with you – you don't want to have to flush a baby away on your own, if it comes to that. Plus I'd stock up on Ibuprofen or get the doctor to prescribe something stronger, the last thing you need is physical as well as mental pain.

*Biza*

**My only miscarriage** happened 11 years ago, and I still think about it now. I was 11 weeks and it was the week after Valentine's Day – my husband and I had just got engaged. I had bad cramps and extremely heavy bleeding. I lived on my own but luckily had good friends nearby, who took me to their house to rest. By the next morning things had got a lot worse, and I had to go to hospital. In the end they did an ERPC (Evacuation of Remaining Products of Conception). They told me that it was just one of those things and the pregnancy obviously wasn't meant to be.

*Ailsa*

**I miscarried our first baby** at about six or seven weeks. I had only just found out that I was pregnant and it was a big shock. It had been completely unplanned and I was full of mixed emotions when I started to bleed and a little embryo came out. Maybe it was seeing this tiny thing that made it real but I was surprised at how upset I was. Getting pregnant hadn't been top of my list of things to do at that time but I was devastated at losing our little baby. My husband didn't really get it because it was a non-event for him but I went through the whole grieving process for that child. I still think about it.

*Harrysmum*

**I was told at my scan** that I had had a 'missed miscarriage' and it was horrendous. I really did not expect to be told that the baby had died a few weeks earlier. I was nine weeks and had only had a small pinhead of blood. I had a two-and-a-half-year-old so tried to focus on him but when you have had a healthy pregnancy first time round, you just expect that the second time will be the same.

*Mima*

**Mumsnet fact**
Women aged between 25 and 30 have a 16 per cent chance of suffering a miscarriage. This rate increases to 25 per cent by the age of 40 and would probably be at least 50 per cent by 47 or 48.

*The Times*

**I discovered I'd had a 'missed miscarriage'** at my 12-week booking scan. I'd had a very, very slight bleed a few weeks earlier and thought very little of it as I'd had the same thing with my first baby and he turned out to be big and healthy. I hadn't realized I'd got so attached already. I keep thinking of the plans I'd started to make for the new baby and it makes me cry.

*Hmonty*

**I miscarried my first baby at 12 weeks.** I had been comparing notes with a neighbour whose baby was due about the same time and the next six months were hard, watching her bloom. We were assured that it was 'just one of those things' and I fell pregnant again fairly quickly. All was fine until about 12 weeks, and again I had some bleeding which was horrific as it was over Christmas. I had a scan and found out that I was expecting twins. I didn't have a good pregnancy with the fear hanging over me that it would happen again, but I went on to have two healthy babies. Just over two years later the same thing happened – rotten pregnancy but another set of girl twins!

I still think about that first baby (I wonder if it was a boy) and that was 19 years ago. The hardest thing the first time round was going back to work and people not realizing and having to explain. Maybe it's nature's way but that's no consolation when you're going through it.

*Twinsmum*

**I had bleeding then two hours** of horrific stomach cramps, then I got the urge to push, went to the loo and out it came, the complete pregnancy sac, about the size of a tangerine and in it my 'baby'. I would not wish that experience on anyone. When I phoned the hospital they said I was 'lucky' that it had come away in one piece as normally it breaks up and the process takes a few days. They said not to keep it as it was only my first miscarriage and tests would only be done if I had a second or third. I just could not bear flush it away and it lay there in the loo for three hours until my husband came in from work. By this point I was inconsolable. I let him see it and we cried and hugged eachother and said goodbye and flushed it away.

Within a few days I went to the chemist for an ovulation test kit and as soon as my period came I started again. I got through the horror because I had the support of a terrific husband and friends and also my son, but I pray that this never happens to me again.

*Croppy*

---

**What the experts say**
In many cases of recurrent miscarriage no cause is found. However, while this is unsatisfactory in terms of explaining the problem, it does not mean the situation is hopeless. In such cases, three-quarters of women will go on, with supportive care alone, to have a successful pregnancy.

Professor Ian Greer (*Pregnancy: The Inside Guide*)

---

**A close friend of mine** was advised to wait until she had a period before trying again to give her hormones a chance to level off and to ensure that her womb was clear.

*Molly1*

**I started miscarrying on October 14th** and according to the dating scan conceived again around November 17th. I say 'according to the scan' as neither my husband nor I can actually remember doing the trying thing – we were, we thought, actively not trying because I wanted to have a period first. I felt lousy all Christmas very sick and tearful, and decided I had some terrible, probably fatal disease (oh, those hormones). No one's even sure if I'd had a period (I bled for almost four weeks post miscarriage). But when I still hadn't had one by late December I did a pregnancy test at the GP's and had an early scan in January and was eight weeks and five days!

One thing my (two) miscarriages taught me is not to take anything for granted until the little bundle is actually screaming in your arms. I think that's one thing the medical profession and others don't really understand is how pessimistic and worried a miscarriage can make you when you do fall pregnant again.

*Nick*

# Dilation and Curettage (D&C) or 'natural' – what's best?

**I was very torn** about the best course of action when I miscarried. I opted for the 'natural' route and although it was quite unpleasant, painful and depressing, it was a massive relief when it was all over and I didn't have to take antibiotics or have a D&C. I didn't see anything that resembled a baby, which was my main fear. The only thing that really shocked me was how painful it was, almost like being in labour. I got some satisfaction from the fact that my body was getting on with the job and doing it properly. If it should happen again, I would definitely try and go 'natural' again although of course it would depend on my midwives' advice.

*Enid*

**I went the 'natural' route** both times when I miscarried. My first was very early, around seven weeks, and felt just like a very heavy period. The second nine weeks was awful, immensely painful, with very heavy bleeding and I had to flush the baby away down the loo. When they gave me the option, 'natural' seemed infinitely better than having to have an anaesthetic, but no one spelt out to me that 'natural' would involve losing a baby down the toilet, something no human being should ever have to go through. By the end of it I wished I'd opted for a D&C.

*Biza*

**I opted for 'natural'** but was not at all prepared for what was to happen, i.e. the whole little foetus coming out intact. It was the worst experience of my life.

*Mima*

---

**What the experts say**
Some doctors take it for granted that a woman who has had a miscarriage should go to hospital for a D&C to scrape out surgically any remaining contents of the uterus, in order to avoid infection. This can be a traumatic experience. Research shows that surgery is no better than waiting, if the amount left in the uterus is small.

Sheila Kitzinger (*The New Pregnancy and Childbirth*)

---

**I had a miscarriage at ten weeks** and went in for a D&C. It was not a very painful procedure and I did not have to cope with seeing quantities of blood or tissue coming out of me. I was left with something like a heavy period, that was all. I physically recovered in a day or two. To my surprise, I fell pregnant again within three months. I then went on to have a normal pregnancy. The midwife told me that a D&C can increase the chances of you getting pregnant by 'clearing you out'. I guess it worked for me.

*Frank1*

**A friend of mine had a D&C** following a miscarriage at 12 weeks. She was also told that it would 'open everything up' and the next month she fell pregnant again and gave birth to a healthy baby.

*ChanelNo5*

**At ten weeks I had a 'missed abortion'** (i.e. the baby had died). I only had two spots of blood and was sent home to miscarry naturally. After 10 very stressful days carrying the dead baby and still having to wear maternity clothes because nothing else fitted, I returned to hospital for a D&C at my request. Physically, the operation was as minor as they come. There was the usual waiting around but I went into hospital at about 1 pm, was given a cannula and had a chat with an anaesthetist, then it was my turn. I lay on a bed, they inserted a tube into the cannula, I felt a very cold liquid go in, and within about five seconds was out like a light. When I came round in recovery a nurse was holding an oxygen mask over my face, which she took off as soon as I woke up. I think I was under anaesthetic for about 15–20 minutes in total.

You had to pass urine before they'd let you go home. I think I got out of bed after two hours, but felt I needed to relax so got back in for half an hour then rang a friend to pick me up. The bleeding afterwards was much lighter than I expected with no pain of any kind, but I bled for a long time. They say two weeks is typical, but I bled for four, stopped for about three days and then got my period. The following cycle I got pregnant again. I can honestly say that there was no pain involved at any stage.

*Amber1*

> **Mumsnet fact**
> It is estimated that a quarter of all women who become pregnant experience at least one miscarriage.
>
> Professor Lesley Regan (*Miscarriage*)

**Many years ago** I had a pregnancy where the foetus died at around eight weeks (I found this out at about 10 weeks) and had a D&C. I didn't have a general anaesthetic, just a local and was awake the whole time (recovery is supposed to be quicker that way with fewer complications and general anaesthetic is always a risk).

The procedure was not painful, not even the local anaesthetic to the cervix, and took only a few minutes. I could not see anything and a lovely nurse was holding my hand the whole time, telling me that everything was going fine and I would be okay. Afterwards, I had to sit around for a while until they were sure I was not going to haemorrhage and was then sent home.

I can honestly say that, apart from being very upset that the baby had died, I felt only relief that it was 'all over' so quickly. For the next two to three days I suffered pain and bleeding similar to a very heavy period and then very light bleeding for about three weeks more. I did not try to fall pregnant again for many years after that.

Earlier this year I had an early miscarriage, at about six weeks, and didn't really get the choice because everything just came out on its own. Fortunately there's not a lot there at six weeks. This time there was also pain and bleeding like a very heavy period but the bleeding stopped in about five to six days. I fell pregnant again right away, before I'd even had a period, and am now 18 weeks!

*Chelle*

# When abnormality shows up at a scan – what can you do?

One of my twins was diagnosed with Down's Syndrome at 13–14 weeks. It was a heartbreaking decision to terminate but we were advised that the risk of miscarriage to both babies was high and I could not face the stress of the rest of the pregnancy worrying that might happen. Fortunately, the rest of the pregnancy went well though I was very emotional and the joy of the baby's arrival was tempered by the fact that there was only one baby and not two.

It was a very difficult time though I have mostly come to terms with it now. We have discussed having another baby but I am still not sure yet if I could go through the stresses again worrying if all would be okay.

*Anon*

**I terminated a pregnancy for Down's Syndrome** at 17 weeks: abnormalities were picked up on the scan at 13 weeks, and it was confirmed with an amnio. My own emotional stages went a bit like this. First couple of weeks: very emotional, but felt very close to my partner, was in wonderment at my eldest child, and was generally fussed over by health professionals. Over the next couple of months I struggled on, hoping things would get better. Then I cracked at about three months and went to a counsellor at the hospital a couple of times, which made me feel a lot better. I was depressed in all the normal ways – couldn't get motivated to do anything, didn't look forward, was anxious, lacked energy. The counsellor told me that 8-10 weeks is a typical time not to be able to cope.

Only my close friends and family knew I was pregnant, it wasn't common knowledge, so in a way that was easier. But some of those that did know about it weren't very understanding – and the way people reacted to the loss has affected my relationship with them. Losing a baby pre-term is just like any other bereavement, but other people don't recognize it as such. People who have miscarried understand that.

Of course, I feel terrible that I didn't have the strength to give our daughter what she needed. However, deep down I know that it was the right decision for us and I would do the same again. I feel very strongly that I shouldn't try and defend my decision to anybody but myself.

In my subsequent pregnancy, I requested an amnio, but this was more to do with putting our minds at rest than anything else. My chances of having another baby with Down's Syndrome are only slightly higher than other women of my age. I now have another baby, who I cherish so much more because of what we've been through, but hardly a day goes by when I don't think of my middle child.

*Anon*

**My sister's child was diagnosed Down's** Syndrome at 30 weeks and she was offered a termination. She was told the baby might not last 5 minutes, he would be floppy and limp, short limbs, etc. I guess they have a duty to tell you all this, but the doctors don't tell you about all the beautiful things. My sister didn't terminate and I won't say there are not problems – there are, lots of them – but he is a lovely, sweet baby, who looks gorgeous, can lift his head up and is looking around the room already. There are different levels of Down's Syndrome, some people have it worse than others, but no one knows how bad it is until the child gets older.

As I also have a brother with learning difficulties I have to say that I am against the termination of a baby just because it is disabled. A disabled child is difficult, hard work and exhausting, but they bring so much joy. This society is obsessed with being perfect: perfect babies, perfect mothers, etc., that anything seen as different is not welcome. Seeing my sister's baby makes me wonder how anyone could not want such a child, however imperfect he may be.

*Anon*

**As a mother of a seven-month-old girl** with Down's Syndrome I would urge any-one not to rush into something you will regret. Even if you don't want your child, there are many couples out there waiting to adopt a baby with DS. My little girl is an absolute joy. She's no different from an ordinary 7-month-old baby and doesn't place more demands on us than her two-year-old sister did at this age (actually, she sleeps through more than her big sister ever did).

She's reaching milestones just like an ordinary baby, has crabby days, days when she's happy, etc. She loves people and is really bubbly and interested. Things have really changed for people with Down's Syndrome in the last 10 years or so – there is no question of whether my girls will both be going to the same primary school – of course they will! And yes, my youngest might need a bit of assistance, but that's not a big deal.

The adults you see with Down's Syndrome nowadays never benefited from education and proper medical treatment, and of course the result is not pretty, but this new generation really has a bright future ahead of them.

*Anon*

> **Mumsnet fact**
> Two babies with Down's Syndrome are born every day in the UK. Around one in every 1000 babies born will have Down's Syndrome.
> Down's Syndrome Association

**My pregnancy was very uneventful until** we went for the 20-week scan and the baby decided that nothing would make her turn over for them to check her stomach, heart, lungs, etc. So we had to return a week later for the scan to be completed. At that point a heart abnormality was picked up. We were devastated as it was quite serious. We managed to get an appointment with a foetal cardiologist. Prior to the cardiac scan we decided that our baby would be born and we would deal with each thing as it occurred. The specialist confirmed that our daughter had a heart problem but not the condition they suspected. She had an Atrial-Ventricular Septal Defect, basically no central wall in her heart to divide the right from the left side, as well as valve damage.

Those first few days were the most difficult of our life. We had been planning for the 'perfect' baby as the media tells us to imagine. However, the cardiac scan provided almost a sense of relief. Her heart defect was very serious but correctable with surgery. The cardiologist also told us that this was a very common heart defect amongst children with Down's Syndrome. He offered us an amnio and we refused – simply because it would not change the outcome. We were given a very detailed scan and there were markers for Down's Syndrome – what they called soft markers. Had our daughter been born without Down's Syndrome it would have been a miracle. But she was born in August 2002 and a few days later they confirmed the Down's Syndrome. It was difficult dealing with the suspected heart conditions and the Down's Syndrome – we found talking about it between us and seeking out reliable information, particularly from other parents, helped so much. Whilst the scans were scary and troubling we never ever contemplated terminating the pregnancy.

Now 13 months old, our daughter is full of life and blossoming after two open-heart operations at 8 weeks old. Every day with her is a blessing. She wakes up with the most beautiful smile and greets the world so happily; at bedtime she is still smiling – though she can still throw hissy fits like the best of them.

Looking at my cheeky, gorgeous little girl now I know it was all worth it. I would not change a thing. I have learnt strength and fortitude from a baby. She continues to grow and develop every day – my friends and family adore her and she is such a blessing to us. She is crawling and working on cruising, standing and scoffing food like it is going to be rationed. She is in mainstream nursery as I have gone back to work full time and she loves it – she is into everything and wanting to do it all. The nursery nurses love her.

Yes, sometimes it was tough and I never thought I would see an end – particularly when she was having her heart surgery and some relapses – BUT I feel it is an honour to be her mother.

*Anon*

**My AFP test at 20 weeks came back** saying I had a high risk of having a baby with Down's Syndrome and I refused an amnio. The last 20 weeks of my pregnancy were really horrendous, every day I thought about it, but I had lost a baby at the beginning of the year and could not bear to lose another one, also to have miscarried a perfectly healthy baby after an amnio was too big a risk for me, emotionally I could not have coped. The hospital told me what I would have to go through if the amnio result showed a baby with Down's Syndrome and I decided to abort, i.e. injection to kill it, labour induced, birth certificate and funeral, and I decided against it.

*Anon*

**I know someone who gave birth** to a baby with Down's Syndrome when it hadn't been detected antenatally (she was in her mid-20s and had normal blood screening). It had a catastrophic effect on both her existing child and her marriage, and culminated in the baby being adopted. She has always said that she wouldn't have continued with the pregnancy if she had known.

I don't disagree with the comments made about how rewarding a child with a disability can be, nor do I think this is an easy thing to go through with. I just think that every situation is different and that you have to make the decision that is right for you. I think if faced with a heartbreaking decision you mustn't add guilt on the part of others' opinions to all the other emotions that you must be feeling.

*Anon*

**I had a termination for Down's** Syndrome following CVS. It is the most excruciating and painful experience. It's a completely personal choice and no one chooses to terminate lightly. If you've made the decision you need support and friendship and not advice about alternatives, well meant as that advice may be. If you feel that a termination is best for you and your family then that's your choice and, hard as it is, you shouldn't feel guilty.

*Anon*

**My baby didn't have Down's Syndrome,** but had a heart abnormality, which showed at the 20-week scan. We were told he wouldn't survive for more than a few days if he were to go full term so we decided to terminate to save the additional trauma of losing a full-term baby. I felt a lot of guilt wondering if I'd done the right thing, and perhaps he could have been operated on, etc, but in the end you have to do what feels right for you and your partner. It is so personal, nobody can advise you the 'right' thing to do, but lots of people try. I had to be induced, and go through labour to have the baby. This is not something I knew until a couple of days beforehand. I had previously thought that you could just have an operation to have a termination, but not when you are over a certain amount of weeks.

No one can prepare you for the experience, but I would not advise rushing back to work. Do not underestimate in any way how much it will affect you. I took about a week off and thought if I kept busy I'd be okay. Not true, and I regret it still after almost three years, and a beautiful healthy child later.

The milk coming in is upsetting, but does dry up quickly, thank goodness. We also had a small funeral, but with no family present, just me and my partner. My friends were fantastic but I wish I'd accepted the offer of counselling – I thought I could cope. My advice is to talk to anyone who will listen without judging you.

*Anon*

**I have a disabled four-year-old** who requires a lot of care; I'm also four months' pregnant and decided early on that if a problem were to occur again termination would be a strong possibility. I simply couldn't cope and felt it would be unfair to my other children and also to a new baby, who needed a lot of extra care.

I spend a lot of time in hospital with my little girl and we decided that to bring another baby into the world who required this type of care was not an option. I'm sorry if that sounds heartless, it's not meant to, but I don't think some people realize what hard work physically, emotionally and mentally it is to care for a child with these degrees of special needs.

*Anon*

> **Mumsnet tip**
> Take someone with you to the scan if at all possible (though not a toddler as they tend to distract you). I didn't take anyone as I didn't expect there to be problems and was told that my son had a cleft palate and it would potentially mean there were other problems and did I want an abortion? It was a lot to take in aged 17 and all on my own.
>
> *Anais*

**With my first pregnancy** they found serious cranio/facial abnormalities at the routine 23-week scan, and we opted for termination. My only advice, looking back, is to read every bit of literature they offer you and then ask lots of questions so that you feel prepared for everything that's going to happen. I was told that from induction to delivery would take on average 12 hours, only for me it was 36 hours. No one mentioned the possibility of needing a D&C immediately afterwards, but I had a retained placenta so needed wheeling down to theatre. Three weeks later I was having another one for yet more retained products that were missed first time around.

What helped me most was being able to talk openly about every little detail with my husband, often over and over again. He was with me throughout, and was a huge tower of strength. We had a very small funeral and cremation for our son, just myself and hubby. It felt almost like closure, yet we still had to await postmortem outcomes and face the fact that we'd been labelled with a possible genetic/recessive trait that may or may not come up again with our next pregnancy (a one in four chance).

We went away for a few days just to be on our own and mourn. We booked a holiday over what would have been our 'due' date, which gave us something to look forward to. It also persuaded me to start living again and that it was okay to have a good time.

Returning to work was hard. People avoided my eye, turned away, and generally ignored the whole issue. I was devastated by this. I wanted to be able to talk openly and have tearful days if needs be but felt I had to do the 'stiff upper lip thing' instead. I wish I'd written to work and explained what had happened and reassured them that I wouldn't dissolve into a puddle of tears but that it would help to be open and up front. I also found some family members were totally incapable of dealing with grief. I found it hard not to judge them for it, but it's such a British thing isn't it? We just don't talk about death/loss/grief.

We planted a tree in the garden in remembrance of our son, and made up a scrapbook of every part of my pregnancy up to the end. It has all the letters of condolences and paperwork from the hospital, plus a photo of our son. It sounds a little macabre but it's all I have left of our baby. Walking out of that hospital with nothing was agony. Having nothing to hold onto or remember him by was just hideous. I hadn't even had the chance to go out and buy him a toy or body suit or anything.

The situation is an emotional minefield. You think that everyone you pass in the street knows what you are about to do and is judging you for your choice. It took me months to accept that the decision we had made was the right one, even knowing from post-mortem results that should our baby have survived to term, he wouldn't have lived. Even now on a bad day I shed buckets of tears for the son I never got to know, beyond the kicks and somersaults of movement I felt whilst pregnant.

On a happier note, we conceived our second son over our 'recovery' holiday. And despite an extremely stressful initial 24 weeks (four scans to make sure that everything was okay) we had a gorgeous baby boy.

I'm glad that everyone persuaded me to see my son. I was terrified that I was going to be presented with some kind of monster, but they'd dressed him and laid him in a Moses basket, and he looked very peaceful. I just remember his perfect hands and feet, and although his face was very misshapen, I could see that he had the most vivid blue eyes.

*Anon*


**There is a charity** for parents who have to make tough decisions after test results called ARC (Antenatal Results and Choices).

*Anon*

## Coping with the loss – what helps and how can you best help others with the pain of miscarriage?

**I was pregnant at the same time** as my sister and best friend. For the first 12 weeks we did everything together and talked about babies all the time, then I started to bleed. I didn't worry too much as this had happened in my previous pregnancy, but two days later I woke with terrible pains, was rushed to hospital and told that I'd miscarried.

I found other people's reactions very difficult. Even my mother kept saying it was for the best and there was probably something wrong with it and I could have another. She was right but at the time this was not what I wanted to hear. All I wanted was this baby. My sister found it awkward to be around me and felt guilty that she was still pregnant, so didn't visit in case she upset me. I was already upset so she could not have made me feel any worse.

I was lucky that I could concentrate on my two-year-old and keep things as normal as possible, but little things like hearing her sing *Rock a Bye Baby* would make me sob. We tried for another baby straight away but nothing happened for six months and I had to watch my friend and sister have their babies. I was happy for them but jealous. Around this time I became pregnant again. This baby didn't replace the one I lost but it gave me something else to focus on.

This is still one of the worst things that has happened to me and almost three years later I still think about the baby and remember him on the anniversary of the day I lost him.

*Del*

**I had a miscarriage** just over six months ago. It was my third pregnancy and completely unplanned. I had just got over the shock of being pregnant – I already had a three-year-old and a one-year-old and was nervous about having a third so quickly – but I was rushed to hospital at 12 weeks exactly. It was very late at night and at around 3 am I was taken for a D&C to help stop the bleeding. I have never been so physically and emotionally shaken in my life.

It took me a while to recover physically and I still have feelings of guilt that maybe I didn't want the baby enough and that's why it happened. Until it happened to me I had no idea how a miscarriage can affect you. I still think about it, but now the due date has passed, I feel better. I was rather hurt that close friends were insensitive about the miscarriage and seemed to think that I should just get over it. I am usually a positive cheerful person but ever since it happened I have become much more irritable and grumbly.

*Bear*

**What the experts say**

Almost three-quarters of women worry that they might have caused the problem leading to their miscarriage...The truth, however, is that it is exceptionally rare for there to have been anything that the mother could have done or not done which would have caused or prevented the miscarriage.

Professor Ian Greer (*Pregnancy: The Inside Guide*)

**One of my friends lost her baby** at 17 weeks. We were all terribly upset when we found out and had a good cry. We spoke on the phone, emailed and went to see her and let her talk if she wanted to. We let her know that we all loved her very much and we would help her get through this and her return to work.

It was difficult for all of us – especially those of us that already had babies. I felt guilty for having a lovely healthy boy. I actually told my friend that I didn't know what to say to her. We had a cry and a hug and she told me all about her daughter. It helped that she gave her little girl a name and we were all able to refer to her as a proper person (that doesn't sound right, but you know what I mean). She has a keepsake box at home full of things that relate to her little girl, which I think is lovely.

If you don't let people know that you have suffered a miscarriage then your friends can't support you. You have to take the lead on how you want to be treated because it's a tough subject to handle. Talk openly about how you feel to your friends and family, then they will be happier talking about it.

It was only after my friend told people that she had lost her baby that other people started to relay their experiences – and it was surprising just how many people had lost babies in late pregnancy. She took comfort from seeing that others had moved on and, in most cases, gone on to have other babies.

*Emmam*

**Realizing that you are allowed to feel awful** and sorry for yourself, even if it's an early miscarriage, is a large part of coping with miscarriage. It's hard because sometimes your partner doesn't feel it as much when it's early and if you haven't told anyone else it can be very isolating. Going back to work helped in some ways, though I found it difficult to actually get stuck in again.

*Lil*

**We all keep our early pregnancies quiet** so we don't have to tell anyone if it all goes wrong, but it's not always something you can hide and 'get over' in a matter of days, yet we're expected to move on and put it behind us. I know that's what we all do, I just worry that there's a lot of pent-up sadness that would-be parents don't acknowledge or talk about.

*Biza*

**I lost a baby in July this year** and my due date is next week. I still feel very miserable most days. I'm not sure that anyone understands how upset I get as I have four children already. I was shocked to find I was expecting another and it took me three months to get used to the idea. I still don't know whether to try for another one. I probably wouldn't have, but now the idea has been planted and it's horrible to finish your 'child-bearing' with a loss. My baby died but I didn't miscarry (it was a 'missed abortion') so I had to go in for an op. This has happened to me twice though not consecutively. We all know pregnancies fail so it's not a surprise, but it is still a loss and I mourn the babies that I have never cuddled.

*Ginette*

**Mumsnet fact**
Despite advances in medicine, the rate of miscarriage is as high today as it was in the 1930s.

mymiscarriage.fsnet.co.uk

**It makes me mad** that in the 'real' world miscarriage is such a taboo. It's so common and yet no one knows how to deal with it. Following the birth of a beautiful girl in October 1997 I thought producing a sibling for her would be as much of a breeze as she had been. We fell pregnant as soon as we tried but the dating scan showed that the baby – they called it a foetus, but it was a baby to me – had died at six and a half weeks. It was such a shock, nothing could have prepared us for that news. One minute we were part of the expectant parents club, but as we left the scan room I felt completely alien to these other women.

Two other miscarriages followed and they are finally getting round to investigating. The appointment for the various bloods they had to take took ages to come through and I had to go to the antenatal department to have the blood taken – sensitive or what! Fortunately I was told that everything is fine, which is reassuring, but in some ways you feel you'd like something to be wrong so you can do something about it.

It occurred to me after a good talk with a gynaecologist that the medical profession is so scientific but a miscarriage is so emotional and whilst counselling is offered in some cases – in my case for one of my miscarriages – it's hard to find someone to really talk it through with. I will talk to anyone and everyone about my miscarriages, it's the only thing that's helped me.

*Lizz*

**After my miscarriage I cried for days.** Nothing anyone said made it feel any better, except perhaps a hug and kiss from my son, who was our rock throughout that period of time. Five weeks on from the miscarriage and the pain has lessened, although I still think about it now and again. A lot of my friends are pregnant so it is pretty difficult being around them. My first period after the miscarriage upset me but at least it meant we could start planning for another baby again. The experience has not put me off, if anything it has made me more determined to be pregnant by my due date.

*Mima*

**I had two miscarriages very close together** before having my two children. I can't believe how much it affected me. Even with my second pregnancy I never had that 'I'm pregnant so I'm going to have a baby' carefree view. I was always on edge waiting for the discharge, dashing to the loo convinced I was bleeding. Before my second loss I went mad trying to find out information but there wasn't that much on offer in the UK and certainly nothing about being pregnant after a loss. I found an American email support group and it was such a comfort to find I was not alone. I exchanged emails with the group until just before the birth of my son.

*Hopeful*

---

**What the experts say**
Your partner...may not have accepted the reality of the pregnancy by the time you miscarry, so it can be difficult for him to understand why you need to mourn. You may find you can talk more easily with another woman who has been through a miscarriage herself.

Sheila Kitzinger (*The New Pregnancy and Childbirth*)

---

**I miscarried at 12 weeks** and I have to say I was devastated. I still get upset about the fact that he or she just went down the pan. My husband and I stood in the bathroom for what seemed an age agonizing over what to do and in the end all we could think of was pulling the chain. It didn't seem right to bury him or her in the garden along with about five cats! I wish there had been something else that we could have done.

A friend who had experienced the same thing said that she always considered the foetus they lost as a baby and hence thinks of herself as having had three children (she has two lovely boys). For some reason I found this very comforting – probably because it recognized that from the moment you know you are pregnant it's a baby inside you, no matter how early on. So I always think of myself now as having had two children – even though I only have one with me now.

*Roz*

**Mumsnet tip**
Make a memorial for your miscarried child. My dad planted apple trees in his garden for all his grandchildren and we asked him to plant an extra one for the baby we lost too – and he said he would. It's a lovely positive thing to do.

*Fp*

**It took me ages to get over my miscarriage** (a blighted ovum at 13 weeks). I had three months of counselling (though I'm not sure if it did more harm than good as I had to return to the same corridor as the room where I had the D&C), but eventually my employers thought that I was being overly dramatic by still taking an afternoon off to go for counselling three months later. Anyway, that was in May and in September our daughter was conceived and, boy, did I ring up at the slightest little thing – I didn't care, I just went straight to the doctor if I thought there was anything wrong – but in fact I had a trouble-free, full term pregnancy.

*Blt*

**I lost my first baby at 16 weeks,** it was discovered at the scan. I had to go through a very real labour followed by a D&C and it was the most awful time. That was 16 years ago. I couldn't face trying again for a long time because I was terrified that I wouldn't be able to conceive, or keep, a baby.

The month after I finally asked for tests from the doctor my daughter was conceived! She was born after an uneventful pregnancy and is now 12. It made all the difference knowing that it can work and there isn't necessarily a reason or anything wrong with you or the baby. I then lost another at seven weeks, like many others, just down the toilet. I kept it to show the doctor – and another D&C. I did not feel nearly so traumatized this time as having one healthy girl made the difference.

A year later I conceived within a month or two of trying and had another healthy girl, now nine. The hard times do fade, although I still remember my two lost ones, particularly the first, whom I was told was a boy. It may sound silly and trivial, but I recommend giving yourself some treats, like new clothes or a weekend away. It won't take the pain away, but a little bit of 'me time' can help you and your partner feel a bit less battered.

*Joyj*

**I actually got round to telling our vicar** a few weeks after my miscarriage and she came and spent some time with me talking, praying and helping me say goodbye. She has no children and yet she was so sensitive to how I was feeling, I felt she was the first person to see this child as a person.

*Nick*

**I have days when I don't think about the miscarriage** and others when I feel really, really down in the dumps, but I suppose this is quite normal. Sometimes I just can't motivate myself to do anything positive. I have found comfort in speaking to friends and relatives who, until recently, didn't even know I had had a miscarriage. It seems quite common for women to miscarry between their first and second baby, so I try to focus on that and be positive. I'm also concentrating on getting myself really well physically – eating sensibly, drinking loads of water, taking folic acid, etc. for when we do start to try again.

*Melly*

**I went through a very difficult bout** of 'low-ness' (I hesitate to say depression, but it must be what depression feels like) about six to eight weeks after my miscarriage. I actually thought I had ME as I was physically very low and constantly ill. I went to the doctors and he said I was thoroughly run down and I should rest and eat properly.

It's amazing how you can fool yourself. I refused to believe that it was post-miscarriage blues and firmly insisted I was physically ill. I had coped very well up until then and then it hit me like running into a brick wall. I had a terrible week when I could hardly move from the bed/sofa and cried all the time.

Finally, Christmas came and my partner had two weeks off work and we had a lovely time and miraculously I felt well and much happier. Then in January I got pregnant again and I could see my 'illness' for what it really was, suppressed grief and sadness. I had a cry in May, which is when the baby was due, but feel that I have put it behind me and although I won't forget, I am looking forward to the new baby and that helps tremendously.

*Enid*

**10**

# Final Thoughts

# I will never get pregnant again because...

**At three weeks post-natal** I wrote a list to stop me if I ever feel like trying for child number four. The list includes: night sweats, sore boobs, piles, the head coming out, indigestion, talking about your body and internals with almost anyone, breast pads, sanitary towels, thrush cream, piles cream, tummy button powder and babies who pooh just as you have changed them.

*Edgarcat*

**Don't forget:** Stretch marks, 'deflated' boobs, varicose veins, sickness, no sleep (before or after), stitches, internals, puffy ankles, feeling emotional all the time... not to mention no booze or Stilton.

*Sb34*

**And what about hideous clothes** and heartburn?

*Babster*

**Day sweats in a summer pregnancy,** carpel tunnel syndrome – I had that pleasure with my second – and the extra two stone in weight left behind by two children.

*Iota*

**All those doctors** talking to me as if I don't have a brain just because I'm pregnant.

*Mo2*

**Rib pain.** Spending a fortune on large bottles of Gaviscon, which I had to lug around in my handbag. People staring at me as if I was a mutant in the gym and worrying over not feeling foetal movement. Losing your own identity and becoming a walking uterus/grandchild-provider and being given 'advice' all the time.

The very worst bit for me, though, was when my milk came in – the dreaded 'day three' – I was in agony. The afterpains were pretty grim too and trying to feed surreptitiously in public whilst my daughter glugged and sucked away noisily was pretty stressful as well.

*Flippa*

**Not being able to get into a comfy position** when sleeping. Waking up constantly during the night to pee. People automatically putting their hands on your bump to feel (without asking). Walking with non-pregnant people – and not keeping up! Seeing people on the train/Tube/bus hide behind their books or papers pretending they didn't see you so they don't have to give up their seat.

*Metrobaby*

**The afterbirth pains get worse** after every baby. The risk of having a child born with problems gets higher. You need a bigger car. There is a disproportionate increase in the noise/laundry level. You will always be pot bellied.

*Lou33*

**The sheer horror** that was my experience of childbirth the first time round.

*Slug*

**I can't afford it** – in terms of health, time, money or sanity.

*Griffy*

**Leaking breasts** – most embarrassing in public. The feeling when the head was coming out – ouch! Piles – ouch! Iron tablets – hideous little things. And stirrups!

*Doormat*

**Sleeping (or not sleeping)** surrounded by pillows and still being uncomfortable. Little feet jammed under ribs for days on end. Having a ten-litre blood transfusion and waking up in intensive care the next day with a very traumatized partner.

*SamboM*

**Feelings of intense disappointment** and uncontrollable weeping when I realized I would have to have an emergency C-section. A C-section scar that itches all the time. A flabby tummy that hangs over said scar. Stretch marks on my boobs and hips (they never told me about those).

*DebL*

**Being repulsed at the thought** of losing your dignity whilst giving birth and being determined not to, then going and throwing all those good ideas out the window as soon as the first cramp hits, then regretting the loss of dignity afterwards. Then there's the lack of bladder control, which they say will probably continue for the rest of my life.

*Meanmum*

**Poohing whilst pushing.** I know midwives claim to have seen it 100 times before but I was horrified! Other minor reasons: resembling Elizabeth I for months after each baby because of spectacular hair-loss and then effectively having a 'mullet' for another five months whilst it grows back. Episiotomy and tearing – sitting on the cheek of one buttock for five weeks because of too tight stitching. Sciatica, pubis symphysis dysfunction, insomnia from 34 weeks, chronic sleep deprivation, the whole breasts containing milk thing, having to wear wire-free bras whilst breastfeeding, breast pads showing through T-shirts. Looking fat, not pregnant, from 3–6 months.

*Molly1*

**Headaches,** ooh the headaches, agony for the first 16 weeks.

*Chiccadum*

**Cracked** and bleeding nipples.

*Girly*

**Insomnia from 20 weeks** because of chronic restless leg syndrome. The only thing that stopped it at night (for about 20–30 minutes at a time) was a really hot bath. By 37 weeks, I was having six hot baths during the night every night.

*Griffy*

**Anal fissure** – ouch!

*Kaz33*

**Because I have a one in five chance,** of having another set of twins!

*Jac34*

**At my age,** I would risk going straight from pregnancy to the menopause – hormone hell or what!

*Frank1*

**The progression into a demented,** fuzzy-haired, tiny-eyed monster with no sense of humour and serious chocolate addiction. And it says something for the sleep deprivation that it took me two months to figure out that I felt like death because I had an infection and wasn't just exhausted (mastitis).

*Gizmo*

**Too much time given over to worrying,** puking over yourself whilst driving to work (perhaps that was only me), a complete inability to concentrate on anything important, a constant need to pee, a constant need to eat, a constant need to sleep, a constant need to puke and worry about where you're going to do it. Going off chocolate, bread and cereal, and feeling ill from the smell of deodorant, perfume and cooking. Waddling, the fact you're not allowed to lift anything, midwives taking pints and pints of your blood (well, it felt like it), finding suitable pots to pee in (and carry to work for most of the day before your appointment). Being constantly kicked in the ribs/cervix/lungs, crying at sentimental songs spun by Terry Wogan. (But maybe I will do it again one day...)

*Philippat*

**With each one my boobs** have got saggier, the varicose veins more prominent and the sex life has deteriorated to practically non-existent. Babies spill my wine, pooh on my carpets, and wake me up just as I have fallen asleep.

*Oxocube*

**I had one child, then twins** – I know I would have triplets if I went on. Cabbage in my bra. The expense. The poverty. The brain-numbingness of being at home. The lack of freedom. Prams on buses. Everyone saying, 'It only gets worse as they get older, enjoy it whilst you can', and you thinking, how the hell does it get worse than this? but it does!

*Custardo*


**<<fingers in ears>>** La la la la...not listening...la la la la...I will have another...I don't care how awful pregnancy and birth were with son...I won't listen...I refuse to remember...la la la la la...

*Ghosty*

## I loved being pregnant because...

**I loved having radiant skin** and really thick shiny hair, the camaraderie between pregnant women and the fact you make new friends. The best bit is going on maternity leave – especially the bit before the baby comes – lots of shopping, swimming and lazing around. I liked getting a seat on the Tube, although I have to say it didn't always happen, even when I was 35 weeks plus and obviously pregnant. I was fortunate that I didn't get stretch marks, varicose veins, piles or morning sickness and although my son was 8 lb 13 oz with a large head, I had a straightforward delivery with no stitches (I loved the epidural). All the flowers, prezzies and cards you get are great, of course, and I'm lighter now than before I was pregnant.

*Flippa*

**I felt really 'special'** when I was pregnant. I loved the thought that a little life was growing inside me.

*Sb34*

**The things I liked were shopping** for baby stuff, decorating the nursery and making sure the house is really tidy – something I previously felt completely unmotivated to do. Seeing the scan pictures. Watching big healthy limbs squirming and jutting around your tummy. Wondering what sex it is and what you'll call it.

*Bobbins*

**Dreaming about what your son or daughter** would look like. Sitting in meetings at work and never getting bored because I could always feel my bump and get healthy kicks to wake me up. The excitement when you feel the first kick, or waiting outside the radiographer's room for your first ever scan, then being told all is well. I was even excited when I realized I was in labour. I knew that I would see my baby soon and I was so ready for it (or so I thought!).

*Mum2toby*

**Being able to wear** tight tops stretched over my tummy for once in my life

*Philippat*

**Balancing a plate** on the bump whilst slouching in front of the TV. Oh and no periods.

*Doormat*

**You somehow erase the first three months.** I loved the rest of it. Feeling a life inside you, everyone smiles and is nice to you, a good excuse to eat more cakes, a good excuse to do less housework, wondering what it's going to be and finally having a cleavage (though maybe that's countered by the hideous maternity bras!).

*Ninja*

**Knowing I was never alone,** that my daughter was with me all the time. Sleeping – I could sleep for England. I would sometimes sleep 12 hours, get up, eat and nap for another couple of hours whilst watching rubbish on TV. My partner could actually Hoover around me and I wouldn't wake up.

*Batters*

**I just loved the feeling** of completeness...I can't really explain...but being all blooming and rotund and people complimenting me on it. Just that glowing feeling. Being pregnant can be so sexy too...!

*Winnie1*

**Listening to classical music** for the first time in many years. Being an incredible ignoramus about it, I had always felt unable to buy any classical CDs, but didn't care when I was pregnant. I bought a few that I liked the look of from the covers, and really enjoyed some of them. My partner offering to do stuff. Suddenly talking to people at work who I've never even been on nodding terms with before. Having an excuse to put my feet up every so often, including at work. Everybody's delight when you tell them. Most of all, looking forward to meeting the new person that's busy developing.

*NQWWW*

**Eating ginger biscuits** in bed first thing in the morning and not getting moaned at about the crumbs!

*Badjelly*

**Not worrying** about looking fat.

*Grommit*

**England losing a crucial** game of football and my husband's depression only lasting until he saw my stomach moving with our baby's next kick.

*Haley*

**That hormonal high** when your little baby's put in your arms for the first time – there's nothing like it.

*Lil*

**I adored being pregnant.** I loved smiling secretly to myself in meetings when no one else knew. The look on my parents' faces when we told them. Rubbing my tummy absent-mindedly all the time. Quitting work a full 11 weeks before the birth and watching the *ER* double episodes every day whilst eating crushed ice and ice lollies. Bizarre dreams, hiccups in the womb. Decorating the nursery and my husband and I spontaneously bursting into tears of joy when everything was finished at the sheer excitement that overwhelmed us. The first images on the screen at the scan and walking around all afternoon saying, 'Oh my GOD! Oh my GOD!' The labour, and the birth being all okay, and hearing the words, 'You have a beautiful girl.' Seeing her face for the first time, and thinking she looked familiar already – I can't wait to do it again.

*Snickers*

# Bibliography

Balaskas, Janet *Active Birth Centre – Birth and Baby Diary*

Balaskas, Janet *New Active Birth*, HarperCollins, 1991

Cooke, Kaz *The Rough Guide to Pregnancy and Birth*, Rough Guides, 2001

Cooper, Dr Carol *Twins & Multiple Births: The Essential Parenting Guide from Pregnancy to Adulthood*, Vermilion, 2004

D'Adamo, Peter J. with Whitney, Catherine *Eat Right for Your Baby: The Individualized Guide to Fertility and Maximum Health During Pregnancy, Nursing, and Your Baby's First Year*, G. P. Putnam's Sons, March, 2003

Douglas, Ann *The Mother of All Pregnancy Books: The Ultimate Guide to Conception, Birth and Everything in Between*, John Wiley & Sons Inc, 2002

Eisenberg, Arlene; Hathaway, Sandee E.; Murkoff, Heidi E.; & *What to Expect When You're Expecting*, Simon & Schuster, 2002

Figes, Kate *Life after Birth*, Penguin Books, 2000

Ford, Gina *The New Contented Little Baby Book*, Vermilion, 2002

Gordon, Dr Yehudi *Birth and Beyond, Beyond: The Definitive Guide to Your Pregnancy, Your Birth, Your Family: from Minus 9 to Plus 9 Months*, Vermilion, 2002

Green, Dr Christopher *Babies! A Parents' Guide to Enjoying Baby's First Year*, Simon & Schuster, 2002

Greer, Professor Ian *Pregnancy – the Inside Guide: A Complete Guide to Fertility, Pregnancy and Labour*, Collins Paperback, 2003

Hunter, Adriana *The Queen Charlotte's Guide to Pregnancy and Birth: All You Have Ever Wanted to Know*, Vermilion, 1998

Iovine, Vicki *The Best Friends' Guide to Pregnancy*, Bloomsbury, 1997

Jamil, Dr Tanvir and Evenett, Karen, *The Alternative Pregnancy Handbook: Complementary Remedies for a Healthy and Stress-free Pregnancy*, Piatkus Books, 2000

Kitzinger, Sheila *The Experience of Childbirth*, Penguin Books, 1967

Kitzinger, Sheila *Homebirth: The Essential Guide to Giving Birth Outside of the Hospital*, Dorling Kindersley, 1991

Kitzinger, Sheila *The New Pregnancy and Childbirth*, Penguin Books, 1997

Leach Penelope *Your Baby & Child*, Dorling Kindersley, 2003

Narter, David *Don't Name Your Baby...What's Wrong with Every Name in the Book*, Cumberland House Publishing, 2002

Nolan, Mary *Being Pregnant, Giving Birth, The National Childbirth Trust*, HarperCollins, 1998

Odent, Michel 'Is the father's participation at the birth dangerous', First published in *Midwifery Today, Vol. 51, 1999*

Odent, Michel 'Lessons from the first hospital birthing pool', first published in *Midwifery Today, Vol 54, 2000*

Palmer Gabrielle, *The Politics of Breastfeeding*, Rivers Oram Press/Pandora List, 1993

Sears, William and Sears, Martha, *The Baby Book: Everything You Need to Know About Your Baby from Birth to Age Two*, Little, Brown and Company, 2003

Stoppard, Dr Miriam *New Pregnancy and Birth Book*, Dorling Kindersley, 2001

Stoppard, Dr Miriam *Your New Baby*, Dorling Kindersley, 1998

Stoppard, Dr Miriam *First Time Parents: The Essential Guide for All New Mothers and Fathers*, Dorling Kindersley, 2001

Wilson, Penny Wipe: *Survival Tactics for Parents with Attitude*, Coronet Paperback, 2003

# Index